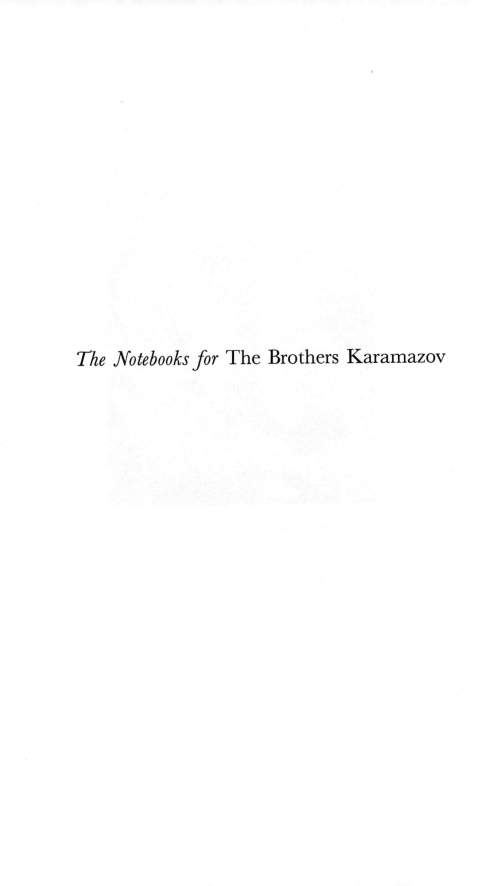

The Notebooks for The Brothers Karamazov

A portrait of Dostoevsky by V. Perov, 1872

The Notebooks for

The Brothers Karamazov

Fyodor Dostoevsky

Edited and Translated by Edward Wasiolek

The University of Chicago Press

CHICAGO & LONDON

International Standard Book Number: 0–226–15967–1
Library of Congress Catalog Card Number: 74–126073

This translation is based upon the Russian edition of the notebooks for *The Brothers Karamazov* as contained in *F. M. Dostoevsky materialy i issledovaniia,* edited by A. S. Dolinin (Leningrad, 1935)

The University of Chicago Press, Chicago 60637
The University of Chicago Press, Ltd., London

Contents

Illustrations

Introduction

I

When Dostoevsky finished *The Brothers Karamazov* he wrote to Liubimov, the assistant editor of *The Russian Messenger,* the following: "Well then, the novel is finished! I worked three years, published it for two—a significant moment for me!" Three years would take the beginnings of *The Brothers Karamazov* to November 1877, and it was in the October 1877 issue of *The Diary of a Writer* that Dostoevsky announced that he would suspend publication of *The Diary of a Writer* with the December issue for reasons of health. If he were actively at work on *The Brothers Karamazov* then, it must have been in a very preparatory and rudimentary vein, for in March of 1878 he wrote to V. V. Mikhailov the following: "I have conceived and shortly will begin a large novel, in which many children and especially young children from about 7 to 16 years of age will take part. . . . Write to me about children, what you yourself know (circumstances, habits, sayings and so forth)." But it was not until 11 July 1878 that Dostoevsky wrote "that the novel has begun . . . it has just been begun." Between March and July Dostoevsky lost in death his youngest son, Alyosha, and out of grief for his son he accompanied the Russian philosopher Vladimir Solovyov to the monastery Optina Pustyn. The real beginnings of *The Brothers Karamazov* must be put in July and August 1878 when Dostoevsky wrote the first four chapters of the first book in rough form. He wrote to Putsykovich on 27 August 1878: "I'm working on the novel, but the thing is going slowly, I've only just begun." By September his letters indicated that the work was going well, and from that point on to November 1880 the work—despite difficulties with particular chapters—went much better than did similar work on the other great novels.

Whether Dostoevsky began *The Brothers Karamazov* in 1878, 1877, or even 1876, as is sometimes suggested, it is clear that in another sense he had been writing it throughout most of his career. There is hardly a character type, situation, technique, device, or idea that Dostoevsky had not rehearsed before. Ivan's metaphysical rebellion has its roots in Kirilov, Ippolit, and even in the Underground Man. The Grand Inquisitor has his prototype in Shigalyov's vision of the happy pasturage of 90 percent of the people and the dominion of 10 percent, and in the Underground Man's revolt against the compulsory organization of happiness. Alyosha has his prototypes in Dostoevsky's meek characters: Makar Dolgoruky of *A Raw Youth,* Mary Lebiadkin of *The Possessed,* Prince Myshkin of *The Idiot,* and Sonia of *Crime and Punishment.* Fyodor Karamazov goes back to the buffoons of the forties, through Lebedev of *The Idiot* and Svidrigailov of *Crime and Punishment.* Katerina Ivanovna has her ancestors in Katerina Nikolaevna of *A Raw Youth,* Lisa of *The Possessed,* Nastasya Fillipovna of *The Idiot,* and possibly Katerina of *The Landlady.*

Despite the ease with which one can find anticipations of what Dostoevsky created in *The Brothers Karamazov,* the novel strikes the reader as an enormous and fateful leap into excellence, more a coronation than a summary, a transfiguration rather than a transformation. The explanation lies in more than what we ordinarily call "art," that is, the refinement of external form and structure. It lies probably in some shift of view of himself, the world, and his material. The vision changes before the art changes. Dostoevsky had always shown great candor and courage in what he dramatized: the Underground Man, Raskolnikov, Nastasya Fillipovna, Stavrogin, and Peter Verkhovensky are all in one way or another representations of terrifying nihilistic views of the world, attacks on the integrity and dignity of man, the sanctity of God, and the stability and performance of society. What his nihilistic heroes attack is what Dostoevsky himself believed in. He believed in God, the organic processes of social change, the glory of the Russian state and the glories of the Orthodox faith, in personal freedom and responsibility, and in the impossibility of altering man's nature and situation by abstract, rational, and external manipulation. He believed in these and similar things with a passion and defended them with aggression and verbal violence. Yet, he subjected them in his novels to constant dramatic experiment and attack.

Dostoevsky had an extraordinary ability to restrain his own aggressions and to distance his violent opinions in the dramatization of his characters. But he was not always able to do so. There are instances in his novels when the ideologue shows through, when the manipulation of the man and the color of his prejudices are easy to discern. Myshkin's outburst against Catholicism serves personal polemic more than it serves dramatic context; Raskolnikov is nudged a bit too easily into the camp of God in the epilogue of *Crime and Punishment:* liberals, radicals, and leftists of all sorts from Lebeziatnikov of *Crime and Punishment* through the Burdovsky crowd in *The Idiot* and the pack of little devils in *The Possessed* are humiliated, ridiculed, and annihilated by polemic and caricature. *The Brothers Karamazov* is, among other things, a summation, assessment, and a confession. To the courage of facing what opposed him from the outside, and perhaps from the inside, he added a deeper courage: humility, the courage to admit he was wrong.

Dostoevsky suspected, I believe, that he too had lied to himself, that not only the antagonists and opponents were at fault, but perhaps he himself. At least this is one of the themes and the prevailing tone of the Pushkin speech, which he delivered when he was writing *The Brothers Karamazov* (8 June 1880), and the content too of many of the reminiscences that he makes in *The Diary of a Writer.* In *The Possessed* Nechaev (Peter Verkhovensky) and the Nechaevists (Liputin, Virginsky, Erkel, Tolkachenko) are vilified unmercifully, but in a reminiscence of his Petrashevsky days in *The Diary of a Writer* he paints them as wrong, but neither insignificant nor laughable. More important, he sees that he too could have become what they were. "I myself am an old Nechaevist," he proclaims, meaning by that that he had stood with the Petrashevsky conspirators in ignorance and illusion, but the Petrashevtsys, and he among them, could have become, depending on circumstances, Nechaevists: "A Nechaev I could probably never have become, but a Nechaevist, I could not swear, perhaps I could . . . in my youth." The seventies bring no change in attitude toward liberals, radicals and toward those who would coerce life by their abstractions, hate, and love, but there is a change in his attitude toward what drives men to believe in what he does not believe in. He grants them increasingly more intelligence (he reminds us that the Petrashevtsys he stood on the scaffold with were talented, cultured, and well-educated), more honesty, sincerity, dedication, and good will. It would be inaccurate to see in this, as Soviet critics have done, any modification of Dostoevsky's basic beliefs. But a desire for reconcilement and understanding appears in his attitudes, and a new humility informs his work. There are glimmers of it in *A Raw Youth,* and much more of it in *The Brothers Karamazov.*

We still get easy caricature of liberals and their self-serving and abstract view of life in *The Brothers Karamazov:* Miusov is so caricatured as is Rakitin. Yet neither is central to Dostoevsky's concern as were the radicals in *The Possessed.* The caricature of Miusov is almost tired and it is surely incidental, and the satire of Rakitin is a foil for Alyosha's pure monasticism and a target for the criticisms of the regenerated Dmitri. In *The Brothers Karamazov* Dostoevsky grants the "other side" more than he had ever granted them before. Indeed by the time he wrote "The Legend of the Grand Inquisitor" he had granted them so much that one could ask, as many did, whether the argument of The Grand Inquisitor was answerable. Many of Dostoevsky's contemporaries feared that it was not, and many more since then have similarly feared. Dostoevsky had said that "all is permitted" if there was no God, at least as early as the *Notes from the Underground,* but he did not quite believe it, or if he believed it, he was eager to execute in one way or another those who believed it. The Underground Man is too fitful, eccentric, and sick for one to take his argument with complete seriousness; Raskolnikov is punished by conscience and God for dreaming of a world where all is permitted; Ippolit is shown to be naïve, vainglorious and egotistical; and Stavrogin is led to self-destruction for daring to permit himself everything. But Dostoevsky dared to permit the Grand Inquisitor almost everything, and he granted him the very qualities we traditionally grant to Christ: honesty, courage, suffering, self-sacrifice, martyrdom, and love of humanity. It was as if he were ready in this last novel—and he was convinced that it would be his last novel—to dare everything and say everything. For if the voices of his nihilistic heroes were also his voice, if his dark heroes were as much a part of him as his light heroes, then he had decided to confess everything in *The Brothers Karamazov:* to let his unbelief speak to his belief, his doubts to his convictions. He had tried to have his say from the very beginning, but it took many volumes and many hurts and many years before he was able to confess what raged in his breast. It was after his return from Europe and the end of his voluntary four-year exile—in the period between 1871 and 1877—that the most direct and explicit preparation for the writing of *The Brothers Karamazov* takes place.

II

The years after his return from Europe in 1871 were in many respects his happiest years, surely the most stable, and the most free from the poverty that had pursued him throughout Russia and Europe and had provoked his miseries and his plaints. There were creditors as usual, but most of them were forced into compromise, delay, and settlement by the determined will and the clever brain of his efficient wife. His health was not good, and the decade was marked by several trips to Ems for his health. Although his reputation was assured, he had no regular income, and this may have contributed to his decision to undertake the editorship of the conservative journal *The Citizen* and subsequently to publish *A Raw Youth* in Nekrasov's journal *The Fatherland Notes.* He was paid 3,000 rubles a month to edit *The Citizen* and despite considerable friction between himself and the reactionary publisher Prince Meshchersky he did not give up the editorship until *A Raw Youth* was marketable. He resigned from the editorship of *The Citizen* on 19 March 1874, but despite the fact that he had published his major novels in Katkov's *The Russian Messenger,* he was not able to come to terms with Katkov. The latter was evasive and vague, and perhaps not entirely aboveboard; Dostoevsky was to learn later and to complain bitterly about it to his wife that Katkov had already promised Tolstoy 500 rubles a printer's sheet (16 regular pages) for *Anna Karenina* and was unwilling to pay Dostoevsky 250 rubles a sheet for *A Raw Youth.*

Financial considerations surely played a part in his decision to edit *The Citizen* and to publish *A Raw Youth* in *The Fatherland Notes*. But something more was operative. He quarreled bitterly with Prince Meshchersky's reactionary tendencies and he was fearful that his association with Nekrasov's journal would force him to compromise his convictions. He wrote to his wife after having agreed to publish *A Raw Youth* in *The Fatherland Notes:* "But even if we should have to ask for charity this year, I will not concede a line to their tendency." He did not have to, because Nekrasov and the editorial staff of *The Fatherland Notes* left him free to say what he would. But the oscillation from reactionary *The Citizen* and the liberal *The Fatherland Notes* and the disgust with the reactionary policies of *The Citizen* and the suspiciousness of the policy of *The Fatherland Notes* seemed to point to a Dostoevsky who was determined to hold on to his convictions and yet quest for new perspectives. The swing from reactionary newspaper to liberal journal was if nothing else a sign of restlessness and an openness to new ideas and influences. Neither association was to bring him satisfaction or the increased knowledge of Russia that he sought. *The Diary of a Writer,* which he had begun as a supplement to *The Citizen,* brought him both. He published it in 1873, and then as a separate and independent publication in 1876 and 1877 and very briefly in 1880. It grew steadily in popularity and Dostoevsky was delighted with its reception and gratified with what he believed to be his colloquy with the Russian people.

The Diary of a Writer permitted Dostoevsky to have his say, and he did have his say on every conceivable subject: on politics, religion, criminals, women, spiritualism, drunkenness, children, and peasant life. He talked about Russia, France, England, the Eastern question; he reminisced, argued, fretted, advised, and even cajoled. He was anecdotal, serious, ironical, and philosophical. He dreamed and he analyzed, wrote short stories and placed them between reportage and philosophical tracts. He roamed the streets of St. Petersburg and haunted its courtrooms, and shared what he saw with his readers. Most of all he wrote about children, for they are everywhere in the pages of *The Diary:* he watches them on the streets, reads about them, pities them, and imagines their lives. He cannot know enough about them, and when he can't learn enough he imagines the rest. After talking to a begging child on a street corner, for instance, he imagines that such children are sent out to beg in the cold by callous parents, who when the children come home empty-handed beat, humiliate, and ridicule them. Most of them, Dostoevsky is sure, leave home, roam about the city, learn to steal, become akin to wild beasts, and lose any idea of who they are, where they live, and why they live.

The Diary of a Writer was Dostoevsky's public forum for what had churned in private reflection. It was his immersion into Russian life, or as close as he could get to it, and he strained to catch its rhythms. Most of all it was the rough draft, the work sheet, the accounting and balancing, the laboratory of impressions, idea, arguments which were to receive dramatic treatment in *The Brothers Karamazov*. Whatever the issue, situation, character, idea—whether important or secondary —one is likely to find some discussion of it in *The Diary of a Writer*. Freedom and responsibility, fathers and children, crime and environment, Satan and Christ; the prototypes of Fetiukovich, the prosecutor, Kolia, Rakitin, Miusov are all to be found there. Even items as small as these are first mentioned in *The Diary:* Kolia's assurance to Alyosha that it is stupid to run away to America finds its anticipatory reference in Dostoevsky's comments on a newspaper article in which two young boys became implicated in a crime in order to get money to escape to America. Or Father Zossima's recollection of a friend of humanity who would betray his cause for his tobacco is similarly first mentioned there.

In *The Diary of a Writer* not only the horrors perpetrated against children, but horrors of parents against children, husbands against wives, and people against themselves are chronicled. Ivan's list of horrors is brief and selected; Dostoevsky's is as broad as Russia and as long as his *Diary:* of peasants beating their wives, starving them, putting bread before them and refusing them permission to eat it, hanging them up by their legs like chickens; of a mother who holds the hand of her fourteen-month-old baby under the boiling steam of a samovar, a mother who threw her foster daughter out of the window to avenge herself on her husband because of his cruelty to her. *The Diary* is a chronicle of every imaginable hurt, physical and psychological, of every manner of degradation and ill treatment, culled by Dostoevsky from reading, trial record, courtroom sittings, and observation.

Dostoevsky spares no details and his reportage is as cutting and acidic as are his dramas. He is appalled at what Russian life amounts to, but he perseveres in exposing a chronicle of cruelty, sadism, and bestiality. And just as he places his pure, humble, and silent Christ against Ivan's and the Grand Inquisitor's canvas of darkness and desperation, so too the faith and purity of the peasant is set against his corruption. The peasant for him is cruel, drunk, slothful, ignorant, and unrestrained in his corruptions. Yet, he is also the savior of Russia, the carrier of the undefiled ideas of Russia and Orthdoxy. Dostoevsky idealizes the Russian peasant shamelessly, but nothing draws his ire more sharply and repeatedly than the idealizations of the peasant by liberal and radical circles. The contradiction is only apparent. The peasant, for Dostoevsky, is a carrier of ideals, but he must not be idealized. The ideal peasant that the liberals loved was a peasant that had never existed, and could not exist, except in the abstractions of the liberals. In loving an ideal peasant the liberals, for Dostoevsky, refused to accept the real peasant: the peasant who was ignorant, slothful, greedy, sadistic, drunk, the descriptions of which Dostoevsky gives us so frequently in *The Diary of a Writer*. By refusing to accept the real peasant, the liberals annihilated him; the beautiful idea was in his view the unbeautiful murder.

The real peasant and not the imaginary peasant had to be confronted, accepted, and loved. But how did one go from the realistic peasant to the pure and faith-carrying peasant? Dostoevsky's explanation is simple and perhaps unconvincing: the peasants are the saviors of Russia because though they sin, they know they are sinning. And in knowing, they acknowledge a judgment and law beyond their judgment and law. Their acts may not be good, but their suffering is. Their humility consists of acknowledging that their lives have a dimension deeper than the depth of their empirical acts, and in acknowledging that they silently acknowledge that their beings—and by implication the beings of others—are beyond their own judgment and the judgment of others. In short they are humble before the sacredness of being, theirs and others. In all this they acknowledge God. One must love one's fellow man, but one must love him as he is. The ugliness must not be the excuse for denying him, nor beauty the conditions for accepting him. Dostoevsky saw the condescension and coercion that lay at the base of a certain kind of idealism and humanism, and he dramatized this condescension and coercion in stark and terrifying form in "The Legend of the Grand Inquisitor."

The historical peasant and the historical children do not enter the pages of *The Brothers Karamazov*. Yet the issue that he argues for in his many discussions of the peasant in *The Diary* survives in *The Brothers Karamazov* and remains to inform the most important moral and spiritual issues: the necessity of loving what is repulsive in others and the impossibility of loving what is repulsive in others without acknowledging what is repulsive in oneself. The historical children, too, of *The Diary of a Writer* enter the novel in a series of structures and relationships that have little to do with the sufferings of the actual children of St. Petersburg cellars. The beggars he meets on the streets and the fates he imagines when they return to their parents become in the novel the premises of universal revolt, of mankind against God. Even the actual examples Ivan uses in his argument against God are of children of past times and other countries, as if Dostoevsky wanted to distance the topical and invite the universal. *The Diary of a Writer* reads like the historical correlative of *The Brothers Karamazov*, yet it seems to have been written so that the history did not have to be incorporated in the novel itself.

Dostoevsky had sought in some of his other major novels—especially *The Possessed* and *A Raw Youth*—to immerse his human and universal dramas in the topicalities of his age. But no vulgar and self-indulgent radicals erupt into *The Brothers Karamazov,* as did the Burdovsky group into *The Idiot*; nothing like the vulgar anti-aestheticism and sociologizing of Pisarev, which is repeatedly satirized in *The Possessed,* is present in *The Brothers Karamazov,* nor for that matter are such topics as the counterfeiting of railway shares and the political program of the Dolgushintsys incorporated into *The Brothers*. One can make a case for Bakunin as the prototype of Stavrogin, as Grossman did, but one is loath to look for historical prototypes for Ivan Karamazov, Alyosha, and Dmitri. Indeed the notes for *The Brothers Karamazov* show us a Dostoevsky who is intent upon eliminating topical references. Anti-Catholic remarks by Alyosha and explicit condemnation of materialistic trends, which are to be found in the notes for "The Legend of the Grand Inquisitor" were eliminated before the final version.

During the seventies Dostoevsky had softened in his attitudes toward liberals and radicals and moved toward more honesty and courage in dramatizing what opposed his explicit beliefs. He moved, in short, toward honest confession. One item in this confession was, perhaps, the recognition that contemporary issues he sought so earnestly to incorporate into his novels and argued so vehemently for were not really what he wanted to say and had to say. As he moved toward what was timeless, he moved toward what was personal and individual. What falls away is what is timely and general, and what falls into place is what is timeless and personal. Dostoevsky put much of himself into the novel: he gave the name of his recently deceased son to Alyosha, his own name to Fyodor; the Chermashnia grove over which Dmitri, Fyodor, Smerdiakov, and Ivan struggle was a reference to a grove by the same name on his father's estate, where he played as a child and which he visited shortly before beginning *The Brothers Karamazov*.

It is after all not the idealogical fathers and idealogical sons that confront each other in *The Brothers Karamazov*, not the generation of the forties and the sixties, but a son and a father fighting over a woman and the inheritance of wife and mother, sustained by no social idea and representative of no special social group. Behind the opponents, circumstances, issues, and programs of history, Dostoevsky confronts something primal, universal, and personal: the Elder Zossima and the Father Fyodor, the spiritual father and the earthly father, the beautiful, kind, unselfish, self-sacrificing father and the ugly, cruel, taunting, predatory father. Dostoevsky had been writing his "fathers and children" at least since *The Idiot*. In *The Idiot* he places Rogozhin against his father, Myshkin in search of his father, Burdovsky claiming falsely Pavlishchev as his father; in *The Possessed* the sons of the sixties are pitted against the fathers of the forties. The sons may be vulgar and stupid—as is the Burdovsky group—or vulgar and clever, as is Peter Verkhovensky, or naïve and confused, as is Arkady of *A Raw Youth*. But the fathers are sometimes shown to aggress against the children. Rogozhin steals his father's money to spend on a woman, and his father beats him nearly to death. Totsky, the foster father, ravages Nastasya; Stepan Trofimovich robs his son of his inheritance and deprives him of his parental care; Versilov abandons the child to marry the mother, and attempts to use the child to gain a mistress. In the notes for *The Idiot*, a father ravages his own daughter, and in the notes for *A Raw Youth* Arkady and Versilov struggle openly for the sexual favor of Katerina Nikolaevna. The sexual hostility that inflames the anger and struggle of father and son in *The Brothers Karamazov* has its foreshadowings in the novels that precede it, but Dostoevsky is more open and candid about it in *The Brothers Karamazov*.

There is in *The Brothers Karamazov* the good father, Zossima, and the bad father, Fyodor, and there is the good God, Christ, and the bad God, the God against whom Ivan Karamazov aggressess. The bad father is repulsive: Fyodor has slobbering lips, a fleshy Adam's apple, and malevolent eyes; he is maudlin, stingy, ruthless, and loathsome. He preys on his sons: he takes the maternal inheritance away from his son Dmitri and uses it to lure Dmitri's beloved away from him; he would have preyed on Alyosha and Ivan too, if one had not already been driven to spirituality and the other to intellectuality. The rage that swells in Dmitri's breast when he sees his torturer panting and slobbering in expectation of Grushenka is understandable and almost justifiable. The God whose world Ivan arraigns in the fifth book is equally repulsive: he tortures his children, as Fyodor had tortured his. In return for a world of cruelty, sadism, and torment he expects and demands not outrage but humility and gratitude.

What Dmitri has difficulty doing and what Ivan cannot do, and what Alyosha does, and what Zossima counsels one to do is to love the repulsive father and the repulsive heavenly father, as Christ loves and kisses in silent reverence what must be abhorrent to him. But one cannot love what is ugly until one has recognized the ugliness within oneself. Dmitri's regeneration begins when he cries to all at the preliminary investigation: "We're all cruel, we're all monsters, we all make men weep, and mothers, and babes at the breast, but of all, let it be settled here, now, of all I am the lowest reptile!" One cannot be the judge of what is to be loved, but one must shower the earth—all of the earth—with one's tears of love and compassion. As soon as one judges what is deserving of love, one annihilates what one considers to be undeserving. This is why the Elder Zossima prostrates himself before the would-be murderer Dmitri in the opening scene: to crush by humility the impulse to judge and consequently to crush the impulse to commit murder in one's heart.

III

The character of the notes that follow is different from that of the other major novels, in that the distance between notes and novels is shortest. The notes for *The Idiot, The Possessed,* and *A Raw Youth,* and to a lesser extent the notes for *Crime and Punishment* show us a Dostoevsky in search of his theme, narrative structure, and the identity of his major characters. They show us a Dostoevsky multiplying variants and trying out character and subject in different modes and different circumstances. Dostoevsky does not have a glimmer of Myshkin's character as it appears in the final version until he has taken him through six plans; he takes Stavrogin through endless repetitions of improbable romantic situations before he discovers that Stavrogin is beyond such complications. Versilov insists on becoming the center of *A Raw Youth,* but only after Dostoevsky insists throughout most of the notes that he is not.

The notes for *The Brothers Karamazov* are not those of germination, quest, and discovery. Dostoevsky knows what he is writing about; the subject is firm, the identities of the chief characters are fixed, and the basic dramatic situation is clear. What the notebooks say and what the novel says are largely the same. Some of the scenes sketched in the notebooks are almost identical, even linguistically, with those of the final version. The differences between notes and novel are differences between schematic representation and dramatic embodiment, summary and amplification, between ideas and the dramatization of the ideas. The notes often read like a stenographic sketch of the novel, an example of which may be seen in the following crisis:

In the notes we have: "Perhaps a four-year-old memory, ray of sunlight, pulpit and mother."

This becomes in the final version of the novel:

> He remembered on a still summer evening, an open window, the slanting rays of the setting sun (that he recalled most vividly of all; in a corner of the room the holy image, before it a lighted lamp, and on her knees before the image his mother, sobbing hysterically with cries and moans, snatching him up in both arms, squeezing him close till it hurt, and praying for him to the Mother of God, holding him out in both arms to the image as though to put him under the Mother's protection . . . and suddenly a nurse runs in and snatches him from her in terror. That was the picture!

The scene in the notes is abstract, fragmentary and undramatic; it has no people, emotions, drama, time. The passage in the final version adds people (the mother and the son), drama and action (the mother holding up the boy to the icon and the nurse snatching the boy from the mother), time (setting sun), space (the corner of the room), tactile pressure (mother squeezing the little boy), and emotions (hysterical sobbing, moans, terror).

The scene in the notes takes on sensuous body and specificity in the novel. In other scenes the passage from notes to novel brings qualifications of ideas, refinement of structure, and amplification of detail and circumstance. In the notes for Book III, for instance, we have nothing of Dmitri's magnificent confession to Alyosha or of the narration of his first fateful meeting with Katerina Ivanovna in his apartment. In the novel the tangle of bruising relations between Katerina and Dmitri, and especially the use of virtue and sacrifice as weapons for hurting, proceed from this first fateful meeting. But tiny fragments —monadic nuclei—which express in very fragmentary form the core or matrix of these relations appear here and there in the notes, such as the following statements that Dmitri makes to Alyosha: "She loves virtue and not me." "Tell her that I bid her good-bye by bowing." and "She wants to save me." The fragmentary phrases catch what is essential in the relations between Katerina and Dmitri. But they are only statements, attached to Dmitri and spoken to Alyosha, but unqualified by circumstance, situation, tone, and descriptive detail.

These notes would seem to suggest that Dostoevsky first seized important scenes, characters, and complex relations schematically, usually in the form of an idea or a key gesture, shorn of the complexities of description and ideational qualification. Something of the movement from disembodied conception in particularization and specification can be seen in the fact that some of the key ideas appear first without being attached to any particular person or dramatic situation. Examples are: "All is permitted," "It is pleasant to take offense," *"Those who love men in general* hate men in particular," and "If there were only intelligence in the world, then nothing would exist." Something of this movement can also be seen in the fact that most of the chief characters at first do not have names but appellations that denote something of their essence: Ivan is "the educated-one" and "the murderer"; Fyodor is "the landowner"; Alyosha, "the Idiot"; Katerina is "the fiancée"; and Dmitri is "Ilinsky."

The interest of these notes will lie in part in the translation of the complexities of the novel back into the monadic simplicity of the notes, and back presumably from what is secondary to what is primary. A great deal of subtlety, psychological and ideational, often intervenes between notes and novel: ideas are refined, structural relationships are discovered, introduced, made more complex; and psychological complexities come to birth with the immersion of the key idea into the world of circumstance and specific context. Dostoevsky seems to know what he is going to say in the notes, but he doesn't know everything that is implied, both in form and content, by what he knows.

Sometimes the scene is rendered almost as fully in the notes as in the novel, so that the change is not one of amplification of detail or circumstance (the usual change), but the discovery, refinement, and adjustment of psychological insight. Things that are not clear to Dostoevsky when he jots down the notes become clear by the time he writes the finished version. In Book IV, chapter XV, "A laceration in a Drawing Room," where Ivan bids Katerina good-bye in Alyosha's presence, Ivan recognizes, both in notes and in novel, that Katerina's love is false, that it is self-serving and that it sustains the image she has of herself as virtuous and self-sacrificial. The notes even tell us that Katerina loves Dmitri because he had hurt her. In the notes we have the following:

> "[And all your life, your whole life, you are going to convince yourself that you love him] and only him since he is the one that hurt you, and in that way you can contemplate your feat of remaining faithful to him, as I have already told you, and consequently you love only yourself."

The novel tells us all of this but it also tells us that Katerina seeks what hurts her and supports her flattering image of herself. She is not the passive sufferer of the bruising relations. In the novel we have the following:

> "You love him just as he is; you love him for insulting you. If he reformed, you'd give him up at once and cease to love him. But you need him so as to contemplate continually your heroic fidelity and to reproach him for infidelity."

In both notes and novel Katerina contemplates her fidelity, but in the novel she reproaches Dmitri for his infidelity. Katerina needs a Dmitri who is abased so as to ensure her own elevation, a Dmitri mired in vice so that her virtue will shine all the more. In the process of writing between the notes and the novel, Dostoevsky saw more and more clearly the active role that Katerina played in pursuing and arranging the drama of hurt and self-hurt.

Although most of the differences between notes and novel are those of qualifications, refinement and specification of content first expressed abstractly, some of the changes are those of content itself. Dostoevsky changed his mind about some things, decided to omit some items and to include others. Such distinct changes tend to be far fewer than in the other notebooks, but many of them are to be found in the crucial chapters of Book V. In Book V Ivan tells Alyosha that he is not revolting against God, but only against his world. One suspects that the distinction is unimportant and only an equivocation of the intellect. The equivocation is not in the notes, where Ivan says: "I would like to destroy completely the idea of God." In the notes, too, Dostoevsky seems to try to find more of the Karamazov insect in Ivan. When Ivan speaks of the power of life and his own attachment to life, the attachment is entertained in the notes as one of "beastly voluptuousness," but in the novel it is softened to aesthetic sensuousness, that is, to "the sticky green leaves." Dostoevsky was apparently trying to find some sensuous bond between father and son: it is strong in Dmitri and nascent in Alyosha but absent in Ivan. Dostoevsky gave up the temptation to link Ivan to Fyodor's "beastly voluptuousness" and wisely decided to reserve for him an "intellectual voluptuousness."

The notes for the "Legend of the Grand Inquisitor" are fuller than those for many other scenes, and although the general conception in notes and novel is the same, some significant differences are apparent. We know, of course, that Ivan is on the side of the Grand Inquisitor, but in the novel Dostoevsky made this point deliberately ambiguous, even though Ivan is unambiguously asked by Alyosha. In the novel, we have the following:

> "The kiss glows in his heart, but the old man adheres to his idea."
> "And you with him, you too?" cried Alyosha mournfully.
> Ivan laughed.
> "Why, it's all nonsense, Alyosha. It's only a senseless poem of a senseless student."

But in the notes Ivan's answer is simple, direct, and unambiguous: "The old man remains convinced as before. And you? I am with the old man's idea because he loves humanity more."

In both notes and novel the Grand Inquisitor, partly directly and partly by implication, charges Christ with acting to increase the torment of man, acting as if he didn't love man. The aggression against Christ in the final version is muted, but in the notes it is stated bluntly: "I have only one word to say to you that you have been disgorged by hell and are a heretic, and that the very people who fell down before you will rake up the coals tomorrow." Even more the Grand Inquisitor in the notes states bluntly that Christ is not innocent but guilty: "They sing of you as Alone without sin, but I say to you that you are alone guilty." Finally, Alyosha makes the point in the final version that the Grand Inquisitor does not believe in God, but in the notes Dostoevsky emphasizes the fact that there is no immortality and that the followers of Christ and even Christ himself found nothing after the grave: "that those who suffer his cross will not find anything that had been promised exactly as he himself had not found anything after his cross." There seems to be little doubt that some of these statements were eliminated or changed because of their shocking anti-Orthodox and anti-Christian character.

In the scene between Ivan and Smerdiakov that follows the "Legend of the Grand Inquisitor," Ivan is less obtuse about his own motives in the notes than he is in the novel. One is hard put to believe that Ivan failed to understand the meaning of Smerdiakov's insinuations and to see his own part in the plan to murder his father. Dostoevsky was probably intent on showing the self-deception the intellect may indulge in if the emotional provocation is great enough. In the novel on the eve of his departure Ivan's sense of guilt expresses itself as a feeling of distaste and discomfort, but in the notes the same scene is rendered as follows:

> And after at night, he leaps up: Does he think, scoundrel, that I will like seeing my father murdered? Yes, that's exactly what he thinks!

For a novel as great as *The Brothers Karamazov* one would wish for notes fuller and more varied than these: large portions of the novel find no reflections in the notes: Dmitri's near-murder and escape from the Karamazov garden find no rendering in the notes; Ivan's chronicle of horrors against children is preserved in a few fragmentary phrases; nothing of Dmitri's reminiscence of his first meeting alone with Katerina is given. On the other hand Smerdiakov's fall into the cellar and his feigned fit, as well as the care given to him, are rendered in more fullness than in the novel. The carousing at Mokroe and the relations with the Poles is repetitiously rendered and indeed Dostoevsky spends a number of pages practicing Polish phrases, not always with the greatest success. The trial too has been preserved quite fully in the notes. One would wish these notes fuller and more representative of the different stages of creation. Yet, that aside, they show us—when taken along with the notes to the other four major novels—a different aspect of Dostoevsky's creative process, and permit us to observe and measure the turns of his craft as he searches for specificity and subtlety, and the refinements of psychological, philosophical, and structural detail.

The notes will serve as a reminder, perhaps, that the Dostoevsky of the magnificent conceptions, Miltonic imaginings, and Dantesque visions was also a writer who had to find the mesh of expressive details, without which the imaginings and the visions would never have found their sensuous embodiment and would never have achieved their magnificent effects. We have in many respects a "denuded" novel in the notes, and the interest in the notes may consist in reminding us how much the details and complexities that Dostoevsky found between notes and novel added to the conceptions and imaginings. It is clear from these notes and from those of the other volumes that Dostoevsky's imagination ran from large conceptions to minute elaboration, from abstract to concrete, plan to realization. Details did not lead him to his conceptions, but his ideas led him to his details. We know from the testimony of other writers that it is not always like that; that is, it is the experience of many writers to find their way to the whole by way of the part. Regardless of the path and the direction each writer must finally make or break himself, no matter how grand the conception, on the rocks and splinters of the minutiae of craft. These notes, more than the others, show us Dostoevsky's handling of craft and circumstance.

IV

This is a translation of A. S. Dolinin's edition of the notebooks for *The Brothers Karamazov* as contained in his *F. M. Dostoevsky, materialy i issledovaniia* (Leningrad, 1935). The Russian edition has been followed in all essential respects; as in the Russian, the notes for the twelve books of the novel have been divided into ten sections. I have added a short introduction to each section.

These editorial devices have been used in the preparation of the text: crossed-out words are crossed out in the text; notes written in the margins, between and above lines and in different ink, are enclosed in square brackets; a few notes that do not fit into the context but appear on the notebook page are included in the footnotes; insertions by the editor are enclosed in angle brackets; and incomplete words or sentences are followed by three spaced dots in angle brackets. Italics, capitalizations, parentheses, and unspaced dots are Dostoevsky's. Numbers on the left-hand margin refer to the numeration of the original notebook pages. Dots between parentheses, such as (. .), refer to undecipherable words; one dot is used for each word. Dates with a slanted line between two sets of numbers, as 3/15 June, refer to the twelve-day difference in time between the nineteenth-century Russian calendar and the Western calendar. Names have been spelled out in full, and obvious oversights such as the failure to supply end parentheses have been rectified. Punctuation, except for changes necessary to conform to English convention, has been kept as in the Russian: omissions of end periods, erratic capitalizations within the lines, commas instead of semicolons, and other unconventional usages have been retained in this translation. No effort has been made to translate the dash as an introduction to a direct quotation into conventional English quotation marks. Dostoevsky uses the dash indiscriminately: sometimes to introduce what are obvious instances of direct discourse; sometimes to introduce what is obviously not direct discourse; sometimes at the beginning of a phrase and sometimes at the end. I felt that interpretation beyond permitted limits would be necessary to translate the dashes into what is quoted and what is not quoted, and I therefore reproduced all the dashes as dashes. Dostoevsky's use of a line between blocks of notes has been rendered in this translation by extra space between such blocks of notes. Finally, I have made a number of comparisons in the footnotes between the version in the notes and the version in the finished novel itself; in all such cases I have used Constance Garnett's translation.

EDWARD WASIOLEK

Books One and Two

Dostoevsky began serious work on *The Brothers Karamazov* in July 1878, but as late as 27 August, he complained to Putsykovich: "I'm working on the novel, but the thing is going slowly, I've only just begun." He finished the first two books, the notes of which follow in this section, in the fall of 1878 and they were published in the January issue of *The Russian Messenger* in 1879.

Most of the notes in this section correspond fairly closely to what we find in the final version, that is, the expository background of the Karamazov past that we are given in Book I and the account of the meeting of the Karamazovs in the Elder's cell that we are given in Book II. The caption "Book Three" appears in the notes, but the notes that follow refer clearly to Book II of the final version. We are told about Alyosha's decision and motivations for entering the holy order, about Dmitri's return to the town to clear up the matter of his inheritance, about Ivan's beliefs, and something about Fyodor's character. In the notes about the cell meeting we have remarks about Ivan's article, about the law of "all is permitted," Miusov's envious pettiness, and references to Fyodor's mock humility before the Elder and his taunting rivalry with his eldest son. The important ideas and situations of the final version are all present in the notes.

What is missing in these notes is the descriptive, dramatic, and situational density that we have in the final version. Many important scenes and dialogues are sketched here in single words or in a few phrases. Important ideas and generalizations such as the idea of "all is permitted," or the generalization about no law of nature compels one to love one's fellow man are unattached to particular persons, or if attached, not concretized in any specific context. Somewhere between these notes and the final version, all the work of dramatic context, tone, gesture, voice, and manifold structural relationships had to be worked out. The statement that there is no law of nature forcing men to love each other is attributed to Ivan in the final version by Miusov;

in the notes this sentiment is not attached at first to anyone, and then it is given to the "murderer." The Elder's comments to Ivan in the notes about the fact that he must be blessed or unhappy, depending on whether he believes or does not believe in God, is stripped of the psychological complexity with which the Elder probes Ivan's spiritual state in the final version, and stripped too of the mixed respect and irony with which Ivan listens to the Elder. The very schematic, abstract, disembodied, and undramatic notes tell us something about Dostoevsky's craft. Ideas—generalized and disembodied—first surged into his creative brain and issue onto his pen, and the ideas bring in their train the dramatic situations and structural refinements.

Although the differences between notes and novel are primarily differences between abstractions and dramatic realizations, there are a few substantive differences. The principal characters are called by different names, and the first notes, too, have nothing to do with Books I and II. They are a series of reminders Dostoevsky gives himself to check on certain things that he will use in the novel: about whether it is possible to lie under the rails when a railway car passes over (something that Kolia Krasotkin narrates in Book X), about whether a prisoner can marry (an anticipation of Dmitri's concern near the end of the novel), and about various facts and queries concerning children.

Memento (about the novel)   <1>
——Find out whether it is possible to lie between the rails under a railway car when it passes over you at full speed.[1]

——Find out whether the wife *of a prisoner* can marry someone else immediately.[2]

——Does the Idiot[3] have the right to take care of such a horde of adopted kids, to have a school, etc.

---

[1] Kolia Krasotkin narrates this in Book X, "The Boys," which was published two years later in the April (1880) issue of *The Russian Messenger.*
[2] This is a reference to Dmitri's situation and query at the very end of the novel.
[3] Alyosha is called "the Idiot" here and in some of the other notes.

———Find out about child labor in factories.

———About high schools. Visit some high schools.[4]

———Find out whether it is possible for a young man of a noble family and a property owner, to retire to a monastery for a number of years (even if it were at his uncle's) as a novice? (N.B. About Philaret whose body began to stink.)[5]
———In an orphanage.

———At Bychkov's.
———At Alexander Nikolaevich's.
———At Mikhail Nikolaevich's (foundling home).[6]

With Bergman.
———About Pestalozzi, about Fröbel.[7] Leo Tolstoy's article about contemporary school education in *The Fatherland Notes* (75 or 74).

———Walk along the Nevsky Prospect on crutches. And if one were to knock a crutch away, what kind of trial would follow and how and where.

To take part in an excursion à la Fröbel. Look up *The New Times,* Wednesday, 12 April, No. 762.

THE FIRST BOOK
<2>   N.B. Look to see if *everything* is there? The straightforwardness of youth.

---

[4] In preparing to write *The Brothers Karamazov* Dostoevsky visited a number of schools and requested information from friends and school officials about conditions in schools and foundling homes.

[5] This is a reference to the putrefaction of Father Zossima's body in the first chapter of Book VII. This book was published in *The Russian Messenger* in September 1879.

[6] A record of a visit by Dostoevsky to a foundling home is contained in the January (1876) issue of *The Diary of a Writer* (chap. I, iii).

[7] Friedrich Fröbel (1782–1852), important German educator. He developed a system of preschool training for children, which was widely experimented with in various countries including Russia. A Fröbel institute for such training was begun in St. Petersburg in 1871. The theory and program of training consisted of teaching preschool children by taking advantage of their interest in games, songs, gymnastics, and sensory perception.

Perhaps that power and glory had an effect on his young imagination.[8]

——He saw how especially old women and a noisy throng flocked around.

And perhaps the little old man had a strong effect on him then with some special qualities of his soul, in any event he attached himself to him wholeheartedly.

——Civil servant.[9]

He believed in the flying coffin.[10] This could not <. . .>

1, 2, 3

How do you dare do such things?

N.B. 1) And it was at that time that the meeting of the three brothers was to take place.

[2 The arrival of his brothers seems to have had a great influence on Alyosha. He made friends with Dmitri, he studies Ivan.]

Two acquaintances:—*the seminarist* and the dreamer.[11]

Alyosha looks on, but is excited more than anything by the idea of the fame of the Elder.

He lived in the Elder's cell; the Elder was very good to him.

Alyosha could leave the monastery. He lived in a cell and wore a cassock, but he did not share the blessings of the monastery.

Description of the hermitage, flowers (slightly)

2) [N.B.] There were also monks in the monastery who were enemies of the Elder, but there weren't many of them.——They kept quiet, suppressing their hate, even though they were important people. One was an ascetic,[12] another somewhat simpleminded, but the majority were on his side. There were some so fanatic that they foresaw an imminent death. He believed also, as he did in the coffin. Many honestly considered him to be a saint, not Alyosha alone, they waited for his death and believed it would be holy. (Silent waiting)

---

[8] Alyosha's sudden and instinctive decision to become a monk is narrated in Book I, chap. V. The next four notes concern themselves with Alyosha's motivations and decision to follow in the footsteps of Father Zossima.

[9] This is a reference in all probability to Father Zossima's past, which is narrated in Book VI.

[10] A legend about a novice who failed to obey the command of his Elder. When he died his coffin—despite a martyr's death—was cast forth from the church three times. The legend is narrated in Book I, chap. V.

[11] Probably a reference to Rakitin and Kalganov.

[12] Probably a reference to Father Ferapont.

Touch on it slightly, only a word. They said that Makarii sees by the eyes.[13]

Fame

<3>　Perhaps a four-year-old memory, ray of sunlight, pulpit and mother.[14]

Perhaps reading from the Bible

Solitude, but love, virtue

Beauty of the hermitage, singing, but assuredly the Elder,

honesty of the generation. Hero from the new generation.

He wanted to and did it—

——moving, but not bizarre.

The Elders.

——Order.

Here 1.

Prefatory Chapter

I said that I wouldn't go into details—But these are basic and fundamental traits.

Chapter—why in the monastery?

Is he a mystic—never

A fanatic—not at all.

The oldest, Dmitri, 27—the other 23 and Aleksey is only 20. He was not at all a fanatic. He appeared a year before [but kind of wildly —with a strange goal, which he did not hide.] The father came back from Odessa about that time. But he came to his father without having finished his studies. He did not come because he had no place to live

---

[13] A reference to Father Zossima, who was able to discern character by one's eyes.

[14] Compare with the following from Book I, chap. IV of the final version: "I have mentioned already, by the way, that though he lost his mother in his fourth year he remembered her all his life—her face, her caresses, 'as though she stood living before me.' Such memories may persist, as every one knows, from an even earlier age, even from two years old, but scarcely standing out through a whole lifetime like spots of light out of darkness, like a corner torn out of a huge picture, which has all faded and disappeared except that fragment. This is how it was with him. He remembered one still summer evening, an open window, the slanting rays of the setting sun (that he recalled most vividly of all); in a corner of the room the holy image, before it a lighted lamp, and on her knees before the image his mother, sobbing hysterically with cries and moans, snatching him up in both arms, squeezing him close till it hurt, and praying for him to the Mother of God, holding him out in both arms to the image as though to put him under the Mother's protection . . . and suddenly a nurse runs in and snatches him from her in terror."

—they liked him there— He came to save the grave of his mother.—
At his father's
[sickness]
[Painful legs Red cheeks.—]
He chattered about all kinds of nonsense and about the feminine sex. About that, however.

Here 2. I. I must say that once he gave himself, he believed fully, despite the fact that he was very intelligent.
prepersonalities.[15]
a secondary matter, most important—the Elder.
Aleksey   money.
Harder than anything is to say something about my hero Aleksey by narration—preface. Before bringing him onto the scene, but I repeat that I can't possibly start anything without that, but I will limit myself to the main points.—
His father did not shock him, but he walked away from the orgies in silence.
Since (.) he was an enemy
At first he reproached <his father> the Father began to embrace him—
He believed as a realist. Someone like him, once he believes, believes completely, irrevocably.
A dreamer ~~and a poet~~ will believe conditionally, a la Luther. But someone like him will not only be troubled by a miracle, but will himself want a miracle.

He understood that knowledge and faith are different and contradictory, that if there are other worlds and if it is true that man is immortal, that is, if man himself comes from other worlds, then there is a tie with these other worlds.[16] There is such a thing as a miracle.

---

[15] A reference in all probability to the theories of Nicholas Fyodorov (1828–1903) whom Dostoevsky knew and to whose theories he was attracted. The most extraordinary of Fydorov's theories was the belief that one's ancestors, "the fathers," could with faith be resurrected!

[16] Compare with the final version (Book VI, chap. III): "Much on earth is hidden from us, but to make up for that we have been given a precious mystic sense of our living bond with the other world, with the higher heavenly world, and the roots of our thoughts and feelings are not here but in other worlds. That is why the philosophers say that we cannot apprehend the reality of things on earth."

And he thirsted for a miracle. But here the Elder and his saintliness, the holy relic.

But he understood, comprehended at least, or felt it, even if <...>

<4> 2. There is much in the world that is incomprehensible, if there are no miracles.

Why shouldn't there be miracles, but then the Elder
Lady, how do you have the audacity to do such things.
The flying coffin:
The institution of the Elders, the monk Parfenii
The monks 2 parties.
The bishop encouraged the institution of the Elders.

HE STILL HAD NOT COME TO KNOW HIS BROTHERS.
MY QUIET BOY.

N.B.

1. If there is a tie with another world, then it is clear that it may and even ought to manifest itself *at times* by unusual facts, which do not take place only on earth.

[The lack of faith of people did not trouble him at all; such people do not believe in immortality and in another life, and consequently cannot believe in miracles, because everything for them is already finished on earth.]

And as for so-called scientific proofs, he did not believe in them, and was right in not believing them, even though he had not finished his studies, it was impossible to disprove matters, which by their essence were not of this world, by knowledge which was of this world. In a word, he was at that time calm and firm as a rock.

cheek.

beautiful.

a mystic.

realism.

a miracle—Foma wanted to believe, and he believed.

I have already said that the love of humanity <was to be found> on this path, on the path of the Elder—

——for the saintly one.

He waited for miracles and has even seen them already.

Lady—you have the audacity.

About the Elder. The institution of the Elders at Optina, old women came on their knees.

Disputes, Monseigneur.

He was a civil servant, sick.

The Elder arranged the day of the meeting, he was interested very much in seeing what state the Elder would be in—

He considered him to be a saint, and he looked forward to miracles. He was a sick man.

The flying coffin.[17]

He would go out.

He came to know his brothers Dmitri and Ivan—and it was at that time that the meeting was arranged. It happened that Miusov *l'ombre d'un carosse*.[18]

Well, go forth my angel and find your way to the truth, and come back to tell us. It will be easier to die, you know that <...> And it will be a pity. Truly, it will be a pity that it's easier.

BECAUSE LOVE WILL RARELY LIMIT ITSELF ONLY TO PITY.

It seems to me that I am constantly being taken for a fool, and because of that I actually become a fool, I am not afraid of your opinions! That's why I'm a fool—from spite and defiance.[19] I am rowdy because of a lack of trust.

It was difficult to decide if he were fooling, or if he actually was depreciating himself.

<THE SECOND BOOK>

The highest beauty is not external, but internal (see Goethe, 2d part of Faust).[20]

<5>

---

[17] See n. 10 of this section.

[18] French: "the shadow of a carriage." Fyodor Karamazov quotes this in Book I, chap. IV, where he discusses whether or not there are real hooks in the other world. This verse comes from a parody of the sixth book of the *Aeneid* by Charles Perrault (1628–1703) with the help of his brothers. This verse was quoted by Voltaire, where Dostoevsky probably learned it.

[19] Compare with the following from Book II, chap. II of the final version: "Indeed, I always feel when I meet people that I am lower than all, and that they all take me for a buffoon. So I say, 'Let me really play the buffoon. I am not afraid of your opinion, for you are every one of you worse than I am.' That is why I am a buffoon. It is from shame, great Elder, from shame; it's simply oversensitiveness that makes me rowdy. If I had only been sure that every one would accept me as the kindest and wisest of men, oh, Lord, what a good man I should have been then!"

[20] Apparently a beauty that Alyosha was supposed to embody. The reference does not appear in the final version.

The idiot explains to the children the position of mankind in the tenth century (Taine).[21]

——he explains *The Funeral Feast* to the children: the evil will have an evil end.

——he explains the devil (Job's prologue)

He explains the Temptation in the Desert.

——he explains the socialism which is rising, new people. Maxime du Camp,[22] the negative, not the *positive*, Russia is the positive— Christians.

——The landowner:[23] What must I do in order to achieve salvation? (on his knees). What is written in the law, how do you read it?

The Elder: most important, do not lie. Do not acquire property, love (Damaskina, Sirina).

——He raises his nose, he says, looks at me insolently, and insults me.—

At the father superior's...she loved much. Christ did not talk about that kind of love, not about that kind. And if he talked of it, he still talked of another kind.[24] Because these words are more beautiful, more seductive...

I am a knight, I am the knight of honor[25]

---

[21] Dostoevsky was reading Taine in the summer of 1878. In a letter to A. P. Filosofa on 8 May 1878 he wrote: "I'm occupied from morning to night . . . I can't read any more here in Petersburg and I'm not going to. . . . I'll take Taine with me until September." Dostoevsky was probably reading Taine's *Les origines de la France contemporaine;* the first part of *L'Ancien regime* came out in 1876.

[22] Maxime du Camp (1872–1894), friend of Flaubert and member of the Academy, poet and novelist. He published a book on the Paris commune *Convulsions de Paris* in 1878 in which he criticized the communards very sharply.

[23] Reference to Fyodor Karamazov.

[24] In Book II, chap. VI of the final version, Fyodor Karamazov defends Grushenka in this way: "That 'creature,' that 'woman of loose behavior,' is perhaps holier than you are yourselves, you monks who are seeking salvation! She fell perhaps in her youth, ruined by her environment. But she loved much, and Christ himself forgave the woman 'who loved much.'" Father Iosif answers him in the following manner: "It was not for such love Christ forgave her."

[25] This phrase is used several times in the final version. Fyodor Karamazov refers to Father Zossima as *un chevalier parfait,* talks of himself in the same way, and Mitia refers to himself as a knight of honor late in the novel.

He knows, however, that no one has insulted him, but he feels insulted to the point of savoring the insult.

The word is expressed by words. Find out about it.   <6>

——*The New Times,* 7 September, Thursday, No. 907.
Among the newspapers and journals, the news about the Archimandrite, who (asked) in his last testament that his body be thrown to the dogs on the crossroads as punishment for the sin of drunkenness, which he could not cure himself of.

——Ilinsky[26] in his cell says that he will not permit them to lecture him aloud about the child ~~and for~~ the orgy in town.

After the meeting in the cell, the landowner wants a church service performed.

N.B. Ilinsky is still counting on receiving something from the inheritance. Most important he needs as quickly as possible 3,000 because he has kept such a sum from his fiancée. In the evening, in the first part, after the scene in the cell. Ilinsky then appears at his father's with the Idiot and proposes a settlement for 3,000. You have them now after all. And then the fight.

——The money is in the package: for my little chicken.
——In love like a dog.
——They think I hid my money in my boots—
——She arose more mad than a dog.
——The ass's ear.
——Isaac the Syrian (Seminarian)
——Spontaneous love. (the little boy and the drowning man).
——The resurrection of one's ancestors.[27] The landowner about Ilinsky: Such a one will not only not resurrect them, but will make it worse for them. Ilinsky gets up: [a shameless comedy.]
——Everything is permitted.
——I am a passionate man.

---

[26] A nobleman in Dostoevsky's *Memoirs from the House of the Dead* who was —like Dmitri—unjustly accused of killing his father. Dmitri is called Ilinsky from time to time, even after he receives his real name.
[27] See n. 15 of this section.

——Grattez le Russe trouverez le tartare.[28]

——La Russie se recueille.[29]

——Take away the stone, a 100 rubles.[30]

——Construct in plaster foot bridges in Germany, 100.

——A certain very important personage in the government. I say, mon cher. And then a most important government personage enters.

——Diderot and Platon. The fool says in his heart that there is no God.[31] He bowed down.

Cement together.

Satisfied with his chapter.

Dmitri Fyodorovich, from now on keep out of my sight!

Yes, I am ready to call you out for a duel.

Ilinsky says to him: You fool, I curse you.

At the Elder's: And Christ forgave her for loving much. She is better than you. As for you: You make a show of your cross.

In the Bible: give away to the poor. But even though we don't give to the poor, still we respect them.

In the evening to the murderer:[32] You know, my friend, I have come to have doubts in something; very simply Christ was an ordinary person, like everyone, but he was virtuous. And he accomplished all that (see △).[33]

---

[28] French: "Scratch a Russian and you will find a Tartar."

[29] French: "Russia draws back upon itself."

[30] The anecdote about how a huge rock is disposed of by digging a hole beside it is narrated by the Youth's landlord in Part II, chap. I of *A Raw Youth*.

[31] Compare Fyodor Karamazov's statement to the Elder Zossima in Book II, chap. II of the final version: "Did you ever hear, most Holy Father, how Diderot went to see the Metropolitan Platon, in the time of the Empress Catherine. He went in and said straight out, 'There is no God.' To which the great Bishop lifted up his finger and answered, 'The fool has said in his heart there is no God.' And he fell down at his feet on the spot. 'I believe,' he cried, 'and will be christened.' And so he was." Denis Diderot (1713–1784) was one of the most important representatives of the French enlightenment, a champion of materialism and realism. Dostoevsky read him in the winter of 1869, and Diderot's narrative manner was in some respects congenial to Dostoevsky. Diderot visited Russia in 1773 and had some influence on Catherine II in persuading her to adopt some progressive reforms. The anecdote about Diderot and Platon is untrue, although it was spread about by some of his enemies.

[32] Reference to Ivan.

[33] Dostoevsky recalled in *The Diary of a Writer* a conversation he had with Belinsky in the 1840s on the subject of Christ and revolution. Belinsky said: "Admit that your Christ, if he had been born in our times, would be one of the

The Idiot received a letter from the fiancée[34] in which she asks him   <7>
to come to see her.—

"The angels of God at God's side. Do not lie."

——*Ci git Piron, qui ne fut rien, pas meme academicien.*[35]

——*Un chevalier d'honneur.*[36]

——Karl Moor and Franz Moor.

Iliusha.[37] I will curse you. You know what a father's curse means.
Lettre de cachet.[38]

Prologue according to the Damascan. Dreams of riches. The devil.

——Lady. Lyosha. *They are too audacious.* The lady and the
daughter. About the fact that she believes, but only a little. A *peasant
woman.* Give 60 k. to someone who is poorer than I . . . [To someone
poorer than I. Thank you mother.]

——The old man has the habit of suddenly beginning to bow down.
on his knees: forgive me . . .

——A word about the fact that Ilinsky had a fight and dragged the
Captain around by the beard.

——Ilinsky helped his brother when he was still at the University.[39]

——A place of fornication. It is very pleasant at times to take
offense.

——The old man has a sick heart.

Job loved other children (the Lady). *The transfer* of love.[40] He did
not forget the others. The faith that we will live again and will discover each other once again in general harmony.

——Revolution never had any effect, except to kill love (better
rights).

——*The resurrection of our ancestors* depends on us.[41]

---

most insignificant and ordinary of people." "No, No!" said Belinsky's friend, "if
Christ were to appear today, he would join the movement and become its leader."
"Yes, yes," Belinsky agreed with astonishing rapidity, "he would do exactly that,
would become a socialist and would follow them." This is narrated in *The Diary
of a Writer*, "Old People," 1873, *The Citizen*, No. 1.

[34] A reference to Katerina Ivanovna.

[35] French: "Here lies Piron who amounted to nothing, not even to an aca-
demician." From the epitaph of the French poet Alexis Piron (1689–1773), author
of many satires, songs, and monologues. French spelling retained as in notebook.

[36] French: "a knight of honor."

[37] Reference to Mitia.

[38] French: "letter under the king's private seal."

[39] This fact does not appear in the final version.

[40] The transfer of love is part of Fyodorov's thinking in his theory of the resurrection of one's ancestors. See n. 15 of this section.

[41] See n. 15 of this section.

About obligations to one's kin. The Elder says that God gave us kin so as to learn to love by their example. *Those who love men in general hate men in particular.*

If there were only intelligence in the world, then nothing would exist.[42]

From Isaac Sirin (the seminarian)

Regierender Graf von Moor.

The Elder was apparently an educated man—was and still is now.

Absentmindedness. The anecdote. Speak of the devil, and he appears. Napravnik.[43]

Rowdiness. A compromising remark given in advance (about the murder of the father).

The educated one[44] about the fact that there is no reason why one should do good.

He grovels on the ground: "I will not leave until I am forgiven." "Do not lie."

——Precision is the virtue of kings.

A pity if nothing more were to occur on this earth. But [perhaps it would be better].

——It is more probable that there will be nothing else.

——Cigars. Here they are, but I'm not going to smoke, out of respect.

——About divorce. Four women. The Mohammedans, better.

——*Humble et hautain comme tous les fanatiques* (V. Hugo)[45]

——*L'ame d'un conspirateur, l'ame d'un laquais.*[46]

——Impossible to have turkeys and chickens at Mount Athos.

——A young lady with her mother, not pretty (The Idiot is in love).[47]

——Get the carriage ready. He brings 1,000 rubles.

<8> The educated brother, it seems, was at the Elder's earlier (later).

The cigars. I gave them up, and I don't smoke.

---

[42] One of the devil's pronouncements to Ivan.

[43] A pun that Fyodor Karamazov makes on the word *izpravnik* (captain of police) in Book II, chap. II.

[44] Refers to Ivan.

[45] French: "Humble and haughty like all the fanatics." This is from Victor Hugo's *Les Miserables* (Part I, Book 5, chap. 5).

[46] French: "the soul of a conspirator, the soul of a lackey." This quotation is from Hugo's *Ruy Blas,* Act 4, scene 3.

[47] This is a reference to the love between Lise and Alyosha.

Notebook Page 8. A fairly neat, evenly spaced page, consisting of disparate comments neatly separated by horizontal lines, represented in the English text by spacing. One quarter from the bottom one will see in large letters the Russian word VAZHNEISHEE, *translated in the English text as* MOST IMPORTANT.

——He asked, during confession, about ranks.

(look up No. 0 △)

——I am a knight of honor.

——I can still conquer any one of them.[48]

Look up No. 0_2, 0_3, No. 0_1

Why do you hate him?

I once did something nasty to him—that's why I hate him.

A touchy woman.

——No. 0. The Elder talks about the prologue, about money-grubbing, and about the person.

——And Nadezhda Ivanovna—she is the progeny of hell.

——One has the heart of Alexander the Great, and the other of a faithful little dog.

——Man is the embodiment of the word. He appeared to know and to speak.

——Old maid (look up No. 0_5)

——No. 0_6

——Look, at the old Man's in the Cell no. 0_7

No. 0_8 Conversations about murderers. Are you acquainted with the murder of von Sohn?[49]

——The boy taught him to put a pin in the bread. For Zhuchka.[50]

No. 0_9, No.$_{10}$—absolutely.

---

[48] This is probably a reference to Fyodor Karamazov's boasting about his success with women.

[49] A real person, the chief of a band of murderers. Dostoevsky learned about him in connection with the von Sohn affair. Von Sohn was lured into a dive on the pretext of being provided with a fifteen-year-old girl. He was robbed and murdered by a gang headed by Maxim Ivanov on 18 November 1869. His body was stuffed into a trunk and sent to Moscow. The baggage ticket was burned. Further murders were planned, but one of the gang confessed and the first murder was discovered.

[50] Reference to the incident that is found in Book X, "The Boys." Dostoevsky originally planned to have the children play an important role in the opening chapters.

——Blessed is the womb that carried you and the breasts that fed you.

[Fyodor Pavlovich calls the landowner Markov, von Sohn,[51] a secret

V. Sohn.]

——MOST IMPORTANT. [Miusov] The landowner quotes from the Bible and is coarsely wrong. Miusov corrects him and he makes even worse errors. Even the educated one makes mistakes. No one knows the Bible. Blessed is the womb that has borne you, said Christ. Christ did not say that, etc.

——The Elder says: There was a learned professor (Vagner)[52] From the Bible "the master praised a clever and thieving steward." How is that possible. I don't understand.

——The Elder, absolutely. But perhaps you yourself did not believe in what you were writing.

——I am troubling you with my liveliness.   <9>
——Oh do not worry and do not be embarrassed, behave as you would at home that will be all the better for me, I will see how you live

Alyosha, don't you dare go to the Monastery! I will curse you!

Ivan Fyodorovich rejected von Sohn

——The old man quieted down suddenly—

——If you had told me before, I would have quieted down long before this, but I thought that you were amused, that's why I made up all this.

At the Kazatyevskaya station of the Myashskaya railroad.

That is plunged in the darkness of ignorance.

The old man—You take a lot, they say

——You have set up quite a number of taverns—

---

[51] See n. 49.

[52] Nikolay Petrovich Vagner (1829–1907), celebrated Russian zoologist and writer of children's stories. Vagner was particularly known for a collection of children's stories, *Skazki Kota Murlyki* (1872). He also wrote a number of articles on spiritualism, and since Dostoevsky was interested in this problem, the reference may be to his work on that subject.

Notebook Page 9. A page of notes consisting entirely of marginal entries arranged in a roughly circular order. As is characteristic, the variants are geometrically situated on the page. Note numbers at the bottom of the page.

The railway car caught fire in the presence of your wives and unmarried daughters (no, there were still no daughters, but there could be.) He grabs him by his mug, by his mug, straight by his mug. Inspiration. A notebook. Who are you? Governmental. The state secretary Prince Murusov got off at the second station. The trip went well.

I don't need any proofs, but I will do it in an administrative way.

He pretended to be Turgenev once.

——Excellent. Sania Kalganov yelled.

Do not lie—

Precisely, permit me to tell you how lying is sometimes really useful—

Otherwise, tell me how I am to defend myself, please

[Little remarks Why does the new year always come on 1 January?   <10:
Answer: Because January is the first month of the year, and December is the last month of the year.]

——They climb down from the porch, and we—there we are.

——And he hits the accursed neck with his sacred fist.

——There was in that talk, so to speak, *plus de noblesse que de sincerité*[53] (and the opposite happens too: *plus de sincerité que de noblesse*).

Smerdiakov He struck her with the knife, she yelled and tried to grab the knife.

[Why live if not for one's pride]

[Mediums][54]

[The Russian language for them is indecent. For him.]

[——This coarse vulgar language (sermons)]

[——Our rotten human race.]

---

[53] French: "more nobility than sincerity" and "more sincerity than nobility." In Book II, chap. VIII, Fyodor Karamazov says the following: "Miusov, my relation, prefers to have *plus de noblesse que de sincerité* in his words, but I prefer in mine *plus de sincerité que de noblesse,* and—damn the noblesse!"

[54] Dostoevsky took an active interest in spiritualism, although rejecting it finally. See an article on spiritualism in the April (1876) issue of *The Diary of a Writer,* chap. II, iii.

[*The carriage driver says:* it is a pleasure to travel with a good gentleman.]

And they took a hundred for a hundred in this matter.
Here is a three-ruble note for you—

Smerdiakov Stinking Liza, ~~small~~ miniscule body, only two arshins, two vershkovs scarcely)

[And so your friend will remain without your head, and you will remain with ~~your~~ head. He was all a-tremble, and I chased him away.]

[Whoever wants to change the head of one friend for another must still pay 10 rubles each time.]

[And he placed his head down with great care and said to his friend: to lie down. And his friend ~~he~~ looked and trembling all over said: I am very afraid Karl Ivanych. Then for a long minute I stared ~~angrily~~ at him and said: "You betrayed your friend." And he said to me: because I'm very afraid Karl Ivanych, and I said <. . .>]

<11> ——Smerdiakov. He fell in love with a slut and was lost by that act.
[And here, the entire lack of restraint of our generals. . etc.]
[She will give something.]

[The Turk, the Persian, Prussian, Frank, and the revengeful Spaniard.]
[Son of Italy and son of knowledge, the German.]
[The son of mercantilism and its merchandise.]
[And enlightenment bringing to all the obliging sun, the Swiss.]
[Before Russia they will rise bowing in series their heads.]
[But Russia hearing their cries will not turn around.]

Smerdiakov. No, I would have kept the woman obedient to me

Book Three

<12> The Elder returns to the cell. The conversation continues without so much as an interruption.
~~The others~~ tell the old man the *theme:* Is there anything on earth that would force man to love humanity?

Or:

Is there such a law of nature that one must love humanity?

——[That is a law of God. There is no such law of nature, right?]

He (the murderer) affirms that there is no such law, and that one loves only because of faith in immortality ~~?~~

The Elder—If you believe that, you are blessed or very unhappy.

The murderer:—Why unhappy?

The Elder:—In case you yourself do not believe in immortality.

The Murderer:—Yes, you have guessed it.

——You haven't settled this question for yourself, and that is why you are miserable.

Ilinsky enters, *bows*—

——Miusov. I disagree most intensely. Love for humanity lies within man himself, and a law of nature.—

Everyone is quiet: "No need to exercise any effort," ~~says~~ mumbles ~~the murderer~~ someone

Miusov. In that case, in case there is no immortality.

[——How define where the boundary is?]

[——The limit is when I harm humanity.]

[——But why constrain oneself—]

If only to live more comfortably. If there is no love, one will arrange things according to reason.

——If everything was arranged according to reason, there wouldn't be anything.—

——In that case, you can do whatever you want.—

——Yes.

The landowner.—Teach me to live. What do I have to do to save myself?

——Do not lie." Property. The person—

——Learn to love. Nose.

Beginning with one's kin—

——I know that he will not come to life again. Karl Moor.

If there is no God and ~~love~~ immortality of the soul, then there cannot be any love of mankind.—

Summarium. 2. Miusov You are not joking. . . . in the church. <13>

Judgment.

——This problem is not resolved for you.

——Will it be resolved?

——May God help you (blessed)

——He went up to him and kissed his hand. The Elder arose.
Alyosha.

——Blessed be the womb. The words of Christ.

——And you do not lie.

(The scene outside)

——They returned, a heated argument, the monks and the
seminarian.

——Rousseau, love, society produced from itself, love.

——*The educated one.* Not wanting to. The Elder enters into the
argument.

——Ilinsky enters—impression, bows.

——There is no duty to love and not to do evil.
The Elder. The nose. He drowned himself in the people, the boy—

——The landowner on his knees, to love,
Property, the person, learn to love one's loved ones, relatives.
Ilinsky is against one's loved ones.
A stormy, brief, remark.
The landowner: He won't resurrect his relatives.
Karl Moor, Franz Moor, Regierender Graf von Moor.
An unworthy comedy.—

. . . .
The whore loved much.
And not large crosses.
The Elder arose, church service.

All things and everything in the world are not finished for man,
and yet the meaning of all things on earth are to be found in man.

——The earth ennobles. Only the possession of the earth ennobles.
Without the earth even a millionaire is a proletariat. And what is a
proletariat? So far, only scum. So that he may be more than scum, he
has to be reborn, and only the earth can bring him to rebirth. He has
to become the possessor of the earth.

——For us what falls, lies there. What once falls, then let it lie.

——Our youth looks for truth, and that is the truth, and I have
agreed with this more than once.

[Is the church a joke or not—]

[If it is not a joke, then how can she agree to permit the state <to
reign> side by side with it, because there is much that is pagan which
has remained in the state from pagan Rome, and belongs to the
Christian society.]

<14>   This opinion is founded on the normality of the pagan order and

consequently of all its institutions. And incidentally, the normality of the pagan penal code. State and pagan are all the same. If the church permits pagan judgment, then it denies its own mission. Not by struggle, but as ideal.

——Elements—theological and juridical, hierarchy and bureaucracy.

That such a mixture of elements will be eternal, that *it is impossible* to bring about a normal order, explain it because a lie is at its base.

233 pages. Not a defined position in the state, but containing within itself the whole state, and if this is now impossible, then it ought to be doubtlessly (desirable), the goal of the whole further development of the Christian society.

236 Social unity <not> in the state, but social unity for eliminating the state, for the transformation of the state into it.

Here Miusov objects: A criminal act.

The murderer—not punishment but excommunication.

Lafargue.

The Elder—But that's the way it is. [That's almost the way it is being done now, already.] As disharmonious as both principles may be, the truth ~~sometimes~~ comes out of the clash (which and so forth.)

Question: has the church reached the end of its development as the society of Christ on earth, has it reached its ideal and its final form, or is it continuing to develop in conformity with its heavenly ideal. This is not the dogmatic side of faith that is being considered, but the moral state of man and society at a given moment.

Not a single social unit has the right to take upon itself the power to dispose of the civil and political rights of its members.

The church—a kingdom not of this world.

If it is not of this world, then it cannot exist on earth whatsoever. This is an unworthy play of words for a man of the cloth in the spiritual world. I read the passage of this church personage in his book which you have been discussing, and I was surprised by it. The holy book does not refer to that. One must not play with words like that. Christ came precisely to establish the church on earth. The heavenly kingdom to be sure is in heaven, but one enters it only through the church. Therefore unworthy plays on words and calembours are impossible here. The church is truly a kingdom and ought to be a kingdom and will be one, and I believe it will have its kingdom here on earth, for so it has been promised. However, lazy churches always confuse this point by their calembours, because the calembour is based on the most important words of Christ.

The penal and civil power should not belong to her and are incompatible with her nature as a divine institution and as a union of people united for religious ends. I am not speaking of the position of the clerics in Eilei. . . . I say that if the church, the whole church replaced the state, then there would be no injustice.

Administration of Orthodox confession.

15>   Miusov—that's ultramontanism.

The Elder—Oh, but we don't even have any mountains

The Elder—A blessed idea, if you yourself believe it. [thirst]

Miusov: Why do you think he doesn't believe? He has gone even further than ultramontanism, he believes that there are no reasons to love, and that there can only be one reason, the immortality of the soul.

The Elder raised his eyes to look at him. Truly, that is why you are blessed if you so think.

——The Murderer (he winces, he talks reluctantly).

——Miusov argues heatedly that people will find salvation without religion.

The Elder I do not think so, the love will turn into a torture.

You are either happy or if you don't believe you are suffering. The process is not finished in you.

The Elder gets up and goes to the people. (The whole scene in a gay and joking tone, as if everyone was testing everyone else)—

He returned, argument—the Landowner on his knees.

Teach me to save myself.

Don't lie

Property

love, nose—

He himself—

relatives

that relative—Karl Moor.

Miusov says to the Elder All of you seem to be joking

The Elder with a quiet smile. No, I'm talking seriously, because, thank God, Russia still believes

And yet the church itself alienates, and why does it?

A peasant woman poisoned her husband, forgive, forgive

——Have the children forgiven?

1)

Summarium

——The end of August.

——They arrived together, those and those. Persons—

——To the monastery through the forest

——Despite the fact that it was not Lent, there were many peasant women. One woman with a daughter

——They do not permit individual women to enter the monastery.

——And at Mount Athos there are not even chickens. You know only that.—You know a lot about that.

——But it is a valley of roses here.—To be sure there are not roses. A thousand pounds of cabbage a week.

——A pale monk. The cell. The father superior of the monastery and Makarii, and also a learned monk. The seminarian. The landowner on his knees.

——He went out with Alyosha, sat down, description of the people. Blessing. I believe. Diderot and Platon.

——I am astonished by your abilities—

The landowner I agree. I am lying. *Je suis humble et hautain.*⁵⁵

~~Napravnik~~ The time is right. Mitia is late, not like me, exactness is the politeness of kings.

——But you are not after all a king,—That is right. *Napravnik.* I'm talking through my hat.

——Makarii to Ivan. And you with your article etc.

Miusov had never seen. The landowner, large signs of the cross.

*Napravnik. Ci git Pyron,*⁵⁶ and he was an educated man. It means that now he is not educated. You are hard with everyone but with me you are worse.

N.B. Two insertions in a half page; insertions in a line.

1) You have <understood?> me just now with your remark: "Don't   <16> be ashamed so much of yourself, because everything comes from that." With that remark you have sort of seen right through me and have read what's inside of me. It is precisely in that way that it seems to me when I enter a room full of people, when I enter ~~somewhere~~ that I am baser than all of them, and that they take me for a fool—well, if that's so I will really play the fool [for them], to show them that I'm not afraid of their opinions, because all of them, every single one, is ~~more of a fool~~ baser than I am! That's why I play the fool ~~precisely~~ from shame, fool, great Elder, from shame. I make a row from mis-

---

⁵⁵ French: "I am humble and haughty." See n. 45 of this section.
⁵⁶ See n. 35.

trust alone. If only I were sure that when I walked in I would be considered extremely pleasant and intelligent right away—my God—what a good man would I be then!

It was difficult to determine then and now, whether he was joking or was really experiencing a change of heart?

Books Three and Four

The notes for Book III were written in December 1878 and January 1879 and those for Book IV were written in all probability about February 1879.

The notes for Book III, "Sensualists," are scanty and few. They refer schematically and fragmentarily to chapters III, IV, and V, "The Confessions of a Passionate Heart," and to Smerdiakov's proof about how he would not be guilty for renouncing his faith in the face of torture, which is recounted in chapter VII, "The Controversy." No mention is made in these sketchy notes of Dmitri's confession to Alyosha about the tangled relations he had with Katerina Ivanovna and especially of Katerina's visit to him in search of money and her father's honor. The only reference we have to Dmitri's relationship to Katerina Ivanovna is a reference to the 3,000 that he had to give back and this significant note: "tell her that I bid her good-bye by bowing." She is not mentioned by name.

The notes for Book IV, "Lacerations," are fuller. The lacerations concerning Father Ferapont, Fyodor Karamazov, Katerina Ivanovna, Lise, and Snegiryov are all represented in these notes, and the differences are for the most part those of descriptive amplification and psychological and dramatic refinement. Something of Dostoevsky's "filling-out" of a rough schema can be seen in how the following note is transformed by descriptive amplification to the final version. In the notes we have the following remarks about Father Ferapont and his perception of devils:

> AND THE DEVILS [one of them is hanging]. I crushed his tail ~~destroyed him~~ by the sign of the cross—he must be decomposed by now.

In the novel these notes have become the following:

> "You—can see spirits?" the monk inquired.

"I tell you I can see, I can see through them. When I was coming out from the Superior's I saw one hiding from me behind the door, and a big one, a yard and a half or more high, with a thick long gray tail, and the tip of his tail was in the crack of the door and I was quick and slammed the door, pinching his tail in it. He squealed and began to struggle, and I made the sign of the cross over him three times. And he died on the spot like a crushed spider. He must have rotted there in the corner and be stinking, but they don't see, they don't smell it. It's a year since I have been there. I reveal it to you, as you are a stranger."

Dostoevsky has added, of course, a great deal of descriptive detail, and the detail is very concrete and specific. The devil of the notes becomes in the novel a devil "a yard and a half or more high, with a thick long gray tail." In the notes his tail has been crushed, but in the novel "the tip of his tail was in the crack of the door and I was quick and slammed the door, pinching his tail in it." The final description also tells us something about Ferapont, for it expresses his eccentricity and queerness. On the other hand the questions that the monk from Obdorsk asks Father Ferapont about the descent of the Holy Spirit in the form of the bird and Father Ferapont's answers are virtually unchanged from notes to novel.

At times details that appear in the notes are suppressed in the novel. These are usually motivations or interpretations which Dostoevsky wishes to eliminate for technical and structural reasons. . The note for chapter IV, "At the Hokhlakovs," where Ivan makes his crucial farewell speech to Katerina, are fairly close to what appears in the novel, although the word "laceration" (*nadryv*) is used with more frequency in the novel than in the notes. In the final version, Ivan understands that Katerina's love for Dmitri is a love from pride, and he has the same perception in the notes. But in the notes he sees that Katerina's humility is a form of pride, that it is worse than pride. This is essentially what Dostoevsky wants the reader to understand from this tangle of relationships, but the psychological insight is made more explicit in the notes and suppressed, for dramatic reasons, in the final version. In the notes Ivan says to Katerina: "You are fighting him out of self-laceration, and this is not humility but pride. The humility is worse than pride." And in the novel he says: "And it all comes from your pride. Oh, there's a great deal of humiliation and self-abasement about it, but it all comes from pride."

Can she really love someone like me? (N.B. in comparison with   <17>
Ivan)?
———But I believe she loves someone just like you.
———She loves virtue and not me.
[Do not worry, she is really good, she is generous.]

———Why have I spent these three weeks with my father?
I know really that I don't have the right to anything.
I would have given him up, but the 3,000 have to be given back.

Ilinsky to Alyosha (in passing)
He keeps sending Ivan to Chermashnia. He is waiting for her.
To Chermashnia?

[I will wear galoshes,] will run after water. No, it's all really finished! He said fatally.

The 3,000 from Smerdiakov, I know.

Tell her that I bid her good-bye by bowing.

I will murder perhaps.
———If she loves, she will forgive—
———She wants to save me.

———Ivan is learned.
Ilinsky, reflectively:
I'm not worth their little finger, but <. . .>

When she comes to my father, this will mean the end of my illusion.   <18>

---

[1] The following rough draft of a letter to students at the Communications Engineering Institute appears on this notebook page: "M. G. I am hurrying to convey to you my sincere regret that I cannot in any way attend the Literary-

How will I marry then?

I will murder perhaps, and will kill myself.

Alyosha: Oh, Dmitri, how unhappy you are!

But really is my mother really his mother, what do you think?

F. Pav——ich became reflective.

19> Oh, you casuist. Look at what you are thinking of. But maybe only the devil knows where you will end up.

Somehow or other he is not really one of us, he is looking at us.[2]

But have you given it up, in your heart? That's it. [That is truly a sin, if in your heart, but not a big sin. Is it really just to punish doubt very hard] What if doubt had fallen in my heart precisely at that moment, for example, from fright, when it was impossible to reason well. How could I be particularly guilty before anyone? For example, before other people? And perhaps there's nothing to give my skin for. It is said, after all, the mountain into the sea. Try to tell not the mountain, but even our house to move to the river, and you will see that everything will remain as before and nothing will move. It means that you, Grigory Vasilich, do not believe [as one ought to], and yet you abuse cruelly others for the same lack of faith. And since no one in our age, no one most decisively can move mountains to the sea, then everyone without exception is the same kind of unbeliever. So, is it possible that the Lord will curse all of them, and in his well-known mercy will forgive no one? And I hope, therefore, that once I have fallen into doubt that I will be forgiven, when I pour out tears of repentance. [And suppose it turns out just so that I always kept the faith and then suddenly fell into doubt before my torturers.] ~~And what if I denied the faith before my torturers? Since I have already sinned and was the same as lost, I consequently had denied really nothing.~~ And what's more I would not be guilty in the ordinary fashion, as

---

Musical Benefit for the needy students of your institute. My doctor, regrettably, has refused me permission to leave my home for several days still. I beg you to convey my regrets to your respected comrades for honoring me with a complimentary ticket for the evening. I wish very much to assure them that I value highly their flattering attention to me. I beg you to accept the assurance of my most sincere respects to you."

Your most obedient servant
F. Dostoevsky

[2] This phrase refers to Fyodor Karamazov's characterization of Ivan in Book IV, chap. II of the final version: "But I don't recognize Ivan, I don't know him at all. Where does he come from? He is not one of us in soul."

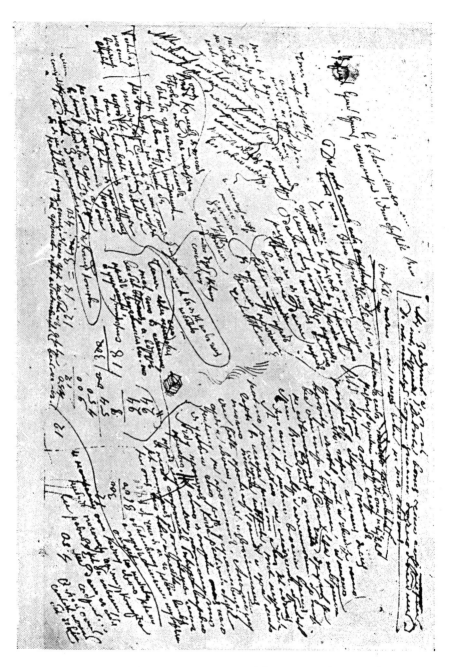

Notebook Page 19. This page contains Smerdiakov's refutation of Grigory's contention that one would sin in denying one's faith. The text is composed of blocks of evenly spaced material, arranged at various angles.

everyone else is guilty, but would have denied the faith before torturers. And if I truly believed at that moment, then would I really be guilty in not taking on the torments for my faith. But I would not have to suffer, if I truly believed.[3] All I would have to do is say to the nearest mountain [or even to an oak tree] to crush my tormentors, and it would crush them all and no one would tear off my skin, [and I would have walked away as if nothing had happened.] If besides at that moment I cried out intentionally [precisely and specially]: crush them, mountain, and it did not crush them. How then could I not doubt? [And if it did not move, then how could I not lose my faith, and especially at such a peculiarly terrifying moment.] [In the final analysis] there would be no special sin here, but only a completely ordinary sin. [And it would be useless to let some Asiatic rascal tear off one's skin, scoundrels who are all like mice . . . Fyodor Pavlovitch laughed a great deal and was very satisfied with himself.]

BOOK FOUR

<20> ——The Elder lean, the rites.
  ——Kiss.
  ——Teaching—
  ——Emotion
  ——Rakitin
  ——Alyosha's friend
  ——Alyosha noticed the young monk.
  ——The young monk and the monk Ferapont
  ——The young monk, on returning, got down on his knees, listened about the miracle [he appeared here and there, but Alyosha did not notice him, he remembered him later, but at the present moment his thoughts were elsewhere. The Elder, suddenly becoming very tired in bed, lifted his eyes and sort of remembered him and called him to his side.]
  ——The Elder sends Alyosha out.
 Father Paissy confirms
  ——He goes out agitated.
 You cannot not communicate, do not have the right, even though

---

[3] Marginal material that does not fit into the context: "You lie, lie, lie, balderdash. Those are your brother. So, anathema, you are cursed and you think that because you are not a Christian they will pat you on the head there in hell for that deed."

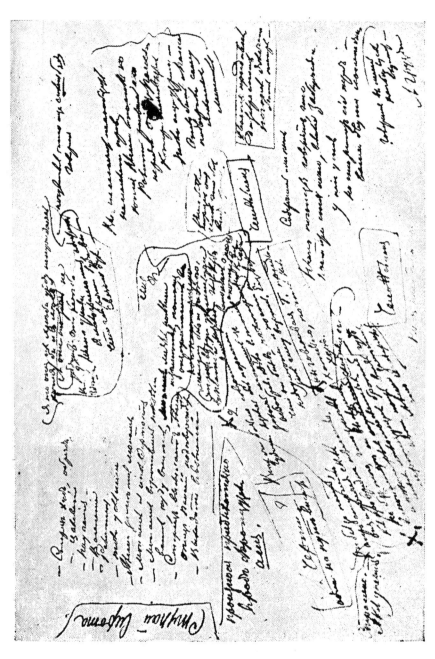

Notebook Page 20. This page is characterized by blocks of material separated by blank space, graphically emphasizing the disjointed nature of the text. Note dashes used by Dostoevsky in the upper left-hand corner to introduce words and phrases; these dashes are reproduced as such in the English text.

Alyosha hurried up, Rakitin told Father Paissy sooner than he whom he had also called out—

——We will see other things still

Therefore Paissy also had come under the influence of the triviality of the other monks.

A visiting monk from Obdorsk was more astonished by the miracle that had taken place than anyone else. The point was that he was more or less in doubt, and practically did not know what to believe. As late as yesterday he was fasting, and he had formerly heard of the institution of the Elders as a harmful novelty. In addition to what he had observed himself, he listened to certain ~~criticisms~~ supporting his own views <which originated from> his superficial and grumbling brothers—and then now again a miracle. Alyosha noticed that he had been poking around.

He[4] astonished the monk more than anything by the fact that he had a strong and healthy appearance.

[You are muddled-headed people. How do you observe the fast.]

[Our cell observed the old monastic rules.]

Do you observe the fast?

Today, pagan rascals say that it is useless to fast so much; a grave error

Our rules

But what is this in comparison with your two pieces

You say that you eat only a small piece of bread—

AND THE MUSHROOMS.

PRONOUNCING IT BY ASPIRATING IN THE FASHION OF THE FRENCH "H." Pronouncing the "G" by aspirating, almost like a "kher."

I will turn away from their bread, I will have no need of it, even if it were in the wilderness. But they ~~here~~ will not give up their bread....

[Who?

Those from around here]

Now they are learned I can scarcely read, but I will get there.

What do they say, as if you were—the Holy Spirit—

AND THE DEVILS [one of them is hanging.]

One of them is hanging from his navel.

I crushed his tail <destroyed him> by the sign of the cross—he must be decomposed by now

---

4 Refers to Father Ferapont.

[But I saw you in a dream]
[Go away]   <21

Is it true that you are in communication with the Holy Spirit?
——He flies down. It happens.
How does he fly down, in what form
Birds, as a bird.
——The Holy Spirit in the form of a dove.

——That one is the Holy Spirit, and the other the holy spirit. The
Holy Spirit flies down in the form of a bird, sometimes as a swallow,
sometimes as a goldfinch, and sometimes as a titmouse—
——How do you recognize him—
——He speaks
How does he speak, in what language?
——In a human language, human—
——What does he say to you?
——Well, today he informed me that an idiot would visit me. You
want to know much, monk
——It is terrible, and terrifying—
Terrifying when he gets angry.

——Red is better, whereas white resembles a hospital—[5]   <22
——If she hears that I had him locked up, she will go to him. If she
hears that he beat me up, she will come to me. Her character is to do
only what is contrary—
[Would you like some cognac? I'll give you some coffee—]
He wants to take Dmitri's fiancée away from him, that's why he is
living here. He told me himself.
——Did he really tell you that? (a troubled feeling. And suddenly
it seemed to him that he might have actually said that, not because
it was true, but to turn attention away from why he was living there.)
——But in that case, why is he living there?—[Is it not that he
wants to butcher?]
——And why not? He won't wheedle any money out of me.—
——Nose.[6] Bruises forming spots. Give out with an evil look. It

---

[5] This refers to the red handkerchief Fyodor uses to wrap his head, which had
been bruised by Dmitri's attack the day before. In the final version, Book IV, chap.
II, Fyodor says the following to Alyosha: "Red's better. It's just like the hospital
in a white one."

[6] This refers to the swollen nose and bruises Fyodor suffers as a consequence of
Dmitri's beating.

seems that he knew that and looked angrily at Alyosha, who was entering.

——The red is better—[7]

——Why have you come by?

——To learn about your health—

——Yes, and what's more I myself ordered you to come. Only: You are troubling yourself needlessly . . . . This is foolishness!

——I will crush him. Cockroaches are crawling.

——Ivan. He has no particular learning, in fact no education either—

——The good cognac is in the cupboard

——I am eating fish soup today

Live for 15 years, live for oneself.—

——So, you have become good.

Not at all, not at all good. Go off with you.

He kissed his hand.

Well, good (bis).

afraid to show emotion

——What's wrong with you (touched, emotion) we'll see each other again. Alyosha! Don't you think we'll see each other again?

[I have had good moments only with you, but I am an evil person]

>[8]   ——I've suddenly had an illumination—
                    (trembling)

——Yes, from the very first you haven't loved Dmitri at all, nor does Dmitri love you at all, but only respects you (yes, he respects you, I know that)."

——What's the matter with you Aleksei Fyodorovich, what's the matter with you!

——I don't know what is the matter with me, and really don't know how I dared, but someone had to say the truth.

What truth [This one (as if throwing himself off the roof.)]

---

[7] See n. 5 of this section.

[8] The fragment of an unfinished letter to K. P. Pobedonostsev appears at this point. The fragment reads as follows:

        Feb. 19/79

        Most respected Konstantin Petrovich,
        I wish first of all to thank you for the news of
        M. N. Katkov's arrival.

——Call Dmitri, and let him join your hands—because you love only him, and yet you are torturing him.[9]

[If you love him, give him your hand, and if you don't love him, then tell him so directly, so that he knows and doesn't hope—anything, because he loves you and is tormenting himself.]

——You are base . . . a holy fool—

Perhaps, perhaps I am awfully guilty. Ivan walks out.

——With Katerina. Ivan. Laughter and tears.

Go, here is 200—

Only you have been mistaken, my good Alyosha: she has never loved me.

A proud woman [like Katerina Ivanovna] does not even need friendship. Revenge against me for what happened yesterday [That's the way it was two months in a row.] I listened to her love for him, but Katerina Ivanovna knew of my love for her, even though I had never talked to her about love. I never talked to you about love.

~~Knowing~~ In this way I provided her with the pleasure of wounding me every day with her talk about love for him. Now I am going away. But know that the more you are hurt the more you love ~~the other~~ only yourself and no one else.

[And all your life, your whole life, you are going to convince yourself that you love him,] and only him since he is the one that hurt you, and in that way you can contemplate your feat of remaining faithful to him, as I have already told you, and consequently love only yourself.

——Ivan! That's not true, not true, at least at this moment this is not true, for she has been hurt too much.

You are fighting him out of self-laceration ~~nadryvom~~ and this is not from humility but from pride. The humility is worse than pride. I am too young, and I'm in love for the first time. But I'm going away forever. And do not be angry at me; know that I'm punished already for I will never see you again. Good-bye, don't give me your hand; you have tormented me too consciously, and I can't forgive you that.

Der dank <sic> Dame begehr ich nich.[10]

---

[9] Alyosha is speaking and calling upon Dmitri to join Katerina and Ivan's hands.

[10] This phrase is used by Ivan in saying good-bye to Katerina Ivanovna in Book IV, chap. V, "A Laceration in the Drawing Room." From Schiller's "Der Handschuh" (1798).

He turned out to be such a charming young man that it does not matter that he knew he was charming.[11]

You are smarter than I thought.
——I thank you for the compliment.
——Oh, good-bye, good-bye. But don't you see that once again I don't know whether she loves Ivan or Dmitri?

4>   And what a child I was. How did I dare, How did I dare!

It seemed to him that he was the reason for new misfortunes—In any case, he had acted foolishly, too precipitously—
Ivan was needed, absolutely, absolutely.
Complication—
An errand near Mitia's apartment—
——There he stopped to think over his errand
He remembered the little boy.

Tavern in the capital—
A good face, a sort of new man said in front of him (his brother Ivan).
——Something happened there about which it is still too early for you to know Lise; everything that can be told to you, I will tell you myself, when I return from Katerina Ivanovna's. . . .

Alyosha and Lise, { Everything that can be known. You protect morality.—
The minister declares that the morality is good.

——Oh.
——And not a word about the rest of the millions of people, it is necessary that all—
——All, all, yelled Lise
——Let's do it together!
If only you knew, Lise, how hungry they are!

——We are guilty (the Elder)
Lise—what are we?

---

[11] The following notes appear marginally at this point but do not fit into the context: "I have a hard time imagining you with a wife." "Such words were actually spoken to those actually present. But why at Brother Ivan's?"

Alyosha. It doesn't make any difference, we will take it upon ourselves, and if no one else takes it upon himself, and only we, well then *not to doubt.* . . .

You will put on new clothes? A velvet frock coat.

A white felt hat and a small rose in the buttonhole. That's very nice. You will be at my side all the time.
——No, Lise, it will not be like that, I've already thought it over. If I have to go in that way, I will naturally go away. We will have lots of time to see each other
——No, it's not that way. It is because you don't love me yet; what's passing between us now, is a marriage by way of reason. The Elder told you to marry, and so you picked me out.
You are cold.
And then: oh, how cold you are!
——He walked and walked and kissed—
No, we don't know how yet—

Kissed.
What's the matter with you?
——I myself think that it is terribly stupid
——Stupid?
——I thought that the fiancé. You say cold—

From mama, on the sly.
——Secretly, secretly, I myself will tell, but you are not to say a word before.—

Do you like my name?   <2
——I can understand perfectly.

Alyosha returned
——Katerina Ivanovna is sick, in a fever, she is raving—she has fallen asleep—

He left Katerina Ivanovna. *I acted stupidly!* too precipitously. (The Elder)
To his brother Mitia's apartment (an errand to the wisp of town not far from Mitia's apartment)
[Perhaps I've even spoiled a great deal.]

[How profoundly had his brother Ivan talked to her, how angry he was, And yet all the same perhaps]

[He needed his brother Ivan.]

He was confident that he would meet his brother Ivan [here].

Afterward Lise went to Foma, *two housewives.*

Smerdiakov—

Ivan in the inn—

He ate his roll.

Wisp of tow—and the boy.

I will whip him

—I will not whip him

cut off his fingers

Papa, papa, what a terrible town this is, papa—

Wait, and we will move to a nice town ~~papa~~ Sasha—

——Because the boy with us is born with a silver spoon in his mouth.

I'll show you a trick, a trick.

——And what will I say to my little boy, if I take 200, I really don't have the right to take them

The small lips tremble. Fly a kite.

That way of obsequious speaking[12] comes from the habit of humiliation.

I am a staff captain.

I began to speak obsequiously

Staff captain obsequious manner of speaking

Snegiryov.

I didn't earn this bread, she says, and she remains hungry.

Our times are complicated.

---

[12] The Russian words is *slovoiersov,* which designates someone who uses words (*slovo*) with the obsequious *s* and the hard sign *ier* after it. This is what Snegiriov does throughout and this word is usually translated by the English word "obsequious."

And he didn't want to Bless anything in all of nature.[13]
You made me cry.
You truly made tears come to me.
My little brood.
If I die, who will love them?
. . . Well then tell, what a wisp of tow it is.

Officer in the Russian army—   <26
Although a dishonored officer, but still an officer.

The wisp of tow does not sell his honor!—
——And if I sold it, what would I tell my little boy?"

A cleaning woman has to be hired, let's say I'm the cleaning woman,
but does that make one a dog, but to hire a cleaning woman you need
money.

——In Russia the drunken people are the best, ~~so that it turns out~~
the best people in Russia are those that drink the most—man [I
love my mama] Nothing you can do about it, you need a budget.
Russia must shine in Europe, Europe must be paid for its education,
and so our best people drink, so as to pay for all that brilliance. The
point is how much money is needed to keep only diplomats. I wanted
to be a diplomat from my earliest years, but it turned out that I didn't
have the mug for it.

You are buffoons, clowns, can there be anything rational about you
—That's the way I talk Varvara Nikolavna; can there really be anything reasonable.—

——Trickster. Something sort of *twitched* in his face.

On the way: I would like very much to make friends with your   <27
little boy.—
——Fine. Permit me.[14]
He cried, ran, papa, papa. We came here. He grabbed me by the

---

[13] This line is a quotation of the last two lines from Pushkin's poem "Demon:"
"I nichego vo vsei prirode/Blagoslovit' on ne khotel."
[14] Marginal entry at this point that does not fit into the context. "Duel. Family.
Try to come to terms with money, Agraf. Alek."

neck embraced me, fell into tears, papa, papa! And I fell into tears . . . We both cried.

You know how children cry when they are deeply hurt—in gushes; he flooded my face in warm gushes, he burst into tears, trembling all over as if in a fever, embraced me, daddy, daddy. God saw it all. Don't take money from him. In school they say that he will give you 15 rubles and <. . .> ~~given~~ When children are silent, proud, they suppress tears for a long time, but once they break out: he trembles like a wounded dove.

We embraced, and we sat there trembling. God saw all of that, saw it, and noted it.

How is it that you, he himself says.

I am weak, I said, and he is twice as strong.

[Who are the strong ones?]

[I say that the wealthy are strong.—]

[——Papa, I will get rich. I will become an officer, I will beat everyone, and I will come back and then no one will dare.—]

——I advise you not to send him to Moscow.

——I will not send him any more, besides he is sick. Cough.

Fyodor Pavlovich became angry and deprived me of his favors. He suspected me of having somehow informed Stepan Mikhaylovitch about his plans for Agrafena Aleksandrovna—

They are introducing Fröbel's[15] system to us. Education. They read, Sing songs.

---

[15] See n. 7, Books I and II.

Book Five

The notes for Book V were written in April and May 1879. The chapter "Rebellion" was sent to *The Russian Messenger* 10 May 1879 and chapter V, "The Grand Inquisitor," was written in the second half of May. On 10 May in his letter to Liubimov, an editor for *The Russian Messenger,* Dostoevsky said: "I was forced therefore to divide up this fifth book of my novel, for even if I had strained to the utmost, I would not have finished it until the end of May; second, this fifth book in my view is the culminating point of the novel and it ought to be finished with special care."

The notes for chapter III and IV, Ivan's confession to Alyosha, are unfortunately scanty. We are given very little of Ivan's justification of his revolt against God's world, and the heartrending detail of the suffering of children are present only in a few fragmentary and schematic remarks, such as: "The general Shoot" and "[The mother of the child torn to pieces]" It is something of an anomaly in these notes that we get the description of Smerdiakov's fall into the cellar in greater detail than we do Ivan's confession and his revolt against God. Ivan's long rejection of a possible future harmony is roughly sketched in the notes in the following manner: "I cannot admit that the future harmony in worth the price. And if it is worth that, then I don't want to admit it. I have too much pity for little children, and I ask that I am freed beforehand from that harmony, I am giving back my ticket."

The notes for chapter V, "The Grand Inquisitor," are quite full and in most respects parallel what we have in the final version, but with some interesting exceptions. The aggression of the Grand Inquisitor against Christ is much stronger in the notes than in the novel. One can hazard that Dostoevsky felt that he had to suppress what was a daring attack on orthodox Christian principles. In the notes— and not in the novel—the Grand Inquisitor speaks of Christ as having been "disgorged from Hell"; he calls him a sinner: "if there is a Single Sinner, then it is you yourself"; and states flatly that Christ had found nothing after leaving the cross just as his followers will find nothing: "those who suffer his cross will not find anything that has been promised exactly as he himself had found nothing after his cross." Most of this is implied in the novel, but it is not stated explicitly as it is in the notes. There is implied in the Grand Inquisitor's tirade in the novel a usurpation of what Christ had claimed and a reversal of what Christ had stood for: it is the Grand Inquisitor who loves the people and not Christ; it is Christ who is guilty and cruel, and it is the Grand Inquisitor who is kind and innocent. It is Christ who demands that men suffer for him, whereas the Grand Inquisitor suffers for men. But in the notes all this is baldly stated. In the notes the Grand Inquisitor says: I LOVE HUMANITY MORE THAN YOU DO. It is true that in the novel we have the following: "we allow them to sin because we love them," but the direct comparison and the bold emphasis is not there. We also get in the notes—but not explicitly in the novel—the Grand Inquisitor's statement to Christ: "I am speaking to you from love of humanity."

There is no mention of Chermashnia in the notes and only one short ambiguous note about Ivan's going away. The notes are confined to Smerdiakov's fear of what will happen between Dmitri and Fyodor and to hints that he will have a fit. In the novel Ivan doesn't want to understand what Smerdiakov is suggesting, and it takes him some time to understand it. On the night following the conversation with Smerdiakov, however, Ivan listens to Fyodor stirring about below and recognizes that "at the bottom of his heart, he thought of it as the basest action of his life." In the notes Dostoevsky is clear about what disturbs Ivan that night: "And later at night he leaps up: Does he think, scoundrel, that I will like seeing my father murdered? Yes, that's exactly what he thinks!" Dostoevsky suppressed this understanding on the part of Ivan obviously to prolong the self-deception that Ivan undergoes about his own motives. The frank explanation of some motive and then the suppression of the motive in the finished version is not an infrequent action on the part of Dostoevsky in these notes or in the notes for the other novels.

——Mme Khokholokova came out troubled: Katerina Ivanovna <2
shut herself in her room, the General's wife, wanted to go home, she
fell asleep. Everyone is sitting around. She locked herself in. I'm
afraid that it is serious (N.B. Decidedly, a fever).

"Sit for a while with Lise. Forgive her. She ~~cried~~ cried that she
had hurt you. Be reconciled, sit here for a while, and I will sit there."

——*A parte:* Aleksei Fyodorovich, don't take offense at her. Don't
bear any grudges: she is good, she is sick. I myself do the best to spare
her. She says that you are her friend from childhood. She feels very
earnestly about that. If you knew her memories about that: There
was a pine tree. Mama I remember that from my dream. [Oh, how
much you did for me Alyosha] And then she told me something so
nice that I cannot express it, good-bye. Sit awhile with her, comfort
her, as you know how to do."

——She went away, Alyosha returned.

——Listen to me (without any foolishness). Mamma told me that
the errand is. To the poor retired officer. And now you tell me that it
didn't come off.—Why didn't it come off; I didn't understand . . .

——Alyosha told her about Iliusha. Vivid impression. How is it
that you did not give it to him?

——I'll give it to him tomorrow. Alyosha's reasoning. Lise's ecstasy.
Arguments together.

——How smart you are I would never have thought up that.

——Lise, Lise, the Elder says ~~about the people: how many poor,
how much sorrow~~ that it's like caring for children.

——Let's watch over together. Put away foolishness. Let's go together. Your Elder is a saint—

——Yes—the People, how many poor, a million.

——Let's go together—[Don't believe, these foolishnesses, that is
nothing but nonsense.]

——Let's go—

——Oh, how happy I am!

——And I am happy. I will remember you Lise: Even in childhood,
you used to express yourself in an unusual way (*Quelque chose dans
un mot*)[1]

You are different from others. You will be chosen—

How happy I am!   <2

---

[1] French: "something in a word."

——Alyosha, I, well . . . (and she can't say it). I really wrote.

——All the better.

—— ~~You are so cold~~

——So much the better? Do you really love me? 15 years old and ¾, etc. [But you are so cold.—What's the matter with you?]

——You (kissed) so coldly, without feeling. You don't know how, [Alyosha how you love. I love you simply,]

[Alyosha. I don't know whether or not I love you simply. In general, I don't know anything about that.]

——Recently, a letter.

——Oh! that means that you understand a lot

——Look and see if mamma is listening in. [Kiss my hand.]

——A velvet suit—[2]

——Liza's rapture.—

——Another kiss.

——Mama listens in.—

——Well, go ahead, go to the Elder . . . etc.

[oh, he's good! Oh he is great!]

He goes out: Mrs. Khokhlokova.—

Once in the world, marriage is necessary. I know that even though I am young.

I've noticed that you have many abilities that I do not have. Then I noticed that you like the poor. Then that you question yourself, and that these questions interest you very much.

——I knew women, but I grew up with you, even though we are different in age, so that you are closer than anyone.

Seated in an armchair, you ought to reflect—

Alyosha: You are better than I am, you are deeper.

——You have a happier soul, you are better.

——You laugh like a little child, but think ~~at times~~ like a martyr.

——You ask very deep questions sometimes.

——I have know you since childhood.

——You asked one question just now.

——I know every one of your thoughts.

---

[2] This is one of the items of dress that Lise wants Alyosha to wear. In Book V, chap. I, "The Engagement," Lise says to him: "I should like you to have a dark blue velvet coat, a white piqué waistcoat, and a soft gray felt hat . . ."

——You don't know how good and pure you are in heart.——
(Recently a letter)
Alyosha, how happy I am. Do you know that I recently, *that letter.*
I'm going to watch over you like mama through the crack.
    ——That is, of course, a prejudice, but you can't help being a
woman, after all. [Do you think that all women spy?]
    ——Alyosha you really don't understand anything about a woman.
    ——Oh, that's true, you are right, only it's not good to listen in.
    ——But I really listen in from love, I am concerned about my be-
loved being.
    ——In practice, doubtless, that can at times be fine, but in principle
it is not.
No Alyosha we're not going to quarrel from the very beginning.
You know that might be really quite bad, but I'm going to do it all
the same.
    ——Alyosha: do it. It's all the same to me really, I'm not concerned
about myself I'm going to act, whatever you might see or hear, for the
most part as I have acted before—as I have decided my duty to be.
What's important let it be
And what is not important?
I'll give in on everything that is not important.
    ——Well, then, I'll give in on everything to you too.
    ~~even in~~
And I'll give in to you on what's most important:
I announce to you that I will not listen in, never, never, because
you are right, and even if I wanted to listen in terribly (But go to your
Elder)
Oh now come as often as possible. Can I now without you? We will   <3
continually talk about how we will live together. We will talk all the
time about that.
[Tsk . . . Mama was listening in, she has just gone away.] I know her
footsteps, I heard <her> go away, go away
When Alyosha left

Ah, yes! What is wrong with you? you told <me> about it a little
while ago.
Ah, Lise, I'm not good enough for you at all, look you just remembered about my sorrow

My brothers are destroying themselves father also, and they are
destroying others and all that is so terrible, and it's impossible to

help, and I ~~ought to give up~~ am deprived of a friend, of my father and must start a completely new life.

and I swear that what you said to me has resurrected me . . . But I have to go—perhaps he is dying.

31>   ——Alyosha about the Staff Captain with Lise.

The man is fearful and of very weak character. He has been overwhelmed by misfortunes and is very good. I have thought about what it is that has hurt him? He has been hurt by many things: first by the fact that he had been overjoyed by the money, No, he really did become overjoyed . . . ~~became overjoyed to the point of~~ . I saw after all that he had a very frail voice, weakened, and he talked to me fast—fast . . . in ecstasy [and cried] . . . so much in rapture that he suddenly became ashamed that he was so much in rapture. I then committed an error . . . He was sick, unnerved, very weak. He was a man who had been hurt, Lise, and the insult *had penetrated his being,* second he did not hide his rapture, [and he treated me too much as a friend]—he took me too much as a friend and trusted me, and third I myself had already let out much, said that we will give more, and that I have as much money for him as he might want . . . Then suddenly he took offense that I also was offering him as much money as he wanted. The important thing was that although he did not know to the last instant that he would trample on the bills, he still had a tormenting presentiment in his rapture about that—the rapture was that strong because he had a presentiment of what he was going to do, he wanted to deliver himself from this presentiment by that rapture. [He wanted to suppress the presentiment by that rapture and free himself] But you know that might have been for the better. I have decided that it would be for the better.

——Why?

—Because to trample on those bills was too tempting, even though it cost him those 200, that is, all his hopes and his happiness. If he had not trampled on them, but had taken the bills, he would have burst into tears on reaching home in an hour because of his humiliation . . . And now he returned proud and triumphant, even though he had destroyed himself. And nothing is easier now, consequently, than to get him to take these 200, because he had already shown that he was honorable . . . and he is sure that he will be taken for a proud man. And therefore it won't be necessary to beg him very long, etc.

Ivan. I will go (to Moscow), but not tomorrow, not this minute, I have to stay here a few days yet, I'm going to try to arrange it so that I won't have to see her, to hide from her. I even have a favor to ask you Alyosha, fib just a little, and say that I've gone, well, that *it seems* that I've gone.

Fyodor Pavlovich's garden was separated from the neighboring <3: garden by a fence. The neighboring garden was ~~rather large~~ as large as Fyodor Pavlovich's garden, [that is, no smaller than a square desiatin.][3] In it there were apple trees, gooseberries, raspberries, seedlings were cared for as much as possible, for several puds[4] of grass were cut—and this was practically the whole revenue of the inhabitants of the pitiful neighboring little house, to which the garden belonged. Fyodor Pavlovich thought once of acquiring this adjoining plot, solely to add to his own garden, but he quickly realized with his sly mind that there was nothing worth acquiring there. The owners of the little house were ~~old woman~~ an old woman unable to use her legs, a widow bourgeois, and her daughter. The house had been mortgaged for some time. There had been buyers. The old woman ~~was taking~~ took 350 rubles from [one of them] for everything, and she took a down payment without telling that the house had been mortgaged long ago somewhere to someone. The buyer, having learned of this before the closing of the deal (she herself let him know about this ~~mortgage~~ sort of through a third party, ~~abuse~~ came running over, quarreled abusively, but the old woman did not give back the deposit, and the matter ended with that. ~~However, she did this thing only twice~~ Fyodor Pavlovich offered a "small" price, but she suddenly became greedy and raised the price beyond measure, haggled, and the matter ended in nothing.

Two years ago the old woman still could walk around, and could still do some work, she would go to people's houses, as a commission agent, she sold things and lent money, but as time went on she made less and less. When she could no longer use her legs, her twenty-year-old daughter Maria Nikolaevna came to live with her; she had lived up to then in the provincial town, as a servant, working in a wealthy house. Even though she had been only a chambermaid there, she carried herself like a lady, and had two or three nice dresses. She didn't know how to do anything, not even to sew. It is true that she

---

[3] A measure of land, 2.7 acres.
[4] Thirty-six pounds.

asked Marfa Ignatievna to get her some linen to sew, but she executed the orders inaccurately, and she was awkward, and that is why the orders practically stopped coming in. It was during the summer and they had practically nothing to eat. The young girl started to go to Marfa Ignatievna for soup, and Marfa Ignatievna would pour them a bowl and give them some bread, and it was in this way that the old woman neighbor and her daughter were able to eat. ~~Smerdiakov~~ Nevertheless, ~~there was nothing~~ there was no air of begging or humbleness in Marfa Nikolaevna when she came with the bowl. She would appear each time as if sent by her mother, enter into conversation, and would announce that she had not gotten used to this fate and was disgusted with it. She took the soup almost haughtily, as if to say: "I dare you not to give it." She did not pawn her dresses, and found absolutely nothing bad about begging. It is true that she had a sprightly and pleasant character, as Marfa Ignatievna would say of her. She would relate a lot about provincial life, about all kinds of gentlemen, about how they lived. Although Grigory would frown at times, he was polite.

But she made one mistake ~~sort of~~ from the very beginning, and she, that is, sort of ~~almost~~ did not notice Smerdiakov, because of some prejudice, or some old story or in general not considering him for some reason ~~nothing~~ worthy of her attention. And Smerdiakov was ~~really~~ the actual cook, and the soup depended largely on him, not only as to taste, but also as to distribution. Marfa Ignatievna hinted to the frivolous girl, and she understood and became extremely nice to Smerdiakov. But he did not give in for a very long time, ~~kept an appearance~~ did not forgive, he gave the soup but with a very grave face. And then? Something happened that one couldn't possibly have expected. Maria Nikolaevna, who liked gentlemen and high society, took a liking precisely to Smerdiakov's stubbornness, precisely to his cold tone, and his complete lack of resemblance to any "man" of the class to which he belonged. Smerdiakov took a liking to two of her dresses, one with a train, and to her manner of shifting the train. At first he became angry at the train, but later ~~later,~~ he took a great liking to it. Each saw in the other people of high class. Added to all of this—Maria Nikolaevna was not distinguished by any special beauty: she was tall and very thin. She was a bit pockmarked, true only a little ~~few,~~ but still it spoiled her face a bit. The good Marfa Ignatievna found her to be even very pretty.

For a long time Maria Nikolaevna kept inviting Smerdiakov to come visit them and get to know them, and ~~speech~~ she expressed herself elegantly: visit their refuge, visit their little corner or their little nest. Smerdiakov always mumbled ~~to himself~~ something in answer, but at least he was not abusive. Still she invited him with a kind of smile and even with a certain kind of easy familiarity. But Smerdiakov still did not go. But then at last she began to invite him without any familiarity and with a directly suppliant expression.

—But why don't you want to go, is it that you don't have the time, remarked Marfa Ignatievna at last, who was very pleased to see the acquaintance of the two young people. If Marfa Ignatievna had added some wrong word, had hinted ~~profiting from her age~~ that well you are young and one's fate is in the hands of God, she would have spoiled everything. Smerdiakov would never have gone to the neighbors for any price, and even would have ceased talking about it. But God dispelled the shadow and Smerdiakov went visiting—not the next day, not the day after, but only on the fourth day. Naturally, he considered this to be more refined.

[I came by, and on the contrary]

[I've seen you for a long time]

[And I saw you.]

[She had enough stamina to swallow a needle and stand it.]

The great crown.   <3·

My little dear (write poetry)

——Why haven't you been to see us? Do you have contempt for us?

——(Freckled) Maria kept repeating that almost always. But he would take offense. He would not appear for weeks—he was uncommunicative, silent, would plant himself by the door. Or perhaps he was seduced by the flattery of his poetic talent. [He composed one poem]—

Smerdiakov's tirade about himself—

Alyosha and questionings about the 3,000—

They *climb over* the fence—Smerdiakov

May I ask how you came across?

Oh, how I love it when someone writes poetry!

——Whatever is in poetry, is pure nonsense

——Why

Poetry is not a serious matter. Whoever talks in rhymes—

How is it then that you wrote about the Russian crown

These are verses. I speak in cadenced rhyme [the crown is powerful by virtue of its beneficent force]

How smart you are—

I would know even more, if it were not for the fate of my childhood.
I hate the Russian people
If you were a military man,
I not only do not want to be a military man, but I would like to
destroy all soldiers.
——Oh, my God. Who would save us if an enemy came"
——In 1812 it would have been better if everything now were
different.
N.B. I think it's very nice to fight a duel.

35>   [The mother of the child torn to pieces]
The rock of faith
——Do you understand me Alyosha
——I understand you very well—
——I have not seen Dmitri
——About Smerdiakov (he has been tormenting himself very
much)
——Does Smerdiakov interest you?
——Yes—
——Brother, are you really leaving tomorrow
——I don't know—a short time ago Katerina Ivanovna.
——Everything about Katerina Ivanovna—I will go away—
——And Dmitri and father—
——What am I the keeper of my brother (Cain's answer).
Are you firm in your intention—Or not—
    Firm or not.

A short time ago (at Katerina Ivanovna's) we were all so very young,
and we were all teaching each other.

Brother, if you go away then Dmitri
Keeper of my brother (I want to live myself)
Brother, you really are going away tomorrow.
I am celebrating my parting with love. That was a very stupid
thing. Alyosha they used to distract me for a whole half a year and—
that schoolgirl.
The most important
Katerina Ivanovna in delirium.
——What's going on there? You were there?
——It's very bad there
His face clouded over. Then immediately, he began to laugh.

I have cured myself (of love)

I will go to embrace my graves[5]

I cannot admit that that future harmony is worth the price. And if it is worth that, then I don't want to accept it. I have too much pity for little children, and I ask that I am freed beforehand from that harmony, I am giving back my ticket.

That's revolt said Alyosha.

Revolt. I would prefer your not calling it that. Can one live in revolt when it is not that *I don't want to* accept it, but I cannot accept it, Can you understand that. Speak.

(He remains quiet)

Alyosha, do you believe in God?

I believe with all my heart, and more than ever before.

——And can you accept.

——Alyosha remains silent

[Can you accept the fact that parallel lines will meet? Can you understand how a mother can embrace the general and forgive him?]

No, I still cannot. I still cannot

——Let's go. It is late. (the bill).

——How can you love sticky little green leaves. How do you want to live.

——In the Karamazov manner.

——That is, everything is permitted.

——Everything is permitted.

I would like to destroy completely the idea of God. If not, in the Karamazov manner, up to 30 years of age a nuance of nobility suffices[6]

——And then—

——Or drown myself in the stink of voluptuousness, or ambition, or cruelty, or get a passion for cards, or . . .

Or?

Or destroy myself.

I have reflected, perhaps one could steep oneself in gambling, in chess, become a banker and play the stock market, become a courtier. But for me I came to the conclusion that I, and you with me, could

---

[5] This line is a reference to Ivan's intention to visit Europe. In Book V, chap. III, "The Brothers Make Friends," Ivan says: "I want to travel in Europe, Alyosha, I shall set off from here. And yet I know that I am only going to a graveyard."

[6] Compare this to the following in Book V, chap. III: "But to hang on until seventy is nasty, better only until thirty; one might retain a 'shadow of nobility' by deceiving oneself."

not do these things. You can't get rid of the idea. It will continue to live like a worm. Only one thing remains: Beastly voluptuousness, with all its consequences, voluptuousness to the point of cruelty, crime, even to the point of the Marquis de Sade. That would carry you for a while. But in order to do this one has to develop within oneself for one's whole life a fire in the blood, but even if you could, it is reptilian, that's why one has to kill oneself. I have come to the conclusion that up to 30 you can get by with the power of life ~~the cup,~~ with the fascination of the cup, that is, with deceptions, and then <one has to> destroy oneself. Up to thirty, that's the way I will live, I'm counting on the baseness of nature. I'm speaking to you straight: If I were imprisoned, or if forced to become a lackey or a slave, and if I were beaten every day, even then my thirst for life would not wear out. I am counting on the baseness of human nature.

How do you want to live
in the Karamazov manner (everything is permitted).
2) Voluptuousness, but perhaps it will be impossible.
——For you *it will be impossible*
Voluptuousness. Steep myself in bestial ecstasies, like my father.
But it is very dirty. It is better to *destroy* oneself.
Would you agree to that. Architect building
——Good-bye.
——Good-bye Ivan. I love you, Ivan.
——And I love you also.

Ivan—And we know really that he did not find anything there. A stupid experiment—I'm even offended by it. That's the way it is.
Inquisitor You are truth itself, you cannot deny it.
Do not curse [HERE]
We have the knowledge (30,000).

You think I'm talking about the poor, about the peasant, about workers. They smell so, coarse, drunken, I wish them the best, but I don't understand how Christ could have come to love them, I do not understand Christ's love.—

the child
If you were creating the world, would you have built it on the single little tear of a child.
Somewhere in an inn they talked about such nonsense. That is possible only in Russia.—

3) Even if there were really a complete illumination, could you agree.

1) I still cannot.

The general
shoot.
yes.

Oh, if even you are saying to shoot. Listen, you'll see something yet Louis XVII

Solely because it is possible to formulate one question. Would you agree to create it thus? [with the aim of finally making people happy, giving them peace and tranquillity

and if it were absolutely necessary to torture to death only one tiny creature, one, for example, that would beat his breasts with his little fists and cry out for God

the tears of a child (I am speaking only about a child) No really, if you are honorable, is the world worth the little fist of a child—if you were creating the world, would you create it on the single tear of a child.]

No.

——Let there be the incomprehensible compensation for us of eternal harmony. Hallelujah. That's why I don't understand the world. I'm speaking only of children, let's suppose that I'm only a louse in mind, but if I'm an honorable louse, then I ought not agree, from love of humanity, I ought not. It's asking too much. I'm returning my entrance ticket as <. . .>"

Life is base. The mind invented the retribution of God, but even immortality is base if I am not there.

Don't come here anymore, go to your Zossima.

Is your Pater Seraficus alive.

"He is alive and he has written down his last word"

[Cut off everyone's head.]

Inquisitor: Why do we need the beyond? We are more human than you. We love the earth—Schiller sings of joy, Ioann Damaskin.[7] What

---

[7] Ioann Damaskin (end of seventh century–754), early church writer. Defended a thesis on the excellence of spiritual power over worldly power. His many theological writings influenced the nature and character of theological scholasticism. One well-known work is *Istochnik znaniia (Source of Knowledge)*.

is the price of joy? With what a flood of blood, torments, meannesses, and bestialities, which one cannot suffer. They don't speak of that. Oh, the crucifixion; that is a terrible argument.

INQUISITOR: <u>GOD AS A MERCHANT.</u> I LOVE HUMANITY MORE THAN YOU DO.

36>   where the serpent loses his sting

The kiss burns in his heart, but he remains unchanged in his convictions.

Christ: the whole world is not worth that thought—invented God. It is so holy, so moving—so true! And all that is nonsense—a stupid effort.

The trial balloon is launched.
Believe what the heart will tell you.

Inquisitor is that really just.
let it be just, but I will not accept it.
secret—that there is no truth, no God, that is, the God that you preached

Despair not tragic, but comic.

He laughs when they took away the base creature, the abject scoundrel from the abject parliament

Alyosha arose and kissed him (he remains silent)
Ivan—Inquisitor! Inquisitor!

They got up and went out. Good-bye, my loved one. About business matters.—

You did not want, you wanted a free acknowledgment. You said, I will make you free.

The idea about the 40,000 of the father's money, this is only Karamazov dirt.

——No, it is not worth it, said Alyosha, still with his half-smile fixed on him.

——If one were to accept life on these conditions—is it worth it or not?

Smerdiakov: they would have got 40 or 50 thousand.

Oh yes he gave his Son, sent him to be crucified—disturbed. Oh, these are frightfully strong arguments, an eternal argument.

Why have you come to disturb our work? I will have you burnt.—

Inquisitor: I am speaking to you from love of humanity—to you who loved him more than yourself ~~understood~~ You alone can understand me, and therefore I am revealing the secret to you. And tomorrow at dawn I will have you burned.—

The stupider it is the closer it is to the goal. Stupidity is always short, and the shorter the closer. I sacrificed my own dignity.

But I don't accept it because no matter how great the idea is, it is not worth this suffering.

Angels will sing. If the mother embraces the torturer of her son, forgives <him>, then that means that something has happened which is so lofty that it certainly will be worth all the misfortunes, but I do not want it—that is revolt—

HERE.

And if I am asked to take part, I cannot take part, pardon me.

Evening party.

Euclidean geometry I will accept God all the more readily if he is the eternal old God who cannot be understood. And so let it be *that God*.[8] This is more shameful.

Will you explain that.

——I began so as to explain. Oh, Alyosha, you think that I'm boasting. No. I began as stupidly as possible on purpose.

Why?

Closer to the point. Listen.

And in the second place—for Russianism. Russian conversations on these themes all take place in that way for all Russian boys, a little <...>

I don't believe that, let, let parallel lines meet and let them embrace

How is my miniscule louse-like mind capable of understanding that parallel lines will meet?

---

[8] The point about Ivan's accepting the "old God" is not in the final version.

LET THEM SUFFER, SINCE HE ATE THE APPLE.

Apocalypse. The finale will express something so precious that it will be worth all these universal sufferings and will redeem them so that one may reconcile oneself to them.

And therefore, the third proposition I do not consider the enterprise as something serious.—

But I do not accept this world, and I do not want to agree to that. That is my third proposition.

Let there be an order of humanity, a touching faith, Death of Christ Something big enough to equal such suffering.

——What is more I must absolutely be resurrected so as to see this retribution otherwise, otherwise it's all just a trial balloon—a trial soap bubble, and nothing else.

That was an impulse of love: at least I will look at them, at least I will go among them, at least touch them.

A force emanated from his raiment.

How did they recognize him? Was he really like us, he was after all the Miracle, the heavenly secret.

We would have guarded the secret, we would have taken the suffering on ourselves; we would have sacrificed ourselves for humanity.

When the powerful and wise spirit, the spirit of death and the spirit of destruction and unlife was tempting you

The mind is a scoundrel, but stupidity is straight and honest. Stupidity cuts at one point, it doesn't squirm, it doesn't go off to meridians, how could it?

37>   Perhaps that is impossible. In any event that will be, because that is the way it ought to be.

[The fallen woman. Let them tear apart. But you don't have the right—I have the truth and then—tear apart if you can.]

The confession of the Elder

——I do not want to leave you in ignorance as I understand it (goes, enters)

——And then Dmitri took it up so naïvely: Yes, perhaps everything is permitted, if the word is pronounced, I do not reject it.

——Portrait—[9]
Why have you come to us,
Why did you come to meddle in our affairs?
——Do not speak I know what you will say, but listen to me and be sure above everything that I will have you burned tomorrow.

I have only one word to say to you that you have been disgorged from Hell and are a heretic,[10] and that the very people who fell down before you will rake up the coals tomorrow—

Did you see the people? What more did you want? You said that you wanted to make them free, and did you see those free ones? Did you see them? This matter has cost us a great deal, and we were forced to proclaim in your name—[15 centuries of fragments, but now it is solid.]

Why do you disturb our work, why do you destroy our work—
——No, if there is anyone who deserves to be burned it is you.
[Man was created rebellious

The most just flee from us into the desert.—We honor them as saints, but they acted like rebels because they did not dare flee from us.

When the wise spirit proposed to you—you wanted freedom—you did not descend from the cross—

Is a free person happy
Stones into bread—
All the wise men of the earth could not have invented anything wiser than what was written [in those lines]

Feed them first, and then ask them.
He tried your inner faith—You did not give in—but is everyone like you—Can they really by faith alone, and the rest, how to protect them from revolt.
The kingdom—

[you rejected the Kingdom that we were forced to accept, and if it *costs blood and whole generations*, then you, You Alone are guilty.]

---

[9] Dostoevsky is probably referring to the portrait of the Grand Inquisitor.
[10] The statement about Christ being a heretic and having been disgorged from hell is not to be found in the final version.

——They sing of you as Alone without Sin, but I say to you that you alone are guilty."[11]

——And we will have to wait a long time in order to construct our Kingdom.

A mass of locusts will crawl out of the ground and will cry out that we are enslaving people, that we are despoiling virgins—but these unfortunate ones will submit.[12] It will end up that even the greatest of them will submit and join us and will understand that we accept suffering in exchange for power. But they, the cursed ones, do not know what we take upon ourselves—we take upon ourselves knowledge—and suffering—

38>   Here.
The Important thing.
——Alyosha—but that is Rome. [You are justifying rapacious Catholicism.][13] And even now you see only greed. That's true, searching. Mass of Gold.

	——You think, said Ivan
	How much contempt in you—
In the 3d proposal	——If only one
Rome proposed to you its	and how sad it must be!
banner, and you rejected it.	So that he, Ivan finishes.
	You do not believe in God
	How then sticky leaves.

Alyosha: I imagined that you would do it differently you criticize only the Catholic clergy—

Ivan: My poem is stupid, but do you agree that the Grand Inquisitor is half right—

Alyosha:—you think so, you think so? you don't believe in God—
Ivan He has irresistible authority. 14,000 and those where?

Alyosha. So for you irresistible you do not believe in God. What does the secret consist of. Can one with the idea of the old man and the happiness of people? Perhaps, perhaps.

The old man remains convinced as before. And you? I am with the old man's idea, because he loves humanity more. Can one about

----

[11] This charge against Christ is not expressed in the final version, although it is implied.

[12] The image of the locusts crawling out of the ground is not to be found in the final version.

[13] This sentiment about Catholicism does not appear in the final version.

idiots. Perhaps one can. You don't believe in God. Sticky leaves. "What secret," asked Alyosha. "You are justifying."

2d Temptation. That you may not stumble—
Yes you had to act like a proud creature. True, you realized that you would have been hurt.—
——But you rejected the authority of the Miracle—and how much we have been forced to struggle so as to correct your work, and if there is a Single Sinner, then it is You yourself.

You proclaimed what men have dreamed of for a long time that they are free, centripetal force, does not belong to the earth, *freedom from miracle*.

You did not descend from the cross, but you are God, you asked too much from the people. The people need miracles, that is, authority. Miracle and mystery. Yes, mystery. Now about mystery. Among us man will die of sickness—

In mankind and the sufferings of its existence lies the task of finding <39: that common thing before which the people can unmurmuringly bow down. Without that, man will not find peace and will not be able to construct a society. The secret is based on the crude imperfection of human nature. Man is given freedom as part of his nature, but his first concern, on receiving that gift, is to give it to someone else as soon as possible. And because of that he creates Gods for himself all through his history, and whoever knows this mystery of mankind's existence, knows how to go about subduing him, and who can, subdues him.

YOU WERE GIVEN A BANNER, SHOWN SOMETHING ABSOLUTE AGAINST WHICH NEITHER INDIVIDUAL MAN NOR THE WHOLE WORLD WOULD EVER THINK OF RISING. BUT YOU REJECTED EVERYTHING IN THE NAME OF FREEDOM.

[Look now at the question, the second proposal, the second mystery and what you did with it]

Question -of conscience- personal, that is, of conscience—how to come to terms with one's conscience. A social and governmental question—an absolute question, an eternal problem before whom to bow down—[for they will never be individually at peace—and will never become a whole]

[——If they don't know whom to worship—]

[In accepting the bread you would have answered the question as to whom mankind should worship.]

You should have come in a way to make him tremble before you, but you yourself proclaimed for him a yet unheard of—freedom.

3d mystery—the necessity of universal unity, for no matter how powerful nations may be, they all dream prophecies of universal union.

40> The public applauds. What? Whom? Because the torturing of an infant has been justified? Oh, I was not there: I would have bellowed forth the proposal to institute a stipend in honor of its torturer!

In general these pictures are charming.

~~Render unto Caesar~~

But among those (and then already, to be truthful, extremely few)

The need to unite into one, Genghis Khan, Timur, Attila, the Great Roman Empire, which you destroyed, for you destroyed it, and no one but you.

For the organization of the human conscience is possible only if you do away with freedom. [For in the beginning people, in order to live, look for peace more than for anything else . . . you proclaimed that life is revolt, and took away peace forever. Instead of firm, clear, and simple principles, you took away everything.]

The 2d thesis, 2d mystery of man's nature is based on the need to organize the consciences of man [<a definition> of good and evil so as to be common for all.] Whoever can show and teach them that will be a prophet.

Whoever comes, like you, to take possession of the people and to make them follow him, must necessarily organize their consciences so as to give them a firm understanding of what is good and what is evil. And so, undertaking such a great piece of work, you didn't know—oh, you did not know that you will never so organize mankind's conscience, and never give mankind peace of spirit and joy unless you take away from him—freedom.

41>[14] But ~~and you thought that~~ did you think that your banner of

---

[14] The following letter appears on the side of this notebook page:
  To Moscow
    Editorial Office of *The Russian Messenger*
      Boulevard of Passion
    I have not received the six books ~~the most humble~~
    I beg you to send them to me in Staraia Russa.
                                              F. M. Dostoevsky

heavenly bread could unite people ~~in their poverty~~ [all together in indisputable harmony.] ~~For~~ But the strengths of mankind are various. There are the strong and there are the weak. There are such that cannot by their very nature conceive of heavenly bread [for he is not for such as they] numberless like the grains of sand in the ocean. Where will you find unity of worship, ~~and can the law and the existence of humanity be fulfilled~~ when most people don't even understand what that is. Instead of a ~~universal banner~~ of harmonious worship ~~I see only strife~~ the banner of eternal wars has arisen,[15] that would not have happened with the banner of earthly bread. But look

That religion is inappropriate for the overwhelming majority of people, and therefore cannot be called the religion of love, that he had come only ~~for~~ for the chosen, for the strong, and mighty, and that those who suffer his cross will not find anything that has been promised exactly as he himself had found nothing after his cross.[16] [That's your] Unique Sinless One, whom you have championed. And consequently the idea of slavery, servitude, and mystery—the idea of the Roman church and perhaps even of the Masons is much more true for the happiness of people, even though based on universal deception. That's the significance of your Incomparable Sinless One.

Because of this universal worship they ~~tortured~~ destroyed each other by the sword; ~~some~~ they created gods and ~~forced all the others~~ strove to make the rest of the people worship them. [They cried out to each other: give up your gods, and worship ours instead, or else death to you and your gods.] And so it will be to the end ~~of the world,~~ even if the gods disappear from the world, [so it will be then, even if the gods disappear from the world, they will fall down before idols.]

In the desert B (.) he will show you all these places

Fall down in worship ~~before him~~ before whom? There is no more <42> constant and more tormenting concern for man, who is free, then to find someone as quickly as possible whom he can worship ~~man is born into freedom and his greatest concern, on receiving freedom, consists in, having been born and received freedom, finding someone as~~

---

[15] The passage beginning with "Where will you find unity of worship" and ending with "eternal wars have arisen" is not in the final version.

[16] The sentiment about the strong and mighty followers of Christ who have, like Christ, found nothing beyond the grave was probably eliminated from the final version because of its blasphemy of the foundations of Christianity.

~~quickly as possible to whom he can give this gift of freedom, which is so tormenting to him.~~ But man looks for something to worship that is incontestable, so incontestable that all other people will ~~accept it~~ agree to worship with him. For the concern of these pitiful creatures consists not only in finding someone whom you or I might worship, but to find someone whom all could believe in and worship, absolutely all together. And so this need for universal worship is a very serious torment for each man individually, [and for all of humanity since the beginning of time]. ~~This is why man creates gods for himself throughout history~~ You knew, you could not have not known this basic mystery of ~~his~~ man's nature but you rejected the [only] absolute banner, which was proposed to you, [so as to force all to worship you indisputably]—the banner of earthly bread and rejected it in the name of freedom and heavenly bread. ~~look, now look~~

Look what you have done further ~~when the second question was proposed to you.~~

43> ——And always in the name of freedom! I say to you that there is no more tormenting concern for man than to find someone to ~~give back~~ give his gift of freedom to, which this unhappy creature is born with, as quickly as possible. But he alone takes possession of the freedom of people who can give peace to their conscience ~~the second thesis, the second question, the second proposal which was asked of you consisted of this~~ In bread you were offered an indisputable banner: give bread and man will worship you, for there is nothing more indisputable than bread, but if at the same time someone takes possession of his conscience, in spite of you, —oh, then he will throw up your bread and will follow him ~~who will explain to him what is good and what is evil~~ who will seduce his conscience. You were right about that: ~~For~~ For the mystery of mankind's existence consists not only in living ~~as animals live~~ but in \<knowing\> what to live for. Without a firm conception of why he is living man will not agree to live and will rather kill himself than remain on earth, even though

44> he might be surrounded by bread. ~~And so~~ That's the way it is, but what happened: instead of taking possession of people's freedom ~~in order to take it from them~~ you increased it for them even more! Can it be that you have forgotten that peace and even death is more dear to man ~~freedom and especially~~ than free choice in the knowledge of good and evil? ~~Look about you, even those in revolt against us are in the final analysis looking only for peace. Why do the godless so love materialism and materialistic doctrines? Precisely because with such~~

~~a doctrine everything finishes so quickly, everything passes by without~~
~~leaving a trace, and consequently brings only annihilation and death,~~
~~that is, peace without the slightest freedom.~~ There is nothing more
seductive for man than the freedom of his conscience, but there is
nothing more tormenting. ~~And so But~~ And so, instead of firm bases
for bringing peace to man's conscience once and for all—You took
everything that is extraordinary, enigmatic, and indefinite, took everything that was beyond the strength of people, ~~and increased their~~
~~anguish,~~ and you acted therefore as if you did not love ~~the people~~
them at all—and who is that: He who has come to give his life for
them! Rather than take possession of the [people's] freedom, you
multiplied it and burdened the spiritual kingdom of man with torments forever. with torments, I say, because despite the fact that they
are unbearable, there is nothing more enticing for man.

You aspired for man's free love, so that, seduced and captivated by
you, he would freely follow you. In place of the firm ancient law,   <4!
man was to ~~decide~~ decide for himself [henceforth] what was good and
what was bad, having before him only your image as a guide,—is it
possible that you did not think that at last he would reject and throw
into doubt even your image and your truth, if he was to be crushed
by such a terrible burden as free choice? They will cry out at last that
truth is not in you, for it was impossible to leave [them] in greater
torment and confusion than ~~you had~~ he did, who having left ~~the~~
~~people~~ them so many cares and unresolved tasks. And so in that way
you yourself prepared the foundation for the destruction of your
kingdom [and do not blame anyone for this anymore]. And yet what
was proposed to you? ~~The wise spirit showed you decisively how~~
~~worthless, weak, base and ungrateful this species was He showed you~~
[There are] three forces, only three forces [on earth] powerful enough
since time immemorial to conquer and captivate the soul and conscience of these weak rebels, for their happiness,—these forces:
miracle, mystery, and authority. You rejected one and the other and
the third, and you yourself became an example of that.

Ivan and Smerdiakov
Scene   <46
——Smerdiakov to Ivan: My position is desperate, I wanted to ask
for advice—
Like every day: why doesn't she come, as if I were at fault.
He had taken out his revolver.

Well, so that she come. I say intentionally tomorrow morning that she will come, when she won't come?

Why say anything?
——He will kill \<me\>.
——I'll say that perhaps she'll come, that she wanted to come very much."
I'll have to tell the master! They are after me like little kids: you are the reason she's not coming (guilty, that is).
He will marry Agrafena Aleksandrovna (that is, Fyodor Pavlovitch)
——That's why your brother has got it into his head to kill: first of all from jealousy, and second in order to preserve his inheritance.
Important
He will take the 3,000, involve me, and I'm afraid I will be implicated: you too therefore are mixed up with him about those 3,000 rubles—
Forgive me, the whole advantage is his: to disinherit
N.B. Ivan: *other steps* had been taken before.
Smerdiakov: Forgive me, he talked so directly yesterday: I will kill him, I will come and kill.—
Smerdiakov about *Mitia:* I need money very much.
He carries a truncheon—
The signal:

. . .

I have shown him the signal.
Grigory will be drunk, he will oversleep . . . the medicine, *he is counting on that,* and Marfa Ignatievna herself always takes some of the drink, and then like a log—It is precisely *tomorrow* that he intends to try it.
Fyodor Pavlovich will be sitting alone and it is agreed that I will knock: Grushenka has come
He will rush out immediately.
——And if she comes I am to knock a second time: "it is necessary" —he will open.
Smerdiakov: I told Ilinsky that she will most certainly come.
But why did you say that?
——He threatened to kill me.
I will become sick from fright—And he will knock without me.
And if there is no Grushenka?

And for the money?

——He won't take it.

——You don't know him.

——Go away.

——How, go away?

Just so the sum of money <isn't connected> with me. So that no suspicion touches me afterward.

——Who will suspect?—You perhaps."

At night after the conversation with Smerdiakov:—

At first: He was laughing at me. Yes, laughing at me

And later at night, he leaps up: Does he think, scoundrel, that I will enjoy seeing my father murdered? Yes, that's exactly what he thinks! (Familiarity is insulting)

(The important thing vaguely, about what's important allusively)

——The devil take it! And perhaps, really, I do enjoy it, hah, ha. Does he really think that I'm in a plot with Dmitri? That could be, he is capable of that—

The devil take it, perhaps he likes the idea of the murder. But that is nonsense, the scoundrel is simply afraid that he will become involved.

The devil take it, perhaps he wants to do the murder.

Ivan still ~~in the conversation with Smerdiakov~~

——All that is nonsense—it cannot be that my brother Dmitri Fyodorovich really has decided to murder with premeditation. If something of that kind happened, it would happen by chance, in a fight, while he would be trying to take Grushenka away.

Smerdiakov. He can look for that sum (3,000)

Ivan. Nonsense

He—He needs money very much.

Ivan. Nothing will happen.

Smerdiakov. Certainly every reasonable man should think that way.

That is why it is said that it is interesting to talk to an intelligent man—

You have to look at his beard. If the beard shakes, and he talks a great deal and sort of gets angry, this means that everything is all right, he is speaking the truth, but if he strokes his beard with his left hand, and snickers—that means that he wants to cheat you, swindle. But don't look at his eyes, never any truth there.—

Gorstkin

and Liagavy

He will put down a down payment, and then will begin about those whores—

And if you are good and *charitable,* you will bring yourself—

Look for him by way of the Piatniksky priest father Ivan—a man of gold.

7>   And F. Pavlovich, having seen his sons to the door, remained extraordinarily content. For two [whole] hours he felt himself almost happy, when suddenly an extremely irritating and unpleasant incident for everyone took place and plunged Fyodor Pavlovich into great uneasiness. Smerdiakov [for some reason] went down the cellar and fell down from the top stairs. It was fortunate that Marfa Ignatievna ~~was in~~ happened to be in the yard. She did not see the fall, but did hear the cry, a particularly strange cry but one very familiar to her—the cry of the epileptic falling into a fit. It was impossible to determine whether the fit took place as he was going down stairs, so that he fell immediately into unconsciousness or whether on the contrary, the fit came about from the fall and concussion of Smerdiakov, a known epileptic. But they found him on the floor of the cellar, writhing and trembling, struggling with foam in his mouth. They thought at first that he had broken something and hurt himself seriously; however, "God had spared him" as Marfa Ignatievna expressed it. Nothing of the kind had taken place, but it was difficult to take hold of him and carry him out of the cellar, but neighbors were called and somehow or other it was done. ~~He was there~~ Fyodor Pavlovich himself was present at all these doings, helped himself, visibly frightened and sort of distracted. Nevertheless, the sick man did not regain consciousness. The attacks would stop for a while, but then would begin again, and everyone concluded that the same thing would happen as ~~three~~ last year, when he had accidentally fallen from the attic. They remembered that they had applied ice to the top of his head. They found some ice in the cellar and Marfa Ignatievna took care of it, and Fyodor Pavlovich decided ~~that if it didn't help during the night, that tomorrow~~ toward evening to send for Hertzenstube, who arrived almost immediately. Having looked over carefully the sick man (he was the most careful and attentive doctor, a middle-aged and respected old man) he concluded that the attack was serious and dangerous, but that for the moment he still did not understand everything, and that tomorrow morning, if the present measures did not help, he would decide to take others.

They put the sick man in an outbuilding, in a little room by the side of the lodging of Grigory and Marfa Ignatievna. Then, Fyodor Pavlovich suffered misfortune after misfortune all day long. Marfa Ignatievna prepared dinner and the soup—compared to Smerdiakov's—turned out to be "like slop," and the chicken turned out to be so dried out that it was impossible to chew it. Marfa Ignatievna answered the bitter reproaches of the master by saying that the chicken was already old, and that she had not, after all, studied to be a cook. ~~Fyodor~~ Toward evening another care came up: he was told that Grigory, who for two days had been ailing, had suddenly taken to bed with a case of lumbago. Fyodor Pavlovich finished his tea as quickly as possible and locked himself alone in his house. He was in a terrible and anxious state of expectancy. The point was that he expected Grushenka that ~~very~~ evening almost for sure, [at least she herself had hinted at it the day before] ~~when he.~~ Yesterday in the morning still he had received Smerdiakov's virtual assurance that she would come. His heart was beating; he walked around the room and kept listening for something. One had to keep a sharp ear out: ~~D.~~ might ~~come~~ Dmitri might be watching out for her, and when she knocked on the window (Smerdiakov had assured him that he had told her where and how to knock), then he would have to open the door immediately so as not to keep her <waiting> in vain in the entry, and so that—God forbid—she would not take fright and run away.

It was trying for F. Pavlovich, but never before had his heart bathed in a sweeter hope. One could say that she would come, for sure, almost for sure, that surely this time she would come.

Book Six

The notes that follow are for Book VI, "The Russian Monk." Dostoevsky considered this book to be the most important in the novel, for in it he confidently expected to overturn the powerful arguments of Ivan Karamazov and those of the Grand Inquisitor in Book V and to allay the fears of his conservative followers, many of whom were afraid that Dostoevsky had gone too far in presenting the arguments of the other side. On 10 May 1879 Dostoevsky wrote to Liubimov to this effect and informed him that "the blasphemy" of the fifth book would be "triumphantly overturned in the next [June] issue, on which I am now working with fear, trembling, and devotion." But as a matter of fact he was still not working on Book VI, since the latter part of May and the first week of June were devoted to finishing Book V, and particularly the chapter on the Grand Inquisitor. He wrote to Liubimov on 11 June that he had sent off the conclusion of the fifth book "three days ago." Somewhere about the middle of June he began serious work on Book VI, but it was not destined for the June issue, nor in fact—as Dostoevsky wrote Liubimov on 8 July—for the July number. Dostoevsky excused the delays by pleading once again the importance of the book. On 8 July he wrote to Liubimov: "I consider this sixth book to be the culminating point of the novel, and I would like to do as well as possible, look it over and clean it up once again; I'm taking it with me to Ems." It was not until 7 August 1879 that he finally wrote to Liubimov that he was sending him the sixth book for the August issue.

To judge from the letters, Dostoevsky worked hard on this book, or tried to work hard on it. He repeatedly stressed its importance, and he sincerely tried to overturn the arguments of Ivan in the fifth book, but the book missed its mark. The writing is pallid, abstract, and lacking in drama; the ideas of Father Zossima read like a list of aphorisms and risk provoking the indifference that banality leaves in its train. Book V appeals with drama and vividness to the universal fount of compassion, suffering. It provokes our sense of justice and injustice; it touches our humanity; it is a call to revolt but also a powerful appeal for human solidarity. Book VI seems remote from human experience, passion, and curiously verbal and abstract. It reads like a sermon.

The notes for this book are—like much of the notes—fragmentary, abstract, disembodied. But the abstractions of the notes of the other books take flesh in descriptive detail and dramatic situation in the final versions. The notes for this book remain disembodied and abstract in the final version itself. It is almost as if Dostoevsky stopped at a preliminary stage, and as such for this section the distance between notes and novel is less. There is amplification, but not concretization; details are added but they are more of the same kind. Both in notes and novel truths are spoken that seem to find no dramatic and human embodiment.

The notes pertain almost exclusively to chapter III, "Conversations and Exhortations of Father Zossima," possibly the most aphoristic and abstract of the three chapters of this section. With the exception of some of the ideas and sentiments that Markel expresses, there are virtually no notes for chapter II, which is, if not dramatic, at least narrative and anecdotal. We have really nothing about Father Zossima's life in the cadet corps, or the visitations of the mysterious stranger. We have some of Markel's thoughts, but no Markel.

As for the teachings of Father Zossima in the third chapter, the main thoughts of notes and novel are the same: all are responsible for all; God has shown the seeds of other worlds on this world; hell is the inability to love; the monastic life or the life of solitude is to be defended against the world's multiplication of desires and superfluities. There are some differences: a condemnation of the clergy for their materialism and slothfulness in the notes is not transported to the novel; concern about child labor is also not found in the novel but is repeatedly talked about in the notes; and there seems to be more emphasis on the undefiled, essential qualities of the peasant, who will overcome the atheistic tendencies of the age.

Many of the notes read like the transcriptions of shorthand, and without the context of the novel they would be mysterious and incomprehensible. We have, for example, the following:

> Salvation in the people. Meeting of the atheists. With the people. Guard the people, educate.

In the novel we get:

> The salvation of Russia comes from the people. And the Russian monk has always been on the side of the people. We are isolated only if the people are isolated. The people believe as we do, and an unbelieving reformer will never do anything in Russia, even if he is sincere in heart and a genius. Remember that! The people will meet the atheist and overcome him, and Russia will be one and orthodox. Take care of the peasant and guard his heart. Go on educating him quietly. That's your duty as monks, for the peasant has God in his heart.

The fragments are amplified, but the amplification is that of exposition and not of drama.

48>   Confession of the Elder
        ——Prologue. Personage—period of people.
avarice 28 800, that eternal dream will lead *to isolation.*
        ——And I saw a marvelous vision, 28,000 men
        ——And I saw *a drowned woman,*
        ——Look up. The Russian solution to the problem.
        ——*Everything is a paradise.* It is not given to many, but it is so easy to see."
The dream about how all are brothers, and not 1/10 against 9/10. *The dream of how at Tikhon's* liberation of the peasants.
        ——Archimandrite, throw the body on the crossroads, for the dogs to tear apart.

    1) Rothschild.[1]

---

[1] Reference to the celebrated French banker. The name appears frequently in the novels of Dostoevsky, especially in *A Raw Youth,* where Arkady's ambition is to become a Rothschild in money and power.

4) Love little children. Why then was I loved. If there were *brothers, brotherhood would follow.*
God's image on man. The masters and Leblaz.

——Self-control, self-domination, work.
We monasteries the picture of that.
On the contrary in the world now: develop your needs, profit from everything.

16) The unbeliever in our Russia will not accomplish anything[2]

——Knowledge of one's country, know one's country

23) Love with a humble love and you will conquer the world.
[If you are an atheist and if you are in doubt, love with an active love and you will return to God and you will see him.]
Shorten, oh Lord, times and periods for the sake of all our children.

25) *He asked pardon of the birds. Everything touches everything . . .*

26) Be an *average* man.
27) Everyone is guilty for all and for everything.
28) I still want to see you strong in the service of others.
30) Prayer; for the sake of children, etc.
Here. 32) And if an infant is killed? Go and take upon yourself the sufferings of another—it will be easier.
(From an individual organism to a general organism)
WITH THE WORDS OF THE ELDER

34) ——Am I worthy of being served by another

35) ——Believe quiet one, believe, dear one.

36) ——It cannot be that the world exists for 1/10 of the people

36) ——Everyone is guilty before everyone. You were a child, and I passed by . . . I was angry . . .

---

[2] Compare with the following from Book VI, chap. III of the final version: "The people believe as we do, and an unbelieving reformer will never do anything in Russia, even if he is sincere in heart and a genius."

9>   37) ——Suffer, pour out blood, all will embrace . . .

The history consists in the fact that *all will be united*—says the sinner, having killed 15 years: I want to suffer.

41) And he who at the ninth hour without fear
> (words before the lamb)

41) About those who commit suicide and those who say *if only the day would pass quickly.*

41) The church—why do we need it, if all would love them, and why should we be angry.

45) Life is a great joy (Lazarus) ~~Suffer, do what you have to~~
The philosopher, it's hard for me, suffer, love with an active love and you will find God.

47) And even if at the very end, there remained only *you two*—give praise, sacrifice, and even if alone—the little tree, the little worm, to all the tombs, and to everything that is beautiful and everything that is evil, a prayer, fall down and kiss the earth, cry, and *love insatiably!* [I've dreamed of only two being left.][3]

Most important, 50) Guilty for all, they corrupted the earth. He could shine as the Unique, Without Sin. *Because everyone can lift his burden, everyone—if he wants* such happiness. He has a human image.

51) You can save the whole earth. Prophets have always been killed. Take suffering upon yourself. (Humility is a very great power).

51) ——All are happy, all are beautiful, all *could create paradise immediately.*[4]

51) Forgive the criminal—the earth forgives and suffers. If you are aggrieved—Look for suffering for yourself.

---

[3] Compare with the following from Book VI, chap. III of the final version: "And if it were not for Christ's covenant, they would slaughter one another down to the last two men on earth." Also, "Believe to the end, even if all men went astray and you were left the only one faithful; bring your offering even then and praise God in your loneliness. And if two of you are gathered together—then there is a whole world, a world of living love."

[4] Dostoevsky describes a conviction of his about how each man carries paradise within him if only he believed that such was the case in *"Zolotoi vek v karmane"* (Golden Age in One's Pocket) in *The Diary of a Writer,* January 1876, Part IV.

51) Do not be afraid of the wealthy or the strong, but be wise . . . be worthy!

51) Love children, and even if you alone on earth were living the truth—do not despair.

51) Guilt for all and for everything, without that you will not be able to save yourself. You will not be able to save yourself, and you won't be able to save <others>. *In saving others, you save yourself.*

52) Nothing dies, everything will be revealed.

[52) Do not believe what others say: It is not necessary to pray. *There is enlightenment in prayer.*]

In every prayer you will feel for an instant a feeling . . . something something new, even for your whole life, for nothing is finished on earth.

52) There cannot be a judge on earth of a criminal until he ac- <50 knowledges first that he is a criminal . . .[5]

52) Love people in their sins, *and love their sins also.*

——*Love animals, the Bear and Sergei.*

53) Charitable works educate the soul. Be *an atheist,* but by way of charitable works, you will arrive at a knowledge of God.

53) Love animals, plants and you will love and see the Mystery of God in them.

53) You will remember at night: I did not fulfill. Arise and fulfill.

53) Be happy, ask *God* for happiness . . . Prayer—enlightens

54) About those who killed each other (Abraham and Lazarus)[6]

55) Be brothers and brotherhood will come; otherwise the tower of Babel.

58) Children, do not look for miracles, faith is killed by miracles.

58) What is hell? The thirst to love again what you had contempt for and did not love on earth.[7]

---

[5] Compare with the following from Book VI, chap. III of the final version: "Remember particularly that you cannot be a judge of any one. For no one can judge a criminal, until he recognizes that he is just such a criminal as the man standing before him, and that he perhaps is more than all men to blame for that crime."

[6] The parable of the rich man and Lazarus is narrated in Book VI, chap. III.

[7] Compare with the following from Book VI, chap. III of the final version: "Fathers and teachers, I ponder 'What is Hell?' I maintain that it is the suffering of being unable to love."

——Those who commit suicide. They have come to despise the gift of life. It is given only once in eternity.

——One instant in a myriad of centuries—

59) The young lady says: I did not earn. To beg. The people have no shame. You are retreating into separateness. Otherwise, aristocrat, no brotherhood, but only *my rights.*

64) Your flesh will change. Illumination of Tabor.[8] Life is a *paradise,* the keys are ours.

65) Remembrance of reading the Bible. The dying soldier. He went to beg forgiveness of a certain woman.

67) About the virgin who drowned herself.

——The little boys in town: Hello, uncle, he gives his little hand.
——The Lord tempted Job—took away his Children—[9]

In the other world: no one can forgive, but *all* can forgive.

1> ——[You fell here before me. Why do you love me? It is Christ that is loved]
——Their anger is cursed because it is cruel.

Order

——The dying brother asked for little birds.

——He began to live: the servants.

——10 percent. No brothers, there will be no brotherhood—

——The duel, love. On the eve of the duel, *the brother* will be remembered.

——Afterward (because of that) paradise.

About paradise. I spoke with the murderer; he would visit me.

——After that I became a monk, began to travel. One has to know Russia, ~~read the Bible~~

---

[8] Mountain southwest of Nazareth, where Christ's transfiguration took place.
[9] Father Zossima narrates the story of Job in Book VI, chap. III. Dostoevsky wrote to his wife the following in 1875: "I am reading Job and it brings me to a state of painful ecstasy; I leave off reading and I walk about my room, almost crying, for an hour. This book, dear Anna, it's strange, it was one of the first to impress me in my life. I was then practically an infant."

1/10 only. How many sins.
Beat his mother.

And I guessed that the whole
world took a different path.

——The boys, the dying soldier, the virgin.

——In hell the just to the
sinners:

——Come, it doesn't matter,
come and we will love you.

——For our Lord has so loved
us, that we are not worthy of
it, and we you.

——Forgive us that we are
forgiving you.

Eternal fire—in that that
we are sinful and forgiven,
and they love us.

in a myriad of centuries,
one instant.

——But this fire will die out,
because they will feel the joy
of forgiveness,

Except for the proud—
eternal blasphemy—

The mystery of God surrounds
man, the mystery of great
order and harmony.

The illumination of Tabor[10]
distinguishing man from food,
blood, from grass.

Read books, *the law*

Socialism
  [Bible]

If the seed does
not die, it remains alone.

——Guilty before everyone
and for everything.

Children, school, what is hell?

——What is hell?

——Love animals, plants and
children.

——Love sins! In truth life
is paradise. Once in a myriad
of centuries it is given.

——Take suffering upon
yourself, seek suffering—

——I began to travel, a great
disturbance; solution of the
problem of 1/10

Christianity is easier than
your (socialism).
The world has gone off on a
different path,

——Knowledge serves only the
proud and the oppressors

——We will become monks—
——No, that is not my career.

And I began to say that life
was a paradise,
    and one man noticed me—

——My little drop of blood.

---

[10] See n. 8.

——And forgiveness of the birds
——Why am I loved, [think on it, and then paradise—]
A fête, a fête took place]
——Little leaves
——Why do you quarrel, Little children.

——Life is paradise.—Well, then what kind of paradise, my friend!
——Because I say that I have paradise in my soul.

——I was not afraid that you would tell about it; you would not have done so.
But how will I be able to look at you? The hate of pride, but only for a moment. My angel conquered the devil in my heart. I left you then.
The black rose

Yes, it is possible that one talks thus, but he acted too passionately.

52> A young man on the river—I see that he has understood. He fell asleep with a light sleep. Then he remembered. Bless the young, Oh, Lord—

My conscience will examine me (he came to kill).

The sculpture of the universe.
and what one can't do with that book. Lord, how the priests are complaining that they can't read, because their salaries are not high enough—

And the people—kind. [Did they come to laugh, would you say. No, not as a joke in the monastery. And this is what has happened to our whole society.]

Lord, may God give peace and quiet to all of God's people!

What is hell? Because if one were to take away this torment, I think, they would become even more unhappy.

Joseph I love you and torment you, torment in loving.
Read this to the peasant, or the prophet Jonas
And not with such a weighty air, but as if you were more sinful than all.

Tormented, tormented while loving, wasted away with love for them, for his country, for his beloved childhood, for his beloved father, and for his dearly beloved mother. All his life he remembered how they sold him somewhere there near a well, and how he wrung his hands.

——Fathers and teachers do not become angry because I have gathered you here to communicate such trifles to you, which you have known for a long time, and which you can teach me a hundredfold more. I am speaking to you from joy, and forgive me my tears.

I sent my orderly away, I was ashamed to look on   <5:
Afterward he met me
father, how can it be you (in a monk's habit). He fell into tears looking at me, we embraced and so joyfully—
What is *hell?*
What is life?—To define oneself as much as possible, I am, I exist. To be like the Lord who says I am who is, but already in the whole plenitude of the whole universe.

And then to give everything
Rothschild.
Christ.
As God gives everyone in Liberty.

Toward the Word
and they return to him ~~and that~~ and fined once again
and that is life

It cannot be that 1/10   <54
——We are striving for that (in Russia).
What does it matter to me that you are great and talented. I myself honor you and *by doing that I respect myself,* that I found the strength in myself to honor you without envying you.

What is there in the universe? Place a pig at the table and it will put its legs on the table—The great man of the future will diminish himself.
And the little person seeing him humility will be touched—
I find the same (pledges) in the man of the people now
did not ~~pay back~~ we will not pay back

——Good day, dear uncle—

And if something kiss the ground
Bear the suffering—

If it is a dream, it is easier to realize it in Christ than without Christ,
because without him it is impossible,
    ——And the whole world is breaking up without him

What is hell.

<5>   The meeting with the Servant (the orderly).

My beloved father, and I see that he still looks at me like an orderly
at an officer, like a servant at his master, but I see too that *our human
oneness* has already come to pass, that our Russian souls had found
something in common. We embraced. Bless me.
    ——But it is not really up to me to bless him.
    [1/10 cannot be. Why such grumbling and dissatisfaction? From
that very fact, unconsciously] (develop one's needs).
    THEIR ANGER IS ACCURSED, BECAUSE IT IS CRUEL.
    About the service of monks to society I traveled over Russia 1/10
Child labor.
    Let that not be, not be. And if one cannot avoid that, then it would
be better for the state to fall and we with it, just so that children are
not touched.
    Our people are God-carriers—be great and I will honor you.—[11]
    If there were brothers, there would be brotherhood.
    [earlier] And without brotherhood, there will be nothing. The
unbeliever in our Russia will not accomplish anything.
    ——Teach that in humility and faith.
    Because our land is saved [only] by the people—
    The people's truth and the atheism of society[12]
    The meeting will be terrifying
    The suffering of the people.
    Children—
    Take guilt upon yourself for everything

---

[11] These scattered and unrelated phrases are found on this notebook page. They
do not fit into the context: "And the orderly with us. Here. I met the orderly. We
live by begging. A proud man does not beg. The death of the Elder. And is it true
that such a small incident? Yes, it shook me. Convinced that paradise will come."

[12] Compare the following from Book VI, chap. III of the final version: "The
people will meet the atheist and overcome him, and Russia will be one and
orthodox."

——And love the earth while shedding tears
——What is hell—
Dream. Christ—much truer—than the tower of Babel.

The next to the last one will kill the last one.

The monk is a servant reserved for a day and an hour and month and year. because the truth of the people up to now is from us, from the holy and saintly, from the fathers who bear God with them.

Keep the image of Christ and if possible picture him in yourself.

——Many will not want to enter paradise and will remain with   <5◀
Satan. We have difficulty in even conceiving of the pride of Satan. We know only that God is life, leads to life and the word ~~and that is death,~~ leads to the fulfillment of life, and Satan is death and the desire for self-destruction. The pride of Satan is hard for us on earth to conceive. And besides we cannot conceive of many of our strongest feelings and strivings while we are on earth. The roots of our thoughts and feelings are not here, but in other worlds.[13] God took the seeds from other worlds and sowed them on the earth, and cultivated a garden of his own, and that arose what could arise, but [all those that have arisen] live with the mysterious feeling of contact with other worlds. That is why [it is said] that we cannot know the essence of things on earth. I believe so.

[But the materialists laugh.]

——They have noted a unity in the attraction of planets, how could there not be unity in the rest. They will say that there is nothing else but the attraction of planets—but that is madness. They were not able to observe everything, but they have just begun to notice. And we are attracted to more than to planets.[14]

——Brother Anfim, one little world only: Lord!

----

[13] Compare the following from Book VI, chap. III of the final version: "Much on earth is hidden from us, but to make up for that we have been given a precious mystic sense of our living bond with the other world, with the higher heavenly world, and the roots of our thoughts and feelings are not here but in other worlds. That is why the philosophers say that we cannot apprehend the reality of things on earth.

God took seeds from different worlds and sowed them on this earth, and His garden grew up and everything came that could come up, but what grows lives and is alive only through the feeling of its contact with other mysterious worlds."

[14] The thoughts of this paragraph are not to be found in the final version.

About the Volga.—

——And father Anfim brought them and gave them with the money from the monastery spice, bread, and sugar.

——Love, oh, love.

——We ought to give much also, remarked the father superior.

——The world has taken a different road. Masters and Leblaz. They suffer it cold-bloodedly. And in the streets, traffic, Carriages, Lord, Alyosha a prayer: all those who have appeared before you . . .

——Liberate oneself from the tyranny of things and habits.

——The family as the practical basis of love.

The family becomes more encompassing: other than relatives enter into it, the beginning of a new organism begins to develop.

57> [and to butcher a living Russia, the living body and blood does not mean anything to him, worse than a foreigner and an outlaw. Exiled from the people—that is their misfortune.]
——And what's more: and none are so full of such materialism as are the clergy. We have the mystery, we make the mystery. Children atheism, and forthwith materialism (the priest in his vestments is respected, but without his vestments, he is a moneygrubber and a despoiler). The laity is materialistic, if a professor he is so [sarcastically]; if he is a civil servant he is indifferent to his work and abstract [full of] plans for he doesn't know life at all. No one piles up money like ~~the priest~~ the priest's son. The priest too ~~would~~ store up money but he has no way of doing so.

——To beg is shameful, one person cannot give up his identity to another, it is so because of our sins, *but we are not ashamed of the people.*
——But there are proud ones in hell, and they will neither forgive or ask for forgiveness.
The fire of love is so powerful. Material fire is only coolness, because a quenching. It is an abstract reflection of the other fire.

——I have always felt guilty for those who commit suicide; always prayed.[15]

——But if all have forgiven everything (for themselves), aren't they strong enough to forgive everything for others. Everyone is guilty before all and for everything, and *therefore* everyone is strong enough also to forgive everything for others, and all will then become the work of Christ, and He Himself will appear among them, and they will see him and will become united with him, and he will forgive also the grand priest Caliphe because he loved his people, [loved them in his own way], he will also forgive the clever Pilate who had reflected on truth, because he did not know what he was creating. What is the Truth? It stood before him, Truth itself.

There will also be the proud ones, oh, they will be there with Satan, they will not want to enter, although everyone will be able to, and even Satan entered, but they will refuse.

——The world is full of beloved dead people, full of great people— They dream of aluminum columns, the queen-woman prostituted.[16]

Before they did not pay any attention to me, and then suddenly ~~they themselves~~ all began to call me. They themselves laugh at me, but they have come to love me.

[Give up tobacco.][17]

<5

[How will I be able to serve, when I can't renounce.]
[*And I will not move.*]

[Formerly,] simple men of action used to leave our monasteries, why can't it be so now.

---

[15] Compare the following from Book VI, chap. III of the final version: "But woe to those who have slain themselves on earth, woe to the suicides! I believe that there can be none more miserable than they. They tell us that it is a sin to pray for them and outwardly the Church, as it were, renounces them, but in my secret heart I believe that we may pray even for them. Love can never be an offense to Christ. For such as those I have prayed inwardly all my life, I confess it, fathers and teachers, and even now I pray for them every day."

[16] This may be a reference to the crystal palace in Vera's fourth dream in N. G. Chernyshevsky's *What Is to Be Done?* (1863).

[17] Compare the following from Book VI, chap. III of the final version: "I knew one 'champion of freedom' who told me himself that when he was deprived of tobacco in prison, he was so wretched at the privation that he almost went and betrayed his cause for the sake of getting tobacco again! And such a man says, 'I am fighting for the cause of humanity.' "

———Monk. Different monks. Great idea. For an hour, a day, a month . . . [because the monasteries preserve. Isolation The freedom of one's needs. There are more things, but less joy.]

———Keep the image of Christ

———Because the people believe as we do

———And the unbelievers in our Russia will not accomplish anything.

[There will be nothing without Christ. That is what must be believed.]

———Russia. Be great and I will respect you.

10 percent.

Afanasy[18]

[*The blood is spilled with anger,* but their anger is accursed.]

———The tower of Babel. The next to the last one.

———Their anger is accursed because it is cruel—

[Without brothers there will be no brotherhood.]

The dream of Christ is truer.

But there is much sin among the people.

Debauchery—of separation.

Drank up all that he had.

Children, drunkenness.

———Salvation in the people. Meeting of the atheists. With the people. Guard the people, educate.

There you have a monk's feat.

[Here 10 percent.] It is not a matter of Jewish gold. We do not look upon even begging as shameful. The feeling of solidarity.

They have shame—they kill themselves.

———The virgin girl—

Everyone is guilty before everyone, 25

Servants. Birds—prayer education (52)

And he will cease to separate himself, to amass money.

The destruction of the great thought of brotherly union.

Then we will not be afraid of science either. We will even reveal new paths for it.

Hell. THE PROUD ONES WILL REMAIN. THEY WILL BURN IN THE FIRE OF THEIR ANGER AND THEIR PRIDE AND WILL DEMAND DEATH WHILE CURSING WHAT IS LIVING.

---

18 The name of Father Zossima's orderly, when Father Zossima was an officer.

One must admit what is odious in Russia—. . . . Kulaks, middlemen, but one must not see only what is bad, or one will miss the precious diamond.

The god-bearing people, how polite.

[10 percent. We are moving toward that.]

With us those who are first, the separation by capital will be over.

——Afanasy.   <59>

——He gave a half-ruble—

——the union took place

——Servants

——I repeat—it is impossible for there not to be servants

——The people: they believe constantly and cry softly.

Afanasy: is it really few. And yet such—

I believe with my living soul

Children, [love one another and do not be afraid of the sins of people—]

Love in sin, *for that is already Divine Love.*

——What is hell? . . . Now I have the knowledge, and though I have the thirst for loving, and [even though I love], the feat will not be one of love, and it cannot be.

For there will no longer be life and "no longer be time."

I can no longer repay love with love—

Hell, the proud. For such hell is voluntary and they are insatiable, for they cursed themselves when they cursed God and life. The evil fill themselves with their own despair [feed on their own envy and hate], as a hungry man would begin to suck his own blood—but they will not satiate their hunger in centuries to come.—

Pray to God for such, it is sin, they say, but pray. God will not take offense at love.

[Ask, and then in such a spirit, as much as possible will be given.]

——The bear is dangerous and fierce, but he is not responsible for   <60>
that.

——Little children ought to be raised with animals—with a horse, a cow, a dog. They will be better and their souls will have more understanding.

"I hate Russia." It has come even to the point of hate. Write whatever you will that is defamatory about the Russian man, and you will be proclaimed as a great man. Write that the Russian is lazy (Oblomov).[19] The Russian, doesn't work?—all that comes from the fact that for two hundred years there has been nothing *common,* the whole herd, millions and millions of them, has been splintered into little pieces. Except for faith, there is nothing in common, and even the faith has been undermined. Do not leave the people. That is a matter for monasteries. Support at least the common work of faith, and you will arrive at everything.

———Children of eight work, at six they lose their innocence. Cry out against that and work. I say thus: If you are bored, great philosopher, because you don't have activity great enough for you, teach a little child to read. And if you want to serve God, love the little child and help him. Only a little is needed at times, very little, and yet a seed is sown forever. [PASSIONATE]

———The clergy cry out that they do not earn enough. And others come and take possession of the flock. But don't think on it, begin with the children, cultivate the soil and you will see how all will come to your aid. What is a priest today for the people? A holy person when he is in church or when occupied with the mysteries. But when at home, he is to the people a moneygrubber. One must not live like that. And perhaps you will not be able to keep the faith. The people will become tired of believing, in truth it is like that. What are the words of Christ without an example? And you will sell him even the words of Christ for money. The ruin of the people, the ruin of faith, but God will save. You cry out that there's too little income: but you should have it worse, go on foot and without shoes, and you will see how your love will increase and also your resources. Is it true, what the unbelievers say that salvation will not come from them [the priests] [that salvation is outside the church]. Perhaps it is true. It is terrible.

61>   I have seen the clergy with children: they teach them the law, what the sacrament is, the texts, catechism. Let the schools do that. But is that what the little country lad needs; read him the whole story of how Jacob went to Laban, how the beautiful Joseph, Alexei, the man

---

[19] Novel by Alexander Ivanovich Goncharov published in 1856. Also the name of the main character, an indolent dreamer.

of God, Mary, the Egyptian—and you will change him for his whole life.[20]

What kinds of books are they—I'll tell you—

——A poor man died on a boat, alone.
——The virgin. The beauty was an obstacle. Who, if not the city, is guilty? It seems to be so. But the city means other <people>. Who is guilty if not you—that's where the truth is.

——Let everything be ready.

——And about the queen Jezebel, and about Esther, and the arrogant Vashti.[21] The tender faces look on, feeling grows and changes in their eyes, and though no one says that they love you, they love you: What reward is greater? When you go to sleep, God's ray lights up bright dreams for you.—Oh Lord, yet another day, bless what I'm doing. Do not think that you have accomplished little, don't think so, oh, do not think so. There are many, many such and room for you among them. How is one to know all the paths of history. . . .

I met a worker on the Volga, we went off together—he was enthusiastic about nature, the night (bear, harmony, nature), forgive me, dear one. Then I met him drunk. He broke into tears. God will remember his tears, but we are the guilty ones, all of us—
But isn't this worker a fantasy. Less fantastic than our economic system.
The truth will shine forth, it is so promised.—
——The world has taken another path, but all we need do is love one another and everything will be accomplished immediately.

You don't believe in God, and so it is impossible for you not to live materially. The more materialistic, on the contrary, the better, for

---

[20] Compare the following from Book VI, chap. I of the final version: "Let him read about Abraham and Sarah, about Isaac and Rebecca, of how Jacob went to Laban and wrestled with the Lord in his dream and said, 'This place is holy'—and he will impress the devout mind of the peasant."
[21] Compare with the following from Book VI, chap. I of the final version: "Do you suppose that the peasants don't understand? Try reading them the touching story of the fair Esther and the haughty Vashti; or the miraculous story of Jonah in the whale."

everything then comes to an end with it . . . There are no limits to materialism, and you will come to the refinements of tyranny and the devouring of one another. And don't dream, materialists, that mutual advantage will force you to construct an order like that of a regular society. This cannot be, for your society will require sacrifice from everyone, but a corrupt desire will not want to sacrifice. A strong desire and great talent will not want to be compared with mediocrity, and since there will be no moral tie, ~~except for capacities~~ except for the mutual advantage of bread, then the great and powerful will arise with his savagery and confederates, and you will begin to destroy each other in eternal enmity and you will devour each other, and that's the way it will finish.

Book Seven

The notes for Book VII are almost entirely about Grushenka, and Dostoevsky considered at one point, as he explained in a letter to Liubimov on 7 August 1879, entitling the book "Grushenka." There are a few notes about the putrefaction of the Elder's corpse, a few more about Father Ferapont's intrusion and indictment of the Elder in Father Paissy's presence, but only fragments of reaction to the rapid decay and putrefaction and about Alyosha's dream of Cana in Galilee. The notes are essentially about Alyosha's visit to Grushenka.

In both notes and novel Alyosha has come to Grushenka from revolt; Rakitin has brought him because he will be paid and because he gloats in the fall of the virtuous; Grushenka and Alyosha find in each other loving and compassionate hearts; the anecdote of the onion is related; and Grushenka narrates her past and the circumstances of her early love for the Pole and her reasons for preparing to go to him once again. But in the notes Grushenka is more open about her intention to seduce Alyosha, as Alyosha is more open about his sensuous longings. In the novel Alyosha's revolt does not go beyond eating a sausage, promising to drink some vodka, going to Grushenka's and having her sit on his lap. But in the notes we are told that Alyosha had been bitten by sensuous feelings for Grushenka and Grushenka states several times that she had intended to seduce him.

Despite the fact that there is a close parallel in content between notes and novel, Dostoevsky adds, as he does often, psychological and descriptive body and refinement to the notes. In both notes and novel Grushenka asks Alyosha whether she should forgive her Polish lover. And in both Alyosha says that she has already forgiven him. Her answer to Alyosha's reply in the notes is the following:

> "To be sure, I forgave. Still . . . But perhaps not yet, perhaps I haven't forgiven. I was lying down and kept thinking when you entered . . . My heart was beating."

And in the novel we have the following:

> "Yes, I really have forgiven him," Grushenka murmured thought-
> fully. "What an abject heart! To my abject heart!" She snatched up
> a glass from the table, emptied it at a gulp, lifted it in the air and
> flung it on the floor. The glass broke with a crash. A little cruel line
> came into her smile.
>
> "Perhaps I haven't forgiven him, though," she said, with a sort of
> menace in her voice, and she dropped her eyes to the ground as
> though she were talking to herself. "Perhaps my heart is only getting
> ready to forgive, I shall struggle with my heart. You see, Alyosha,
> I've grown to love my tears in these five years. . . . Perhaps I only love
> my resentment, not him . . ."

The drinking of the vodka and then the breaking of the glass are
more than descriptive details. They are a dramatic embodiment of
what Grushenka is saying. She drinks the vodka in one gulp as she has
drunk the poison of forgiveness and the throwing and breaking of the
glass is a gesture of violence against the act of forgiveness. Also in the
novel Dostoevsky provides us with an explanation of why she has perhaps not forgiven her lover; that it is the resentment and not the
lover that she has loved for five years.

‹2›   Extreme unction (Is extreme unction repeatable?)
——Rite.
——Communion. Rite.
——Funeral. Rite
Water. Oil. Holy cloth Cloak Slippers. Coat. Cowl with a cross. On
the wings of the cherubims, coat. Black cover, and the open cloak.—
——How much time in the cell before the taking of the body to
the church?
——Who reads over the body?
——The priest-Monk. The Bible. The priest-Monks and the monk-
deacons.
Chapter, Grushenka
‹3›   [The story of the frivolity and thoughtlessness of people.]

Much about thoughtlessness. The Elder, *repugnant to describe.* But necessary because something happened that had an influence on the soul and *significance* of one of the heroes of the tale (Alyosha). and began to yell. An impatient one who had run in after Father Ferapont on the stairs from . . .]

——Khokhlakova—she did not expect that from the Elder (such an action).

——Grusha. The little onion.
——The seminarian stands up for the priests.

2) Grushenka: Why hasn't anyone spoken such words to me before?

——The people will not want. *The Seminarian.* Get rid of the people.
5) The other one is too saintly, but in Grushenka there is a vitality that corresponds better with my corrupt soul. (N.B. Seminar. To Alyosha *when they are going to Grushenka's.*)

12) The monks about the Elder: Why didn't he open the letters? And others: why did he open them . . .

16) Alyosha would have been horrified, *last night sensuous feelings* for Grushenka bit him! (But he goes *with the seminarian*)

21) *Seminarian* To Alyosha: you say that I'm dishonest. And he says that I am liberal old bag without talent (the priests guard the secrets. For the priests) (*when they are walking to Grushenka's*). *At Grushenka: But why should I love you?*
22) Grushenka about Katerina Iv. Mitia related that she was yelling: whip her. But I would simply spank her. I would invite her and give her a whipping. What's more, a good spanking.

23) Grushenka. She wanted to conquer. She invited me and the girl vanquished me.

49) The smell of corruption. Alyosha in the forest. He lay down in   <64
the copse. What difference does Iliusha, or Mitia make to him. Rakitin finds him.

53) Rakitin and Alyosha. God is just but I don't accept his world. The elder was a shining example and now . . .

——*Rakitin:* Can it be that such a bit of stupidity (how he smelled) made you lose your senses (separated <you> from God?) They didn't give him a promotion, and you're in revolt.

——And you wouldn't have revolted?

——Drink a little vodka. Come on

——At Grushenka's reminisces about animals, about his childhood; astonishes

——*Who rocked you in the cradle, who sang over your cradle?*

——Rakitin: The Russian people are not good, because they are not civilized.

54) I went about barefooted (Grushenka) He seduced me. I became bitter and I became vile. Play a little on the piano. (Champagne. Rakitin) cries out: let's have some Champagne, I brought him! She promised a bottle.)

——Alyosha. Forgive me for crying over you.

Grushenka. He is a king and you are a toadstool.

Rakitin. I'll show you still (got angry)

——(he took 25 rubles; Grushenka he betrayed you. I promised him 25.)

55) *Alyosha* to Grushenka. I am guilty for you.

Grushenka: You are a little boy, what are you guilty for before me? To Rakitin: "Don't laugh, you imbecile. You never said that. He's talking seriously."

Rakitin. I'm not going to start talking nonsense.

55> ——23) When the cadaver began to smell Alyosha began to doubt for the reason that Ivan had so clearly thrown out: "The Elder is holy, but there isn't any God."

——Alyosha to Grushenka: You *turned me* back to God.

——The seminarian had *an air of having been insulted* when he left.

28) Alyosha, instead of teaching, looks for *peace* from Grushenka: give me peace. My sister.

——And I am guilty before you as before birds.

——Who are the righteous. If we didn't have them, we would all be brothers, and you are everyone's sister.

——For Grushenka tears and laughter mingle:
——Let's go and pray to God for all. [richer]

——29) Accusations against the elder by the monks.

30) Stellar glory.

——32) The monks about the Elder, he ate jam
——Ferapont: The institution of the Elders is a novelty, he will
go to hell. A hunk of bread every week.

——33) The monks about the Elder. Why the bad smell, the body
was small. Windows. God wanted to show a sign on purpose. [It
means] God's judgment is not man's. *I am uneducated.* The land-
holders and the protectors.
——34) *The monks:* He abused the sacrement of confession.
——Grushenka. She gave A LITTLE ONION.

36) You were a little child, and I passed by
Grushenka But you weren't even born yet,
The world for 1/10 of the people.

——43) The father Joseph: *On Mount Athos—yellow bones.*

——45) The monks: he taught that life was joy and permitted himself sweets.

46) *Alyosha to Grushenka* Why are you unhappy, from now on we
will be happy.—Everything that is true and beautiful is always full of
universal forgiveness.
——Stellar Glory.

59) Grushenka, you are good, protect me.   <6(
——No, I'm not good, I was getting ready *to eat you up,* do you
understand? I did it from spite.

68) You were pushed that way from childhood. No mercy was
shown to you.
Grushenka. You are really speaking the truth.
——Let me cry a little. . . . It's good to cry; the old woman and the
vicious one.

70) Why, cherub, did you not visit me? . . . . I have waited for that all my life . . . I knew that someone would come . . . I had faith that someone would come to love me, disgusting though I was, *but not for the shame alone.* [*I will tear my face apart*]—

72) Gave a little onion. But everything else was sin . . .

——They still think they are at war with the Turks and have forgotten everything.

——Rakitin: but is it possible that you believed in relics of a saint's body?)
Alyosha: I believed, and I believe, and I want to believe, and I will believe.
[Yet, you are still educated.]
The Monks—open the windows: it was understood that there could be no question of smell from a saint's relics. *A thin one.*

——Grushenka to Rakitin: Don't you dare use the familiar address with me. (pig)—Whaaaat?

——Such an immediate expectation of something extraordinary is a frivolity that is excusable for the laity, but inappropriate for us . . . Rakitin. The little monk from Obdorsk. Alyosha (was crying in a corner). What's the matter with you, we are joyful and do not cry . . . But then cry, cry, with softened heart and joyfully. The tears of a softened heart are a rest for the soul, the joy of the heart which resides in heaven.

[Ferapont to the dying sun. To the dying sun—]
——Alyosha heard. Although Paissy could not hear what Alyosha heard, still he guessed everything. He understood the situation completely, and watched over it with a piercing, sober, and tranquil gaze.
There was no smell from the body of Father Leonid [for years], nothing, nothing, he kept the fast.
Accept it and suffer for him.[1]

---

[1] This paragraph belongs to Book VI, chap. III, "Conversations and Exhortations of Father Zossima."

——Rakitin had an irritated look, but he still restrained himself. <67
He is a little Polak, and so forth—and suddenly gibes; you converted,
—Enough, don't get angry said Alyosha.
——Oh, go to the devil, And you too. From now on I don't want to
know you.

At Grushenka's.—Rakitin was standing and was astonished at them:
why was everything so extraordinary between them. And truly before
the meeting each of them had an unusually heavy heart, almost beside themselves (excited). [Her lover had arrived, and Alyosha's Elder
had left him]

——When they entered Grushenka's place, she was in an extraordinary state of excitement. And *among other things,* she cried out
when she saw Alyosha (but joyfully). Well, you didn't arrive in time
with him, I've got something else to think about now.

Grushenka cries out after Alyosha: And tell Mitia from me, with
my words: Goodbye, Mitia, don't think badly about me and don't be
angry, I loved you for a while, but it is not for you to know the
diamond that I have guarded. It's for another . . .[2]
(And up to then she had not mentioned Mitia during all that time,
thought Alyosha).

Cana in Galilee. The texts as he goes to sleep.
——[And here is Cana in Galilee, there is the marriage,] here is the
young and wise master of the fête, leans over the fiancé with a good
and sly smile.
Cana in Galilee, Zossima among the guests, a thin old man, cloak,
an eight-branched cross, but the face unveiled. What a joyful face.—
I gave a little onion, quietly laughing, and his delicate lines quivered. To Alyosha: Why are you astonished, I gave a little onion and
here I am. And all here gave only a little onion. Let's go. Do you see
the sun, do you see our Sun.

---

[2] Compare with the following from Book VII, chap. III of the final version:
"Alyosha, give my greetings to your brother Mitya and tell him not to remember
evil against me, though I have brought him misery. And tell him too in my words:
'Grushenka has fallen to a scoundrel, and not to you, noble heart.' And add, too,
that Grushenka loved him only one hour, only one short hour she loved him—
so let him remember that hour all his life—say, 'Grushenka tells you to!' "

——I see it . . . I am afraid, whispered Alyosha.

Do not be afraid of Him. He is terrifying in his majesty [before us ~~terrifying in~~ terrifying because of his loftiness,] but he is infinitely merciful, [as if all he had done] was give a little onion just like us.

> From love, he has made himself like us
> like a guest, a fellow-conversationalist
> he attends upon the marriage festival
> he changed water into wine
> so that the joy would not be interrupted
> look, they are passing about the cups—
> There he is, you see him

Something burned in Alyosha's heart, was bursting, but his heart was fainting with love

——Where is he? someone's voice rang out, another one woke up, and it was as if the whole universe was reflected in Alyosha's heart—

68> You are afraid of him, of such a little chicken?

Grushenka. He's a little chicken for you, [that's what I'm afraid of]. Do you believe, Alyosha, that I love you, that's what. And not in a shameful manner, but I love you like an angel of some kind. [Truly Alyosha, I've had my eye on you for a long time. I keep thinking that it is my little son that is going by there, and how truly he feels contempt for vile me. And I am ashamed. Do you believe that at times I simply think about you and I'm ashamed . . . Because . . . because I nourished another thought about you.] And now it was that I began to think about you and when I started, I don't know and I don't remember.[3]

---

[3] Compare with the following from Book VII, chap. III of the final version: "And now, Alyosha, I'll tell you the whole truth, that you may see what a wretch I am! I am not talking to Rakitin, but to you, I wanted to ruin you, Alyosha, that's the holy truth; I quite meant to. I wanted to so much, that I bribed Rakitin to bring you. And why did I want to do such a thing? You knew nothing about it, Alyosha, you turned away from me, if you passed me, you dropped your eyes. And I've looked at you a hundred times before today, I began asking every one about you. Your face haunted my heart. 'He despises me,' I thought, 'he won't even look at me.' And I felt it so much at last that I wondered at myself for being so frightened of a boy. I'll get him in my clutches and laugh at him. I was full of spite and anger."

Rakitin—Oh you shameless hussy. She is declaring her love.

Grushenka. And so I love. And the officer in Mokroe. And so what about the officer. I don't love him at all in that way. But why are you so sad (and she fell on her knees). Surely you will let me go (on her knees), surely you are not angry. Why do you look at me so pleasantly?

——[I can't explain what is the matter with me. Zossima.]

Alyosha. Save me from myself.

[I'm telling you that his master began to smell.]

. . . Grushenka. Don't be sad. To Rakitin. Play Rakitka. Don't speak about the soul, Rakitin. There, they're bringing the champagne.

Alyosha swallowed a mouthful: no, there's nothing better.

Grushenka. Well, and afterward. I don't want to either. Drink along Rakitin. No it's better. Good-bye Alyosha. You are good.[4] [You gave a little onion.]

Grushenka. I am good. I'm carnivorous (again about the young lady). [It is not fitting for me to sit on your lap. Forgive me. I wanted to seduce you. Kneeling down. And you say that I'm good.]

Alyosha . . . And I also thought of you.

Grushenka. What, what did you think about me.

Alyosha. About her beauty and her soul. Dithyramb. He ends up about Zossima. Began to cry. Rakitin is witty. Be quiet Rakitin. [You are a toadstool, and he is a prince.]

Rakitin. Pay up—

Grushenka. She brought out 25 rubles. Do you know that he sold you, Judas ~~don't dare~~

——You don't like us.

Rakitin. —Why should I like you—

Grushenka. Love for no reason at all. [*She gave a little onion.*]

—Rakitin.—

Grushenka. Don't you dare use the familiar address with me. He is a prince and you are a toadstool

Little onion.

Alyosha. Who sang over your cradle?

Grushenka. Confessions. I lay down feeling nasty and I got up more vicious than a dog.

Alyosha I passed by perhaps.

———————————

[4] The gender of the adjective indicates that Alyosha is calling Grushenka good.

Grushenka But you weren't even born then

Alyosha. Another doesn't matter. All are guilty before all.

Grushenka. Reflectively: that was well said—(then, about the cradle. You are pure and generous in soul)

Grushenka. I am corrupted. *Alyosha.* The years will pass and you will find your heart—

[[(You see, Alyosha, he is coming: forgive him or not?)] Well, tell me. I was lying and thinking of who would tell me.

He is coming. I want to be pure. ~~Forg~~ (Rakitin again). Forgive or not, Alyosha—

69>   *Grushenka* . . . Alyosha, will you believe me?

Alyosha I will believe you.

Grushenka (moving away with a smile) Will you believe me really in everything?

Alyosha I will believe you in everything.

Grushenka I was afraid that you would have contempt for the scoundrel that I am—

Grushenka. (On her knees before him). His eyes Rakitin, what eyes. I noticed his eyes a long time ago.

——Rakitin about the fiancé, And where will he come?

Grushenka. Perhaps here, and perhaps in another place at first. They'll let me know.

——When?

——Perhaps any moment. I've been waiting since yesterday from hour to hour.

——Rakitka, tell me, etc.

Grushenka. I wanted to corrupt you. Rakitin here kept wanting, he kept putting me up to it. I am ashamed of myself before you.

——You are good.

——We are drinking the new wine, of new joy, of greatness.

Here he sits ~~humbly~~ gentle toward us, humble, and merciful, he sits in our human form, as if he himself had only given a small onion—

——*Grushenka.* At times I lay for whole days, nasty . . . At times I think that I will go to work for all the people.

Grushenka. At night you go to sleep full of anger. *In the morning* you get up more furious than a dog.

——Alyosha: But the people will not permit that.

——Well, then, destroy the people, curtail them, make them keep quiet. Because European enlightenment is greater than the people ... (fell silent). [No, it is clear that serfdom has not disappeared, uttered Alyosha.]

But the devil with you and the people. Go away! I don't want to know any more. (he turned around and went away angry).

——Rakitin went away angry from Grushenka's. Alyosha was silent. But Rakitin began to talk: "Everything can be done without religion, enlightenment. People are becoming more humane, More educated, and more humane. Ignorance. Religion is too expensive. You ought to read at least Buckle.[5] And we will destroy it.

——The people will not permit it.

Nakedly, without preparation, suddenly as when one expresses extreme statements in anger and rage, just to express oneself.

The most important, Rakitin was irritated that Alyosha was silent and was not arguing with him. They had exchanged crosses.

You are an aristocrat, Rakitin.

——I am not an aristocrat but a priest's son, but the hell with you, and he went away, etc.

You took offense and talk that way.

——At Grushenka's. I took offense! Oh, you, bastards! He went away.

The devil take it why I got tied up with you! I don't want to see you again.

But if one were to tell all the truth, he became friends in the hope that Alyosha had influence in the monastery.

——Rakitin and Alyosha come in: <7(

Grushenka. Oh, oh, well! You've picked a pretty time to come! (she laughs)

---

[5] Henry Thomas Buckle (1821–1862) believed that "the progress of every people is regulated by principles ... as certain as those which govern the physical world." He equated the progress of civilization with the advance of knowledge. His *History of Civilization in England* (1859–1861) appeared in a Russian translation in 1864–66. There is a reference in *Notes from the Underground* to Buckle's belief that civilization becomes softer with the passage of history and less adaptable to cruelty and war.

Rakitin. Did we pick the wrong time?

Grushenka. I'm expecting guests.

Rakitin. What kind of guests? Here.

Grushenka. Well, here or some other place. I'm troubled, and you bring him. Even yesterday would have been better, but to bring him here at such a time. But, no matter. I'm glad anyway. Perhaps it's even better. I am really glad to meet you any time [Why did you come]. Why I'm happy on your account, I myself don't know—because before *I wanted* you to come *for a completely different reason.* Do you believe that? But sit down, sit down. I'll give you a good time. Rakitka. Now, I'm good. Sit down, Alyosha dear. You sit down, too, Rakitka, oh, you've already sat down. Do you know Alyosha, here he is sitting and taking offense because I didn't ask him earlier to sit down. so How did you lure him here, not, no, how is it possible that such a treasure should come here: without doubt you were passing by.

Rakitin—He is unhappy. No promotion. He stank.—

Grushanka. So the elder Zossima died. Lord and (she crossed herself piously). But what a moment to bring him here.

[And I who was thinking, etc. But what foolishness and I'm still sitting on his knees, jumped off. What are you afraid of. Sausage.]

Rakitin. Bring on the champagne. He's going to drink champagne. He was about to eat sausage. He's ready for all kinds of sins.

Grushenka. Why so? [ALYOSHA FIRMLY]

That's all nonsense, I don't understand anything.

[That's enough Rakitin. I feel better looking at you, and you, Grushenka. I haven't revolted Rakitin.]

Rakitin. I'm telling you he stank. And that's why he revolted.

Alyosha did not revolt, he sat down sad and covered his face with his hands. Grushenka went to him with compassion. And then: I'll make you happy, I'll make you happy. Truly, although I'm stingy, I do have a bottle of champagne. Mitia left it.

[You'll permit me really on your lap, you really won't get angry?]

Rakitin. You know she promised a bottle of champagne for you, Alyosha. If you bring him, I'll offer a bottle of champagne. That's why I'm asking for it.

Grushenka. Well, you are something! I'll not give it to you. His eyes. I (to Alyosha). Though I'm happy, though I'm waiting for guests, I want to have a good time.

Rakitin—But you have done up your hair [as if you were waiting for us to do your hair], and you've dressed yourself up.

You can sit down, you can. Ah, but it is not the moment for it now.

Grushenka.—He is coming. The officer in Mokroe.—

Rakitin. Why in Mokroe?—.—I suppose that Mitenka, now.

Grushenka. Don't remind me of Mitenka. He broke my heart completely. I don't want to think about anything right now. I'm looking at Alyoshenka now But, smile. See, he smiled. How affectionately he is looking. And I thought, you know Alyosha, that you were angry with me? (at the schoolgirls) . . . No, It wasn't good. I'm carnivorous I invited you. But I was afraid that you were angry.

Rakitin.—Really, she was afraid of you. She's always afraid. But of what

Rakitin: Well, have you *converted* her? Have you *converted* the <7] sinner? ~~Happy that~~ ~~Devil~~ Drove out the seven devils. Happy because of that.

Here were revealed 22 years, ~~young~~ the impatience of youth. Youth's lack of restraint.

Grushenka. And I wanted to seduce you. *I haven't given my sinful body to anyone* except to that old man, but *I wanted to give it to you,* and so I had decided to seduce you . . . Base, I am base!

——We are drinking the new wine (miraculous)—

MUST NOT FORGET—CANDLES—

Must not forget—as if?—

——Rakitin was surprised by their enthusiasm, by their apparent ecstasy. But [for both of them] everything that should have shaken their souls united them: for one, the death of the Elder and everything that happened that day, and for the other the news she had just received of the arrival of that man, so fateful in her life, to whom she had, as a young inexperienced girl, given her love once, and who had thrown her over coarsely without pity, who had married and outraged her, and who now, having become a widow, remembered her, and if he remembered her, it must be then because he was in love, for now he was coming, had almost already arrived, had announced himself, and although Grushenka knew about his coming long ago, even though he had reminded her and announced himself two months ago, still the news that he was already here must have shaken her soul terribly—and she was in a state of violent emotion. But Rakitin was unperturbed. [But he continued to be astonished and was even maliciously angry at their ecstasy.]

[They went out. He is a Pole, I wouldn't want to be in his shoes . . .]

[—Oh Rakitin—]

[—You're angry because of those 25 rubles doubtlessly you have contempt for me—]

[——Alyosha. I was not even thinking about it—]

[——Oh, the hell with you.]

——Forgive or not.

——But you have already forgiven him.

——To be sure, I forgave. Still . . . But perhaps not yet, perhaps I haven't forgiven. I was lying down and kept thinking when you entered . . . My heart was beating.

[You're bragging, Rakitin maliciously reproached here.]

——Why did you get all dressed up? Rakitin asked maliciously.

——Don't reproach me for the dress, Rakitin. You don't know my heart. If I want, I will tear up these clothes, you don't know why I've gotten dressed: Perhaps ~~THE BODY OF THE DECEASED MONK FATHER ZOSSIMA~~ I'll show myself to him, and I'll say: you have seen me, am I beautiful or not? ~~Well, be satisfied with that~~ I'll seduce him, and I'll astonish him, after all, he left me as a 17-year-old, thin and consumptive! I'll say, you've seen what I am now. Well, then be satisfied with that: it's a long way from cup to lips. [I'll see at first how he himself is] (laughs maliciously). I am violent, Alyosha, and malicious.

——The cradle—

She began to cry.

But what did you tell her.

——[I'll tear it up—]

[Rakitin got up, enough.]

[Well, where are you going?]

——Alyosha, do I love him or not, speak!

——You love him, Grushenka, you love him very much

Alyosha smiled.

——It is true, Alyosha, I'm vile. If he calls, I'll run to him like a dog. What a vile heart! Drink a cup, Alyosha: For my vile heart!—She drank the goblet and then broke it.—

And yet perhaps I don't love him, well we'll fight it out, [you see, Alyosha, I love the tears of these five years. I love my dreams of all those years. I love my hurt]—

——Well I wouldn't like to be in his shoes.

——You won't be, Rakitka, you'll never be in his shoes. You'll sew shoes for me, Rakitka, that's what I'll use you for, a woman like me will never be for you. But perhaps not for him either.

I'm carnivorous. I wanted to eat you up. *Sinful body*. And you came at such a minute.

The news came. I'm coming! 5 years, 5 years! God!

He is, to be sure, a Pole. But why not love a Pole?

I got drunk, like a regular drunk. Goodbye Mitia, I loved him also, he pleased me for a little while, pleased me very much. A scoundrel will have me, but not he, who is noble.

Let him suffer Rakitin cried out.

Rakitin (leaving) He's a Pole, it seems? A Pole, perhaps. And you know everything, Rakitin. Alyosha. Rakitin! Rakitin cried out.

Paissy to Ferapont. Go away, father. It is not up to men to judge   <7
but God. And you are a man. It is possible that we are seeing a sign here that we cannot understand. embrace. Go away, father, don't upset the flock. By my authority, I am telling you! [He doesn't observe the fasts, fills his stomach with sweets, and his mind with reasoning. Forgive]

——You are driving away the evil spirit, but perhaps you are serving him. And who can say about himself: "I am holy." Your words are thoughtless, father. I pay respect to your fasting and your asceticism, but your words are thoughtless, I say to you, go away father, and do not trouble the flock . . .

——Do I raise myself. [He has a Helper and a protector.]

Ferapont.

Casting out, I will cast out.

Wise, I have become ignorant, and now I have completely forgotten.

Paissy to Alyosha: Can it be that you too (have fallen into doubt). Alyosha wanted to say something, but he laughed and waved his hand, almost as if without respect.—What is the matter with him! Paissy thought looking after him. But Alyosha left.—You will come, said Father Paissy to himself and he began to read.

——The glass, he drank a half of swallow: enough Grushenka.

And I too have had enough, I won't drink

Rakitin: not me, I'm going to. Champagne is not so easy to get.

Grushenka. That's because I promised to give champagne if he brought you.—(She jumped up on his lap).—

——*Rakitin.* And why should I love you. Tell me simply why I should love you?

Grushenka. But for no reason at all, love—that's the way you should love.

Rakitin. Nonsense! Who loves without advantages and reasons.

Grushenka. (by the way) No one has ever loved me . . . (and she began to cry) barefooted, he seduced and went away. And now he writes that he is coming. He treated me shabbily, but ~~he'll call~~ whistle only, and I'll run to him immediately.

——That's another matter. And then there's a reason why you'll run to him.

4> ——Grushenka says to Rakitin: you haven't spoken such words to me?

——By what did he say to you so special?

——I don't know, but he said it! My heart felt it.

Grushenka says to Alyosha, (she went to sit down away from him) What are you doing to me, no tell me, what you are doing to me? (she folded her arms on her lap and lifted her eyes into the air.)

——Alyosha goes away. Grushenka cries out in anguished astonishment: But why are you leaving, why are you leaving me now alone? (shook up and tormented) and leaving <me> in darkness.

——Alyosha (in the vision of the Elder, he remembered that he had not seen his *brother*. And about Iliusha).

Leaving Grushenka, he remembers.

SUGARINESS

Here X

~~Your brother Ivan has not gone away~~

~~And can it be that you, educated as you are, broke into tears.~~

~~Ate or drank?~~

~~Do you want some vodka? he asked lightly.~~

——~~Give it—Alyosha said grimacing~~

——~~No, wait,—let's go~~

——~~[Let's go] whenever you want—~~

——~~Not, not wherever you want, To Grushenka's, as if Rakitin suddenly thought of it.~~

~~without a goal (advantageous), didn't do anything.~~

Suddenly he heard his voice, and then he was stretched out before him without a word with an icon of the Savior on his chest.

AND HE FELL TO THE GROUND,—he felt . . . etc.

STELLAR GLORY.

As if the threads of all the numberless worlds of God's creation had suddenly come together in his soul, and his soul trembled *"at contact with other worlds."*

He fell to the ground "blessing life and loving his ecstatic tears." [HERE]

Her guardian Angel stands [says] there and thinks: <7!

What good action of hers could I remember in order to tell it to God. He remembered and ~~goes~~ says to God: She pulled out a little onion in a garden and gave it to a beggar.

And God answers him: Take that same onion and tender it to her in the lake and let her be pulled by it. If you are able to pull her out of it, let her go to paradise, and if you can't pull her out of there, let her stay where she is.

The angel ran to the old woman: ~~began~~ he tendered her the little onion and he began to pull her out carefully, and he had her almost out of the lake, but the other sinners saw that she was being pulled out, and they began to grab hold of her so that they too could be pulled out with her. But the old woman was a nasty, a very nasty woman and she began to kick them. [That is my onion, and not yours, they are pulling me and not you, but as soon as she said that, the onion broke. And the old woman fell back into the lake and she is in torment there until now. And the angel broke into tears.]

A smile ~~still on~~ of joy on her swollen face, from tears.[6] Well, I am like that old peasant woman. In my whole life I've *given* only that little onion, and as for the rest, I've only done nasty things, but I still hope—

Grushenka. [You lie, God knew that one can forgive all sins be-

---

[6] Scattered on the page are fragments of variations of the legend about the onion, as follows: "The other sinners in the lake. When they saw that she was beginning to be pulled out of the lake, they began to clamor to be pulled out." "The old woman says grab hold and pull and he began to pull her out carefully." "But the old woman was nasty and she began to kick with her legs—" "As soon as she said that the onion broke." "And the old woman fell into the lake and burns there to this day." "And on <her> knees crawling after him."

cause of that one little onion, as Christ himself promised, but he knew
~~that~~ in advance that it was impossible to pull out that old woman,
because she would do something nasty. That's the purest of truths,
that's what! You are lying, poison-tongue. What kind of saint am I,
I'm a wench.

~~wench~~

6> Should I go to him, [Alyosha,] to him who hurt me, speak!
——Go.

I'll go. He'll call and I'll go. You know that during these five years,
you sleep at night and you wake up in a rage. Ah, I'll give it to him!
And when I remember that I'll not do anything to him, I throw myself
on the pillow and ~~drown myself~~ drown myself in tears, [in the morning
I'll wake up angrier than a dog]. And now he is coming, perhaps he's
already come, he'll call and I'll run to him like a little dog, I'll run,
run, Alyosha, I'll run to him. Forgive him, Alyosha, or not?

As you wish—my dear.

——He's a Pole. But I'm dissolute, I'm no longer what I was. I'm
violent now. Yesterday, a young lady and now

But why are you sitting there, Alyosha, so downcast—

They didn't give him a promotion.

——No it's not that . . . Alyosha broke into tears—And then, to
Grushenka: You are better than all of us. *What you could have been*
And you will be, will be, I see it.

——Why do you see it?

——You are good and generous. You forgave him.

——No I haven't forgiven him yet. *The heart is only getting ready
to forgive.* Or is it that I have forgiven?

——My sister, there is so much love in you, love me, soften my
sorrow. I am in anguish—

——It is he who is asking for me.

——You are better than all of us. And you will be. Your angel and
Guardian is taking care of you.

As with the old peasant woman, he is crying over me.

It would be good if he resembled you, why then cherub did you
not visit me.

[From now, I'll never be bad, I'll always be good!] Goes down on
her knees and repents: I was vile—I will mutilate myself, my beauty.
I'll burn my face, cut it up, I'll go begging. I'll no longer go anywhere
to anyone. I won't go to the merchant, I'll send back his furs, his
money.

But what is it that you said to me, say it to me: What is it that you said to me [I gave you a little onion, gave you only a little onion] that so completely changed me. You were the first to pity me, that's what. And, you know, I have been waiting for someone like you ~~my whole~~ life, I believed that such a one ~~he~~ would come—it is not for nothing that the first time I saw you, I thought of something of that kind. And yet I wanted to seduce you. And yet you say that I'm better than anyone.

You are better than all of us to be so grateful for a little word of mine. And me? Lord, what did you give me? How much have you given me. And what was I today? How I grumbled. You strengthened me, Grusha, my dead sister.—Why are you on your knees, why have you withdrawn your hands from mine—

But she had broken into sobs—

They go out and, and someone had driven up: he has arrived, arrived!

Book Eight

These notes were written sometime near the end of September 1879. Part of Book VIII was published in the October issue and the larger part in the November issue.

The notes to this book are by and large close to what we have in the final version, and it is clear that they were preceded by an earlier and rougher state of experimentation. There are no notes whatsoever for the most important chapter of Book VIII, "In the Dark," that is, the chapter which deals with Dmitri's leap into the Karamazov garden, the near-murder of his father, and the hurting of Grigory; the chapter "Kuzma Samsonov" is touched on only superficially, as is the chapter "Liagavy." The chapter "Gold-mines" in which the frantic Dmitri appeals to Mrs. Khokhlakova for 3,000 rubles and is advised to go to the gold mines is treated more fully. But the chapters dealing with Dmitri's visit to Mokroe and his dealings with the Poles are treated at great length, in some respects in a more detailed fashion than in the final version. Dostoevsky goes over details of the dialogue with the Poles again and again, and he experiments with turns of Polish phrases by transliterating them into Cyrillic characters and translating them into Russian.

The differences between notes and novel are differences of emphasis and of explicitness. Grushenka is a little more drunk and more wild in the notes than in the novel: Dostoevsky returns again and again to her desire for wine, the effect of the wine on her, and her desire to dance. In the novel she is already morosely disgusted with her former Polish lover, but in the notes this is not so clear and there is at least one remark that she is flirting with them at the inn. The moral meanness of the Poles is as clear in the notes as in the novel, as is their pettiness in refusing to drink to Russia. Dostoevsky's old resentment at the "imagined" superiority of Western countries toward Russia comes out baldly in a note that does not appear in the final version: "The Poles: The Russian people cannot be good because they are not civilized."

There are the usual summary statements, which are dramatized and amplified in the novel, such as the following: *"About the blood, where and who saw the blood on Mitia."* Characteristic, too, is the addition of explanation and reasons for what is depicted. The following two passages are very close in expression; the first is from the notes and the second from the novel:

> "Come here, kiss my lips, harder, *beat me, torment me.* Oh yes, you must really torment me. Listen: Don't touch me, yours . . . later, but now don't touch me. [I love you. It's good on earth.]"

> "Kiss me, kiss me hard, that's right. If you love, well then love! I'll be your slave now, your slave for the rest of my life. It's sweet to be a slave. Kiss me! Beat me, ill-treat me, do what you will with me. . . . And I do deserve to suffer. Stay, wait, afterward, I won't have that . . .

But a short time later when Grushenka asks Dmitri not to touch her, Dostoevsky adds the reason for her request:

> "Don't touch me . . ." she faltered, in an imploring voice. "Don't touch me, till I'm yours. . . . I've told you I'm yours, but don't touch me . . . spare me . . . With them here, with them close, you mustn't. He's here. It's nasty here . . ."

Officer, in speaking of that I am anticipating very much.   <7

Although he was not thinking about the officer, he felt that he had sort of to give in. So that perhaps his soul, in its essence, was a lot broader and more just than the portrait that the reader has probably already formed of him, solely as a consequence of the clumsiness and weakness of my story.

THE REVELATION OF SO MUCH PURE LOVE IN SUCH A NAÏVE AND COARSELY JEALOUS PERSON MAY APPEAR TO BE IMPROBABLE TO MY READER.

I WILL PUNISH MYSELF FOR MY WHOLE LIFE, I'LL PUNISH MY WHOLE LIFE!

A strange thing: it would seem that he was in deepest despair,—but he was not in despair.—It seemed to him that things would work out.

That's the way it is with those who spend and do not ~~know how~~ have a conception of how hard it is to make and obtain money. He was an officer, he didn't know work—But he thrashed about.

Fantasies.

Samsonov didn't want to receive him

But he saw that he was beside himself. In order to get rid of him, and perhaps to have some fun—he pointed out Liagavy. He might perhaps take up the affair, he said.

We, your worship do not handle such matters. Lawsuits follow, lawyers—it's a mess!

It is difficult to imagine it, but as it appeared later, he did it for fun. But the unfortunate Mitia took it for truth and he left the old man in ecstasy.

Liagavy began to curse. [2d chapter] Another time Mitia would have beat him up, but now he got into <the carriage> and flew off. On his return, he was in an inconceivable state. On the road he began to imagine that Samsonov was hand and glove with Fyodor Pavlovich and sent him on purpose to the Liagavy in order—

One fact after another.

[*How did you get here?*]

[A little present prepared Let's go, I'll show you]

[Mitia thought that he was <referring> about the money, and an unbearable and impossible rage suddenly boiled up in his heart.]

. . . .

And at that time Grigory Vasilich was thoroughly drunk.

78> I don't know anything.

——Leave me alone, leave me alone, for Christ's sake, I say, leave me alone.

——Show the law—

Who are you?

You are lying.

No, I'm not lying. The son of Fyodor P. Karamazov

The dyer—I don't know any Karamazov.

And it was only at the end of an hour that he suddenly realized how stupidly he was acting.

He went out in a sombre mood, sat down and pressed on terribly,

He accompanied Grushenka—

What terrible tragedies realism constructs for people.

Irritated

Crushed—

With a lost idea.

Fate is a monster murmured Mitia.

There was something senseless

realism, realism, repeated Mitia, harvested fields,

What despair, what death everywhere!

——I am an experienced doctor, Dmitri Fyodorovich.

——Well, if you are an experienced doctor, then I am an experienced sick person.

With your mind and your energy, you will find many mines quickly.—

Khokhlakova I will tell you the idea ~~you should pursue~~

You will return and [will be a man of action,] and you [will direct us] and move us toward the good. And everyone will be extremely happy. Russia will be the gainer and no particular person will lose— Everyone will give banquets and will help the poor, and when they die they'll go to heaven.

I don't have any money and I don't lend anyone money I promised myself I wouldn't, because we would quarrel, but even if I had money I especially would not give you any, because I love you, I would not give you any from love I wouldn't give you any in order to save you.

[I told you: mines, mines, mines, that's your goal, your true destiny, your calling!]—

He slammed <the door> it was a tragedy.

He left Khokhlakova's

His lips quivered and he broke into tears

Suddenly, he bumped into <somebody>

—Oh, good fellow why are you pushing so?

True, Othello is not jealous, as Pushkin said: He is much too calm   <7⟨ in searching for details, in running about, in looking for secrets, in vile spying. His soul and entire life are simply crushed by the fact that his ideal has been destroyed, but he doesn't hide under tables. Jealousy is not like that: with the purest love, with love full of forgiveness and sacrifice one can hide under tables and come to terms with the dirtiest of dirt, with open spying, and proved betrayal—if only *she* returns again. That is not Othello, etc., did not come *to a certain limit*.

Such a jealous man will forgive eagerly embraces and kisses, if she will swear that she will not go further, and he will accept everything you please, if only it does not come *to a certain act*. It is precisely the jealous ones who forgive everyone and everything very quickly if only they are assured that the past is forgotten, and everything will be different. Ideals have little to do with it.

Do you want money? later

——[No, brother, you are lying, you put forth your qualities too nakedly.]

——[But I am not doing any harm to anyone.]

——[Fine, fine, wait a little, later perhaps, later, but now wait a bit, restrain your passions.]

But that tirade

Sublime love appeared—self-renunciation and self-sacrifice.

[And that] Blood did not cry out after him: it has been written, *I will punish.* But there was another torment, no less than the blood, that is at least <considering> the character of Mitia. This torment was: *This money,* this champagne, all this carousing . . . You are a thief, you are a thief, after all! He would have talked to himself that way every minute, if yesterday or the day before he had begun to dissipate the money. He spoke that way even now, and knew that he was a thief and scoundrel, but without the burning torment of conscience, [without malediction, because the judgment had already been rendered, *I will punish* my life. Tomorrow at dawn the punishment— and nothing will remain.]

>   ——*Mokroe, Grushenka.* We are going to love God. . . . and then we'll have our fling forthright.

I am a rebellious woman!

Carousing: Mitia is in ecstasy before Maksimov: I respect you, I bow down before you. Everyone is base in something. You are simply base.

Splendid! yelled Kalganov.

——Well, do you want, do you want I'll give you a ride piggyback.

——Carry me, said Maksimov—

——Sit down

——You won't beat me up

——I won't beat you, but maybe I'll whip you

——No, then it's better not to—

——But then I will do it from love, from love [don't you understand.]

——Yes from love, but it can still hurt even more ~~I was once whipped from love.~~

Oh, let him alone, yelled Grushenka ~~come here~~ (behind the curtain).

Dance: Grushenka looked curiously, smiling sourly, but she was not very gay. Nevertheless, Mitia remained terribly satisfied, believing that Grusha too was terribly pleased.

——Well, enough (to Maksimov) Do you want a little cigar perhaps?

——A cigarette.

——Do you want a drink some sweets, some caramels.

——Give me some chocolate to nibble on.

——Take it, take it.

——Vanilla, preferably.

——What a guy you are.

——Listen (he took him to the side). This girl, Maria, how could I.

——Oh, brother, you want a great deal! [No brother, not that: we permit only songs, but did you really believe that? Grushenka, tirade, tears. Why am I so good ~~I dance~~ I dance.]

——Kalganov: don't bet.

——Pan—[1]?

——Pan or not pan, I don't want him to bet. Don't bet, I'll tell you why later.——

The Poles went away; Grushenka: Oh, how shameful, shameful, shameful for me, Mitia, how shameful . . .

——It's not very amusing,

——To the health of one bright falcon.

I won't say whom. To Kalganov: come here.

——How nice he is!

Mitia: We ask the seigneur.[2]

Mokroe. The Pole shows that he wanted to give 3,000 yesterday.—— Hasn't he then [hidden] money somewhere in town.

——Hidden, hidden in the city

(district police officer)

[*Drinking champagne*] But you may very well really shoot yourself, <8 I won't give it,

---

1 "Pan" is the Polish word for "Mister" and "Sir."
2 Spoken in corrupted Polish and transliterated in Cyrillic characters.

you won't have enough time to ⧾ I'll go and tell someone. [I swear I will tell]. You won't have enough time, my friend, you won't have time enough, the globe will blow up. Let me kiss you.—

You're sort of crazy

I—order, there's no higher order in me. There has been very little higher order in me

[you know, even though you are kind of wild, you've always sort of pleased me!]

———[Thank you, brother. You say I'm wild. Savages, savages! I repeat only this that we are savages. There's no order in me, higher order.]

To Mokroe.

But why to Mokroe

———Grushenka flew away

The civil servant: ah, ah, ah, that's what it is, that's what it is

I understand now, but, old fellow, you will work some misery there

No, I will stand aside.—Let's go together. Let's go have a drink at Plotnikov's let's drink

———But do you remember me?

———How could I not remember, why do you ask such nonsense, as if you were in a delirium.

[They walked together gesticulating, recited verses.]

[To Mokroe? Why should I go there.] It's far—

we'll have a fling—

we'll drink champagne

Perhaps I'll want to go to a tavern

What fool were you fighting with. Whom did you fight with? You want to with everyone. It's like the time with the captain.

A hopeless little old woman on the road—I crushed her.

the little old woman?

———No, the old man—

———[Without trouble, however.

———Forgive me now,

Forgive now.]

———*The bullet.* You think that death doesn't mean anything to me. I want to live, I want life.—

———They drink champagne. Long live life!

Forgive me Andrey, yes, forgive me for everything—

It would be necessary to prevent you—

(in a whisper), you won't have enough time—Phoebus will not yet have risen and I will be there.

——But are you drunk or not.
——[And am I drunk now?]
——[Worse than drunk]
——[I'm drunk in my soul]
Sitting down in the carriage:
——Pardon me Fenia, I forgot to ask your forgiveness a little while ago for having run in and having insulted you, but then you have already forgiven me—

About the civil servant with Andrey. [He's a good gentleman.] <8
A steward?—
——A steward, sir, steward, miserable steward.
Will I enter the kingdom?
You? Will you enter because of your simplicity?
My good fellow, Dmitri Fyodorovich, resolve my doubts about what Fyodosia Markovna spoke and what she was asking about ?
——She went with Timofei—
——Oh, sir, I fear I'm taking you <there>—
——Can one live in one hour—
Forgive me!—
Forgive me alone for everyone.

Hell groaned. Do not groan hell, you will henceforward be filled. The great lords, the high judges and rich men will enter you . . . That is the way it is, that was the word that was given, such a word was given. People's wisdom. [Many, sir, do not believe that, but I will tell you only the truth.]

[To Fenia's.]
[Late.]
[Game.]
[Third game, he put down the cue and went off to Fenia's.]
[I'll knock until someone answers, he said to himself.]
[And Mitia galloped]—
Will I fall into hell for three thousand?
——I don't know, my dear, that depends on you.
——Even if I go to hell, will you forgive me Andrey. No, you alone will forgive me Andrey. [Andrey, man]

Notebook Page 82. This page is a good example of "compartmentalized" chaos. On close examination, one discovers almost a geometric symmetry in the disposition of the notes.

I am afraid, I'm taking you to

Whip the horses, my friend, whip them. You'll get rid of me and you'll cease having fear.

Drive me faster, faster. Whip them, my friend, whip them, that's it.

But isn't it already eleven-thirty—

Thought about the old man left behind.

He had decided to step aside.

——About her—I'll give her a clear road. One must give everyone a free path, Andrey. I have been in the way of others, I am spoiling the life of others . . . Because I have loved life too much. Cure yourself with what has hurt you. Thought. My heart leaps toward her.

[He, galloping along, remembered how he flew once with her, woke up the gypsies and got the peasants drunk.]

What does a peasant know (about champagne).

Timofei, But suppose they're gone to sleep? Mitia cried out suddenly.

——They have surely gone to sleep . . .

——Mitia fell into thought. And suppose they really are asleep. A nasty feeling boiled up in him.

Go on, go on! he suddenly yelled.

Ring the bell. I'm coming [Drive up smartly, jump, threw down 50 rubles for his services]

In the middle of the road, a ferry

Small river—

Do you remember, remember [Mitia said in ecstasy.]

It was Timofei who was with you then

Yes I had forgotten Timofei—

His heart was aching for Grushenka.

THEY ARE NOT SLEEPING, YELLED MITIA

[What, sleeping—they are not sleeping! We've got here ahead of time, and there's Mokroe, I see lights.]

Why not read Chichikov. Mitia was happy to have bothered to talk.

Gentlemen, a passerby may, a traveler, sirs, a traveler may.

——There are other rooms also (apartments). . . .

I don't want to compete I want to say good-bye, he took out some money. WELL, LET'S HIDE. BLINDMAN'S BUFF, DO YOU WANT TO.

——THEY PROPOSED CARDS (MAKSIMOV).

Girls, perhaps

——All your acquaintances, it seems, are sitting here—

83> ——Lord, accept me with all my sins but do not judge me. Don't judge, because I have judged myself, don't judge—because I love you Lord, I'm vile, but I love, if you send me to hell, I will love there too, and from there I will cry out to you that I love you, but I am base and vile, [Andrey, forgive my soul, my soul, he groaned]
will you forgive me or not.—

[MOKROE] And why did I not do something for you, didn't restrain my passions, didn't conquer myself— Lord, you know everything— but don't judge, look, I plead—don't judge—let me pass by I plead Lord, but don't afflict my heart. I don't dare . . . don't dare . . . I pray, and yet I don't dare pray. [This heart belonged wholly to humanity, even though I didn't do anything] For I love the queen of my heart, I fall down before her, you are right in having passed by me, but I worship you [and now let me love you permit me to love you here for five hours, only five hours have remained.]

Adoration churned in his soul—
Strange: blood—but he didn't think—
However ~~something~~ something vaguely did not give him any peace
—And suppose they are sleeping?
——A bottle of champagne for Andrey, I gave offense to the peasant—Afterward Andrey said: he comes, carrying the money in his hands (did not distinguish the blood in the dark).
A timidly-joyful countenance
Well, what's wrong with him (that is, Maksimov) The ecstasy of a little dog.
What nice little eyes he has (Kalganov's)—
Tomorrow—to the gold mines.
Mitia—I'm ready even to carry you all: Sit on me, pan, on my back, I'll carry you—
Grushenka's confession on the bed about the money. Both are drunk. I am a thief—*Katia's*. A pig and scoundrel. ~~I didn't reveal that to Alyosha~~
Grushenka: not Katia
We will go, we'll bow down, give back the money, we'll ask for forgiveness we'll go away . . . Take the money
You are a falcon
To think that I was such a scoundrel.

Grushenka not to Katia's we'll bow down . . . I will work . . . We'll make a lot with you . . . I won't cry . . . The end to tears (that is about the officer), about those miserable five years! (with hate and rage) Take me and carry me far away from here . . . ~~And~~ Let the bell ring and [I will be your faithful and obedient one]

My last night, I will mark this day with my joy.   <84
We became acquainted here.
Mokroe. I'm leaving! I'm leaving! I'm leaving for good, forever!

Realism

——Toast, Cards. And after the cards, girls. The Pole, having understood that they saw him cheat, protested against the girls: other apartments. And Grushenka yells: I don't want to, I have not been bought. The Pole hints that if that's the way things are, he will go away and will not marry her. Grushenka says: go away then, that's the way I want it. Then Mitia takes him into another room and bargains with him for 3,000. They return. They announce that they had been bargaining. Grushenka yells: But it's not necessary to give money. The Pole calls the proprietor and protests against the girls ~~that trick,~~ the proprietor says that he had cheated. Oh, it's shameful, yells Grushenka. The Pole *insults* her. Mitia grabs him and pushes him out. Grushenka asks for songs. I want to be gay, I want an orgy. Suddenly, a passionate speech with tears: look at whom I loved! 5 years I loved him and he is ridiculous. I was a fool, was a fool! Go to it Mitia. Songs, drinking, dancing. Grusha is Mitia's: Come here, you loved me, you falcon. You ~~mine~~ are better than anyone, etc. I want to dance. Dances. On the bed, Mitia at her feet [Here the scene *au naturel*]

Another charges straight ahead and all his life is like that. No stopping him.
Straight ahead—straight into hell?
They are sleeping.
There's an officer there of some kind.

Oh, we drove with Timofei then. Yes, with Timofei. A good man, Timofei. What is that, sir, doubt.
What was Fyodosia Markovna demanding
——Give way. You are a coachman and you give way—
——True, sir—But not everyone gives way.

Hell—

[And hell groaned. Because it thought that no more sinners would come to it.]

[And you will be filled in that way for centuries and centuries until I come again.]

[And so, sir, that's whom hell is for, but you, sir][3]

Mitia laughed stiffly

And will I go to hell?

You. Because of your simplicity.

Go on.—

Now only thoughts about her. See her for a moment. Timofei, you can after all live a lifetime in an hour—

Forgive me—for all—

How strangely you are talking, sir—

50 rubles. 3 rubles.

85>   64)—MITIA 64 examine

80) *Mitia.* Appearance in Mokroe.

Grushenka became afraid. Maksimov

The Poles. Mitia yells: But, I have nothing against it, nothing! The Poles become encouraged and *the fiancé* makes *a heavy and solemn* speech, that since he wants *to honor* Grushenka with his *hand,* then how disagreeable the appearance of *former people* is for him. Grushenka's outbursts again *this speech. In opposition Grushenka* accepts Mitia with joy, and Mitia suddenly takes on courage. That begins with Boileau.—

And then a small game of cards takes place. They brought Champagne. Girls. They squandered 3,000, Squandered, we are witnesses.

The key word: *former people,*—

——Grushenka—how stupid you are.

——At first the Poles were against the group of girls, but the group came just in time *for the dispute.*

——About the 4 dozen bottles of champagne.

He took a lot remembering the other time.

——The revolver. *Grushenka:* I don't want you to kill yourself and it won't happen.

---

[3] The following fragments are found on the left margin and do not fit into the context: "But not to the station. But at the Plastunovs at the inn. They have a free station. I know where from before—cards are played there. Doubt."

N.B. *Grushenka:* The Poles were chased out. *I won't say whom I love*, first drinks—

N.B. Grushenka on the bed, Mitia on his knees:—Not worthy of the happiness, I would like *to experience great unhappiness.*

——I didn't know, I didn't know that I love you so! exclaimed Mitia.

——*The Pole.* To my beautiful sovereign. And he kisses Gru-   <86
shenka's little hands.

——But do you love, asks Grushenka.

——Afterward, suddenly after the pompous speech of the Pole, Grushenka suddenly begins to say: "No, that's not the way it should be. In my opinion it should be different." Says about love: *gaily and sarcastically. Preference for Mitia.* She begins to flirt and to enrage the Pole.

——Grushenka *interrupts* Mitia when he, at first, began to say that she was pure and is radiant: You're saying stupid things, don't you dare ask forgiveness for me.

What I want to do, I do, I'm not sold after all.

Here, Grushenka: I want girls. About distractions. Proposes cards.

——Well, let's go, pan, let's go! Mitia—already happy and in ecstasy that Grushenka is well-disposed toward him and *takes his part.*—

Here. Before he was gay, and now he has become a pedant. Uniform.

——I was not pure because of virtue or because I was afraid of Kuzma, but in order to be proud before you, so as to have the right to call you a scoundrel.

——Someone is knocking   <87>

Open the door

Give <me> a chair, armchair

Pan you are very much in a hurry

——what, peop-

——What can I propose to you.

——What do you like more

---

[4] Notebook pages 87, 88, 89, 90 are almost entirely in Polish transliterated in Cyrillic characters with the Russian translation in parentheses. The translation is often wrong or incomplete. Notebook page 91 is in transliterated Polish without a Russian translation.

—— ~~have to~~
Have to do what is possible.

——What do you want?

——Here I am.

——I thank you very much.

——Aren't you standing on ceremonies?

——I am ready

——sit next to me

——Don't make noise

——Not very good

——Splendid

——Late

——It is still early.

——I know him very well

——That is completely probable

——All the worse for others

——Good-bye

——As for me, I will not wait a minute longer

——If you want to come with me, let's go, but if you don't then good-bye

88> ——I thank you

——I thought so.

——Give her my respects

——But why?

——More quickly, I don't have time to reason with you

——I am ready

——Fine, but how much trouble was necessary

——One can't help but have an attachment for one's country.

——From time to time.

——Don't you need anything yet?

——That's impossible

——Your truth

——Here's your check

——Didn't you make a mistake

——This way please

——So much the better

——It seems like a lot of money

——That goes without saying

——That's perfect.

——That's the best thing

——Only, don't deceive.

——You can count on that.

——As you like,   <89

——There is no room

——Have to wait

——Please be seated, gentlemen.

——That's good.

——You did well

——I thank you and accepted

——Absolutely; interfere; speak; and (not to obey); punish, gold silver

——Dishonor; room; listen; would break the door.

——lucky, —unlucky.

——I was very astonished

——Be reasonable

——Be honorable

——So that they will be faithful

——So that I would be blind

——happy

——Sad

——Ungrateful

——Not modest

Deal the cards

Wouldn't we be comical

——Love

——Kill

——Steal

——Willful

What an odd fish, was he like that before? And I cried for him? I spent five years crying about him. But he's not at all like that! It must   <90 be his older brother. Oh, what I fool I've been, what a fool!

But speak Russian, before you knew how to speak Russian, speak Russian.—

I'll fulfill my promise

The bank had a million

Tomorrow

Today

——You're joking, pan

——Improbable

I can't be insulted any more

That is very unpleasant

——Phew! Phew!

——Shameful!

——Aren't you ashamed?

——How dare you do that

——Stop it.

——I want   keep quiet

——Keep quiet—

Half-past one

——What to do?

——I heard that . . .

——I am not saying

——I am not saying anything

Grushenka behind the curtain. Guess who I love. A kiss for Kalganov. Beat me, pinch me. Mitia, shoot oneself. She kisses Mitia's hands, tormented herself for five years. Why is he that way. That's his brother, but not him. I am good. Why am I so good. It is because I am so good that sometimes I get into a rage.

I dance. Let's become reconciled to him. He will come. I will forgive him and will love you.

91>   Pan father and Pani mother.

——Holy, Priest, Sun.

——[those cards are from here, the proprietor's]

——A Polish zloty, pan

——It will overcome

——It seems

——I am listening, pan. Honor kingdom.

——He adds.

——We cannot not.

——Inconstant. I protest.

——Wife. Take the road for, entirely.

——Primitive. From the beginning. Village tavern.

——Pan, welcome. When he arrived.

——I fall to your knees. Saintly mother of Zestochowa.

——To your health, pan. Impossible, pan. Farm.

——Farm. To the woods. Old vodka.

——Auxiliary. Schismatics Schism. I understand.

——Pan, scoundrel. Dog. Dog's blood. A slave's faith.

——It will be quiet everywhere, what is it. Devils.

——Everyone. Let it be, pan. The republic.

——Base. I beg your pardon, pan. Poland.

——Irrevocable. Impossible. I show. Subordinate.

——He will be able. A certain. There is truth.

——A parasite. Carnivorous. You are lying, pan.

——A million. Not suitable. Needed. White.

——Fruit. What town. Which. Of money.

——Do you understand Pan Wrublewski

~~Mitia~~ Private—

[Don't have to give him money.]

——[I gave my heart. But miss . . . Either get rid of the girls or I will go away.]

[Grushenka, in a frenzy, yells at him.]

That's it!

What time is it? What is the weather like?

——*Twelve o'clock has not yet rung*

——It is night

——I think

——I do not think

——As best it can be

——As usual

——I am very happy about that

——They are knocking

——With all my heart, pan.

But what is he afraid of, I think. But you have become completely afraid, afraid. Not of them certainly, can it be that you are afraid of someone.

Card game. They sit down, sour. Before you came Mitia, they were all quiet, and swaggered about me. I was riding. . . . I was thinking. . . . And there they were.

——Pani, pani po. . . . everything is ready. If you please, pan, ask for cards.

Because of Piron   <92

But, look, to begin with I have begun to talk in epigrams.—

[A certain epigram.]—Is that you Boileau,[5] what funny dress.

And they became angry [became insulted.]

And then you are Sappho and I Phaon.[6]

---

[5] Reference possibly to the first line of I. A. Krylov's "Na perevod 'L'art poetique' " (For the translation of "L'art poetique"). The first line is: "Ty l' eto, Byalo? Kakoi smeshnoi nariad." (Is that you Boileau? What a funny dress!)

[6] In Book VIII, chap. VII Maximov relates how he recited the following poem:
Yes, Sappho and Phaon are we!
But one grief is weighing on me.
You don't know your way to the sea!
Epigram to the poetess A. P. Bunina by K. Batiushkov from his "Madrigal of the new Sappho" (1809).

This is a very well-known and biting epigram. They felt hurt all the more, considered it aimed at them, and I then unfortunately told the story about Piron, and how they did not elect him to the Academy, and how he in revenge had a gravestone made for himself *Ci gît Piron, qui ne fut rien*.[7] As soon as I said that they opened and whipped me. Because of my education. Why did I display my education to them.

And when I said *Ci gît Piron qui ne fut rien* that about Piron. They took me and whipped me.

——Because of Piron.

——Yes, because of my education. People don't need much of an excuse to whip, but we became reconciled shortly afterward.

[but,] more, but Nosov only kept yelling and kept urging him on
I said that I myself was coming.

——No, he is truly, truly, he is a sincere scoundrel!

——Well, did they still whip

——What a way to put it: *whipped.*

——Insulted? Well, whipped. I had just praised.

And I with the stakes, stakes
With smaller stakes it's better

Here. Mitia: Well, what should we do? What should we do?

Kalganov Yes, boring. Couldn't we play at forfeits?

Mitia. And are we going to play forfeits (looking at all of them), or not?

Maksimov. At bank, it's late, pan, he said suddenly, the pan, as if against his will.

Grusha.

[*Mitia.* I'm losing a lot of money to you.]

[Pan]

[Sit down.]

[Answered.]

[Pan listened to Podvysotsky]

<93>   I looked out after you, I studied even your way of walking and I made up my mind: This man has to go to the gold mines [and he will find many gold mines.]

---

[7] French: "Here lies Piron who didn't amount to anything." From the epitaph of the French poet Alexis Piron (1689–1773), author of many satires, songs, and monologues.

——According to my walk, madame!

——[Almost by the manner of walking. What, you aren't really denying that it is possible to tell character by one's walk.]

——But I'll go, madame, I'll go . . .

——You are going, I knew you would, that you would come to that decision. (Icon of Barbara the Martyr)

——Three thousand? rubles? Oh, no, I can't give you 3,000 rubles.

——. . . Madame, but how can you.—

——Oh, no, no, I can't under any circumstances [give you] any money—

——You will construct buildings and different kinds of enterprises.

——You will become known and indispensable to the Ministry of Finance.

——Then you will find a beloved person, I know that you will find her. She will be a girl with all the perfections, gentle and tender . . . I am not at all averse to the current female question, Dmitri Fyodorovich, the development of women and even the political role of women. That is ideal. I wrote to Shchedrin[8] about this, *that* writer has shown me so much, showed me so much about the significance of women. You know, I wrote him an intimate letter: in two lines: I embrace and kiss you my writer in the name of the contemporary woman.

——I am not averse to the woman question, but I am little understood in this respect. I have a daughter, Dmitri Fyodorovich, and I have the full right to demand the development of women.

——No—No no and no, not for anything. You will be happy from another point of view, from the point of view of the mines—

——For the Ministry of Finance, which has such a great need at the present time. The fall in value of our ruble keeps me from sleeping, Dmitri Fyodorovich. [People don't know this side of me.] From now on, after the whole business of the monastery I have become a thor-

---

[8] Reference to the polemic between Dostoevsky and Shchedrin in the sixties, the details of which may be found in S. Borshchevsky's *Shchedrin and Dostoevsky* (Moscow, 1956).

ough realist, Dmitri Fyodorovich, and I want to fly from ideals to contemporary life. I'm cured Dmitri Fyodorovich. *Enough* as Turgenev said. . . . to Shchedrin; and I register myself: a Mother, A contemporary mother.

)4> ———I have a cousin, her husband, a horse-breeding farm. You surely have some idea of horse-breeding. Dmitri Fyodorovich.

———You are making me cry.

———Cry, cry, that's good, that makes things easier, but then you will be glad and you'll make a special trip to thank me, [from Siberia.]

———I wanted to sign myself Contemporary mother, but I hesitated, and ended up signing simply mother: more suggestive and poetic. But contemporary mother will remind them also of *The Contemporary,*[9] a bitter memory for them, Dmitri Fyodorovich [considering the present censorship].

———Have pity, have pity on me, madame, have pity.

———Mother: more moral beauty, Dmitri Fyodorovich.

Mokroe—At Mokroe Dmitri confesses to Grushenka about the money on his chest and that he is—*a thief.*

Mokroe—I wanted, wanted—to kill my father.
Perhaps you yourself don't remember how you struck.

Grushenka. (Drunk) ℰ No, tell me: Why am I so good? No I am good. My heart tells me I'm good.

———And I wasn't drunk before: about the Pole: while riding, here, I kept thinking: how will I meet him, what will I say. God knows, I thought, what I will say. And here seeing him was like being drenched with cold water. He speaks like a teacher. Every-

---

[9] Possibly a reference to the troubles that Michael Evgrafovich Staltykov-Shchedrin was having at that time as editor of *The Fatherland Notes* and the similar troubles with the censors he had as editor of *The Contemporary,* which was closed down in 1866.

thing so pedantic, so pompous, he met me so formally that my tongue was tied. ~~and now everything~~ I can't get a word in edgewise. I sit looking at him <and wondering> why is it that I can't talk, I'm speechless in his presence . . . Mitia.

Whom do I love?

Nice legs, nice hips. Tail flourishing. A mouth as wide as his ears, <9.
though.—

Mitia vodka for Andrey. My heart is pained.

Grushenka—But why does it hurt you, be gay, you see that I'm happy, I'm happy, my lady Sovereign. Want me to carry you on my back—

Maksimov [THE WHOLE CAVALRY]. A lieutenant had granted her to me. He brought her. I, to do service. She was lame, but she hid it. I thought she was scampering about, but she was lame.

——I am an educated man.——

——~~2~~ But that was the first, the 2d ran away.

—She scampered about from playfulness [Polish girls scamper about on their knees.]

——From joy that she was marrying you?

——Yes. But it turned out that she had one leg shorter than the other She jumped, supposedly, across a puddle and broke it.

——Kalganov: I like him, and you know, he is really telling the truth. [Grushenka contradicts the Poles]

——When I heard that your wife . . . ~~ran away~~ (Mitia)

——No that was already the second one, yes she ran away.

——Yes, I had that misfortune.

3d wife ~~took the property~~ unlawful, took away the property, you say you are an educated man, so you'll find a way—

You know he often lies said that they whipped him—

Nozdryov.[10]

---

[10] Kalkanov says the following about Maximov in the final version: "Only fancy, he claims (he was arguing about it all the way yesterday) that Gogol wrote *Dead Souls* about him. Do you remember, there's a landowner called Maximov in it, whom Nozdryov thrashed. He was charged, do you remember, 'for inflicting bodily injury with rods on the landowner Maximov in a drunken condition.' Would you believe it, he claims that he was the Maximov and that he was beaten! Now can it be so? Tchitchikov made his journey, at the very latest, at the beginning of the twenties, so that the dates don't fit. He couldn't have been thrashed then, he couldn't, could he?" (Book VIII, chap. VII)

[Grushenka saw that he was not liking it, and kept up the conversation on purpose—]

You know he is lying about that. Look, we praised him, and he has begun to lie. And you know not from a corrupt feeling, but from a good one, so as to give pleasure.

Nozdryov.

One is ashamed with him.

God bless him!

——Well, that's enough cries out Grushenka.

Play forfeits.

——Yes, I'm ready (Mitia)

——How about Faro

Mitia ran off to give orders, girls. Candy. Maksimov 5 rubles. The girls gathered about.

[20 years ago —at the time of my youth]

Grushenka, slightly fault-finding, irritated.

[They took me and whipped me out of patriotism for speaking French]

[and Piron—he was an academic. Well that too did not please them.]

96>   ——Pure and glistening (Don't dare ask forgiveness for me!)

——I was not pure from virtue and not because ~~afraid merchant~~ I was afraid of Kuzma. (2)

——But I'm not saying anything, anything, what's wrong . . .(64)

——To my beautiful queen (2)

——Gentlemen, one can for someone passing by, for a traveler

——Gentlemen, travelers have other rooms [for that].

Why other rooms (357)

——I don't want to argue about it, I want to say good-bye (he took out money)

——Why didn't I do anything for myself. My Queen.

This heart has belonged completely to mankind.

——At least until tomorrow, until tomorrow, until dawn (money) (they bring in the chorus) Oh, how gay!

My last night, I will commemorate my day of joy.

——[Stop, don't bet! Kalganov]

[We'll drink! cries out Mitia]

You're really crazy, pan—yelled Mitia, I'm sorry pan, sorry

Scoundrel—got up and went off a little.

——But why are you asking pardon, look at him walking like a rooster

The fiancé makes a speech, about old lovers.

She's pure! I say it to a scoundrel—

Pan, yelled Mitia, in another room—

Even though Mitia cries, pardon me, pan, he had already come out of his former contemplative state. For a long time already, it had seemed to him that Grushenka (disgusted look) and so forth. He became more energetic, more impetuous.

[Podvysotsky]
[Grushenka. Well, that's something, it's true then.]
[*Mitia.* They have nothing in the kitty.]
Mitia observed things for a minute and he understood something.

——Mitia was not jealous of Samsonov. AB   <97

——Three foreheads bumped.—He is not jealous *of the former one.*—If he did not find me there, then he went there and was there.

The broken casket. (Timofei you are driving a murderer).
Why was it necessary to say that he had spent the whole 3,000.

——He had threatened to kill him in the cell, and then at home when he was beating the old man. Testimony of Grigory. Grigory speaks to the inspector:

From that point on I began to watch him.

He was good at everything (right words)

345. Today's criminal is not tormented by the pangs of conscience.

[I'll give him his what for
3) *Mokroe:* Even though I am not guilty of that, what fate is punishing me for, still I am *completely guilty.*

5) *Mokroe.* Savages! savages I repeat only one thing: savages!
The garden is completely beautiful, etc.

5) POLICE OFFICIALS

6) Glory to the most high in the world, glory to the most high in me. *Not poetry, but a tear.*

10) I will kill him. He bragged that he would kill (Grigory)

13) I am in agreement with Ulysses: the feminine nature is credulous

I will give him what for

14) I am a Russian by conviction. The resurrection of the dead in Robert.[11] Seizes the soul.

16) *Forgive me, forgive me,* but if you don't forgive, it doesn't make any difference.

19) Russian hearts. Angels sang in heaven.

98>   ——21) There's no discipline in me, no higher discipline! I break my own sword and go into the pit of vice and shame.

28) Let's go to pray to God for everyone.

32) *Grushenka:* I'm guilty for everything! He did it because of me.

53) The Poles: the Russian people cannot be good because they are not civilized.

55) Cast-iron paperweight. Maria Kondratievna heard him brag.
58) Court session in the town of Gdov, etc.

63) Sound of chickens—chick, chick (Maksimov)
Grushenka—I want to frolic. God will forgive
If I were God, I would forgive people everything: sin my loved ones, and I will love you.
Dance hut, dance stove.

66) Mitia riding to Mokroe, conversation with the driver (Moscow, piebald horse, all the girls). It is not Timofei who sat down, but they put an old man half-drunk—all the girls. *He's not from around here.*

65) Grushenka here. I'm base, I'm corrupt, and everything else.

---

[11] Perhaps a reference to the opera "Robert le Diable" (1831) by Jacob Beer Meyerbeer (1791–1864).

She became charmed by Mitia because he gave away to him who was indisputably the legitimate one (But for himself a bullet in the forehead the next day)

66) Grushenka, drunk,

67) The arrest of Mitia. Prosecutor and so forth.
Question: Where did Mitia take the money? Because he had visited Samsonov, *had asked for it in connection with Chermashnia.* The latter pushed him toward Gorstkin, and he had renounced all his rights to Chermashnia for 3,000. *They laughed* at him.

67) *About the blood,* where and who saw the blood on Mitia.
[100 gave to a girl.—]

They found a letter from Father Ilinsky on Fyodor Pavlovich.

67) Mitia: God found me. Grushenka. Oh, sorrow, my sorrow. Writhes at his feet. Yes, it is you, he says. District Police officer.

68) The legal investigator *hinted* that he wanted to kill himself <99. *because of his crimes.*—No. judges, cries out Mitia: you are mistaken: I wanted to kill myself from passion, and not from disgust with myself. And I wanted terribly to live, even though as a scoundrel! That's the way we Karamazovs are.—Yes, in essence all the Russian people now are like that, said the police officer suddenly.

N.B. 68) Take me from here anywhere, as long as it is away from here forever. We will work in the fields.—Tomorrow off to the monastery, but now let me dance.

———Perhaps I did kill, Grushenka, and if so we will perish together.

[Grushenka]—But perhaps I loved one person—your brother Alyosha.

[N.B.—I love someone perhaps. Whom do I love?]

69) I want to be good, dance stove, dance hut, everything is turning, turning, *(she cannot form phrases)* guilty, weak.

———Come here, kiss my lips, harder, *beat me, make me suffer.* Oh yes, you must really make me suffer. Listen: Don't touch me, yours . . . later, but now don't touch me. [I love you. It's good on earth!][12]

69) Don't you want to become reconciled, as if you weren't people, I, look, love everyone. Look at how I dance . . .

---

12 Grushenka is the speaker.

70) The same with Grushenka.

——Mitia silver *watch for two rubles*

——I'm a thief, I stole 3,000 (remembering Katerina Ivanovna's money) he says out loud in Mokroe.

70) Weak, forgive me, wine doesn't give any joy ~~peace.~~ And peace. I want to ask for forgiveness. Before everyone.[13]

> 70) Bribing of the Pole in another room. The 3,000 appear again.

71) Grusha, *drunk.* [Wine does not bring tranquillity.] It's good on earth, even though we are vile, but it's good on earth, etc.

72) After the failure of the bride, *shooting* through a handkerchief. Tomorrow, I will shoot myself. *2 pistols* loaded with me. Grushenka cries out:

Oh, put that away!

Hey, you Podvysotsky and others. Pan scoundrel. You are worse than a scoundrel

72) On the bed: Don't touch me. Even though you are an animal, you are honorable. A wretch like me wants to pray to God. Give me some champagne. No, don't, don't do it. Don't give in even if I plead. [Wine doesn't give peace.] Delirium. *Sleigh bells.*

73) Hire a troika. It's ringing and I am dozing.

I saw a dream, I drove away with a nice guy.—I was embracing him, kissing him, and the snow was sparkling and crunched, and the moon was shining, and it was *as if I were no longer on earth,* and so forth.

73) Mitia in the kitty. The whole conversation with the Poles. *If you had not served, it would be better.* You have a priest.

73) Pan Colonel—In return, you have young ladies! and so forth. Maksimov. Is that you Boileau, what funny dress.[14]

Keep quiet, I'm preparing to go to a Masquerade, that is, to a bath.

You are Sappho, and I'm Phaon

You don't know the way to the sea.

[çi gît Piron qui ne fut rien.][15]

74) Scoundrel, don't beat them and so forth.

——Bribing of the Pole and the offer of 3,000.

---

[13] Grushenka is the speaker.
[14] See n. 5 of this section.
[15] See n. 6 of this section.

Out loud: You want 3,000. I happen to have 3,000 on me.

Von Sohn.[16] Where did Fyodor Pavlovich get that.   <1
—Well then you really didn't know him.
——I knew him as well as you could know him and so forth.
Mitia: Don't talk to me about the old man. I almost killed the old man . . . (another old man in blood) I have come to kill myself. But today, have a good time. Poles, I'm a cosmopolitan.—I'm drinking—72 years. Faro, bribe in the other room. Chase them out and don't give them any money. The proprietor was cheating at cards, fight. Songs. ~~Grushenka~~ Little chicken. Grushenka is drinking. Maksimov fell asleep in the armchair. Grushenka and Mitia together on the bed. The little bells. Investigation.

> After Boileau [and von Sohn] Grusha sat down next to Mitia. Gayer next to him.
> Solemn and somberly tragic monologue of Mitia, I'm giving way! I will shoot myself! Buy.
> Abroad 72 Faro. Proposed a bribe. *Don't give it* and so forth.

3,000 Mokroe: Perhaps shoot.—

——Maksimov: and I dance the clog dance.
Kalganov. Oh, no, he's kind of queer. It's shameful to be with him.
——Nozdryov whipped. *Kalganov* says with contempt that he invented all that on purpose to please, and whatever you say to him, he takes it all on himself.—No *Maksimov* objects that all that had happened, only it was not Nozdryov but another. *Kalganov* in ecstasy embraces him and cries out that he was wrong.

N.B. Suddenly, I will awake and my loved one is near me, so good,   <1
Bell,

74) *Grushenka.* Don't give him any money and so forth.
Throw them out, quarrel.
N.B.—To Grusha: Goddess. He used to say also: Goddess!

——You can like him as a man, but as a Russian you cannot.

---

[16] See n. 48, Books I and II.

——No, as a Russian also.

——What kind of a Pole would you be after that?

74) Grusha on the bed. Don't touch. Little Bell. I like people like you . . . and so forth.

——Mitia . . . Oh, I'm afraid for the old man.

74) The proprietor of the tavern about the marked cards.

75) Grusha. I love such senseless ones.

75) To the colonel. The countesses jump to their knees. Podvysotsky and Mitia: Podvysotsky.

75) The investigator: You were telling someone here a little while ago that you killed your father.—You told her.

——Oh, I did!

75) The money is here on my chest, a long time to tell about it, but then it doesn't make any difference. He loses coherence *"He is drunk."*

75) You saw your father then. Through the window. Who opened it? I don't know. And then, recollecting: but I didn't go in. *Smerdiakov* was lying sick.

76) I want to suffer.—

——To stop and to whip.—

——Then the old man is alive— Thanks to you Lord.

——There are honest Poles, and there are such as you, etc. 3,000.— I squandered 3,000 here last time.

The proprietor.—You squandered it, old man, you squandered it. We are witnesses.

——Is it true that I'm a vile person? Whoever has made up his mind that I am vile doesn't know me.

——Here on the chest.

——True, I am a thief I carried the judgment that I was a thief here on my chest (a reckless fellow, but not a thief).

)3> 77) I'm cosmopolitan, I drink first.

The Pole does not drink. To the Russia of the frontiers of the year 72.

——You are a fool, Pan.

About Poland and Russia (Ivan's delirium).

77) The revolver loaded in the morning. He had redeemed it, the servant and the merchant saw him

Why had he taken the pestle [at Fenia's]? Why does one carry a stick? and so forth.

3,000. 77) Bribe, 3,000. Take 500

77—He loads a bullet into the revolver. Thought. In the presence of Fenia.
He arrives at Mokroe, 25 for vodka. Andrey doesn't take it. Give a little ruble.

78) About Grigory. The little bell rings: 10 years just as long as he lived. He insulted *Aesop,* etc.

78) To the investigator: I'll tell you the whole truth. I knocked with the signal He opened: Is it you Grusha. I ran away.

——The Investigating Lawyer: There's a sea of facts, but the conclusion is clear.

79) The money was sewn here on my chest.—Where did I get it from? I won't say, it's too base.—How much money was there, 3,000.
—Yes, there were three, and then half that much.
The Police Captain: Yes, of course, at first 3, and then there remained half that amount.

3,000. 79) Bribe. 3,000 and so forth. Scoundrel and so forth.

80) 100 rubles in the toilet. If they were *yours,* you would not be throwing away 100 rubles.

——You don't know her heart, police captain—
I am in revolt—
I accept:
N.B. The Police Captain: He killed in a fit of passion. He killed from passion.

04>   80) Grusha. She yells (she had lent an ear): If he really says that he didn't do it, then *he didn't do it,* he's honest.

82) in playing whist. Martian Krestianovich. *Experiments with sick people.* He gave them all up and attached himself to Smerdiakov and so forth.

80) A revolver for 2 rubles. The merchant heard of the catastrophe and reported the 2 rubles. *At 5 o'clock* he was still looking for two rubles.

80) Grusha. Do you remember how you broke the bottle? and so forth.

80) Smerdiakov and Martian Krestianych.

Maksimov:
They thrashed Nozdryov was drunk.

Maksimov recounts how Nozdryov whipped with birch rods. We then drank *brüderschaft.* It was the lieutenant Kuvshinikov who pushed me to register a complaint. We became reconciled for 25 rubles. I lost them to him at odd and even.
Mademoiselle *Fenardi.* (Some kind of tale with Fenardi)—

05>   ~~You are a little scoundrel, pan, and that's all I have to say. Goodbye. Be calm~~——

DELIRIUM

~~5 years~~
~~——Pity, Mitia, shameful Mitia!~~
~~He had a presentiment of happiness.~~
~~And I love someone——Grushenka began to say~~
~~At times she calls him, at times she sends him away.~~
~~No I'm very good, I'm very good~~
~~——He was happy then Mitia and young. So Young He sang songs, and played a guitar for me~~

[The investigating lawyer has little thin hands with a ring.]

——The proprietor refused to drink, but he came in often and did not go to sleep

~~No, not a thief, not for anything a thief~~

Investigation: Grushenka in another room. Oh misfortune, my misfortune! leaped up and rushed into the room. Please, you can take the testimony now, In fact you must

—How much did he dissipate? 3,000

Investigation: Mitia refuses to say where he got the money from, for a long time. But suddenly he says: I will tell <you> where I got the money? He has everyone leave the room, *speaks*. They don't believe him. Was quiet for a long time (invented). Did you tell anyone this before? No one. Testimony of the Poles. 100 witnesses—

~~thief, thief! and blood blood!~~

~~Good for you Mitia! Grushenka has wicked little lines <on her face> Give me wine to drink Mitia. How is it that they aren't drinking. A chorus of Jews. [I'll marry, I'll marry. Let them drink] An orgy began. Jews Delirium Mitia had a presentiment of his happiness. He looked at his pistols. [He glanced at the curtains. Tears.] He started to press his head. I don't want to think <about it>.~~

~~He did not leave Grushenka's side: How did you get here? But how did you enter. Look Kalganov is sleeping. Kiss. I love someone, I love someone here. Grushenka became gay.~~

~~——Why were you yelling that it's my last night.~~

~~——I'll go and dance by myself.~~

~~——I'm suffering! What is bitter for you? Be gay. Dance, a small piece of chocolate. He turned around and Grushenka was not behind the curtain: Mitia! (she yelled) I loved him. He played on the guitar for me 5 years. Away with regret. You know whom I love. Beat me. A frenzied kiss, [but she tore herself away.] Rushes out. I want to scream. Champagne. A kiss for Kalganov. [I'm good.] Give me more champagne. I'll go to a nunnery tomorrow, but today I want to revel. If I were God. Announced finally that she wanted to dance, etc.~~

N.B. *Numbers, the most fortunate thing.* [25 rubles.]

~~Up to the curtain [Andrey, the proprietor does not drink] (Calls and sends him away. She sits down at the door. Songs. Introduction [Andrey]. Hors d'oeuvres arrive. Drinks. Pistols. Mitia goes out. She calls him. Bitter for me. — by gay, Dance, vanilla, behind the curtain)~~

~~After the curtain (give <me> wine, I'm drinking my third glass, and I'm still not drunk. A kiss for Kalganov. I'm good. Alyosha, I'll go to a convent. But today I want to dance~~

~~Kalganov looked on with a certain curiosity, but did not like it Calls three times:~~

1) When you came in a little while ago (well then go) Surprised that he knocked. So then you've given me up? [You didn't want to accept happiness she looked at him in a beatific fashion.]

2) He wanted to shoot himself (no don't shoot). Wait, I'll tell you something yet.

3) Why are you sad? (But Mitia just then was laughing.) No, I see that you are sad.—Do you see? It's bitter for me. Go and be gay. (Then Dance) (In the corner: I'm a thief, blood) He returned, she wasn't there.

N.B. Each time that he goes away—then songs, [description.] Then the food came. [The proprietor is gloomy,] then Andrey and the dance. Mitia drank up, his head was turning, he gulped down a glass of champagne, and for the first time felt himself drunk, he felt good, everything was turning around.

Grushenka, Mitia give me some more wine. Three glassfuls, She had become tipsy and she: Beat me

63 If I called you scoundrel that doesn't mean yet that I said everyone in Poland was a scoundrel.

Mitia to the judges, when he is in prison: *I agree.*
This matter will clear itself up tomorrow, tomorrow, and then you will see . . . you will see all . . .
THE OLD MAN IS ALIVE THEN? Oh, thank you, God! I thank you God! [(To her)] He used to carry me in his arms.—

Why am I good. Don't blame me for the wine.
I wanted to end my last night in the way we first became acquainted, to remember that happiness and to remind you of it, and about morning end it all.
Poselkovich. What is that, I beg your pardon, sir, I beg your pardon pan father and pani mother[17] Aleksei Mararych began to expose his knowledge in the Polish language, but what is good about them is the little lasses.
——Well true, true, there are no queens on earth more beautiful than Polish girls.
——The colonel writes poetry, put in the investigating lawyer, not knowing a verse of Pushkin's.
The colonel: But look at how things take place there: she dances a

---

[17] In Polish and in Cyrillic characters.

Mazurka with a Russian officer, and then suddenly sits on his lap—
In front of everyone, in front of everyone! We wouldn't dare but that's
their custom. He softens, of course, and the next day they get married.
In that way our whole cavalry has got married there.

Pole: Pan Colonel has been in Poland?

No, my brother served there and got married there, answered the
Colonel morosely.

~~Bow down to Katia to her feet.~~

~~Why money~~

~~He will spend the money~~

~~Will you love~~

~~Forever, forever faithful~~

~~And if you throw me over, I will drown myself.~~

~~But don't love Katia. I'll tear her eyes out. Don't love her The
little Bell. You hear, the bell is ringing—~~

Book Nine

The notes for this book, "The Preliminary Investigation," were written near the end of November and the beginning of December 1879. Dostoevsky first thought of including the arrest and arraignment of Mitia in Book VIII, but on the advice of an important prosecutor he decided to expand the arrest and preliminary questioning of Dmitri into a separate chapter.

Some of the characteristic changes between notes and novel are the following. The following note does not find its way into the novel: "And never heretofore did a man enter prison more filled with hope, thirst for life, and faith." Dmitri glimpses the possibility of regeneration only after considerable torment and doubt, and what is stated about him at the beginning of his imprisonment must be separated in the novel.

A good part of notebook pages 114 and 115 is concerned with a conversation between the prosecutor and the investigating lawyer. They analyze Dmitri's motives and character in a fairly crude fashion and confess frankly and eagerly to the profit to be gained from the celebrity of the trial. Much of this in one way or another appears in the novel, but the tone is less crude. The self-deception of public service and pursuit of truth are permitted to cloud the self-serving motives of the prosecutor and the investigating lawyer.

During the interrogation Dmitri attempts to explain to his questioners why it was impossible for him to go to Katerina Ivanovna for the money he needed to take Grushenka away. The differences between the two versions are significant. In the notes, Dmitri says:

> "She might have really given me, given that money, gentlemen, and I would have taken it too . . . and then . . . all my life, oh God!"

And in the novel we have:

> "Yes, do you know that she might have given me the money, yes, and

she would have given it too; she'd have given it to satisfy her vengeance, to show her contempt for me, for hers is an infernal nature too, and she's a woman of great wrath."

Between note and novel has intervened a greater consciousness of the hurt that Dmitri and Katerina inflict on each other.

After the preliminary hearing is over—or Mitia thinks it is over—he makes a speech in which he says that he is glad that the blow has fallen because he would not have raised himself by his own efforts, and though innocent, he accepts suffering and expects to be purified by the suffering. The version in the notes and the version in the novel are essentially the same, although details differ and the version in the novel is fuller. The version in the notes ends with the note *"hands,"* which is perhaps a note Dostoevsky makes for himself to have Dmitri offer to shake hands with the investigating lawyer. In the novel Dmitri thanks the questioners and offers his hand, and the investigating lawyer hides his hands behind him in nervous and embarrassed movement. "Mitia instantly noticed this, and started. He let his own outstretched hand fall at once." Gesture in the notes becomes psychological and structural refinement in the novel.

——*Undressed*—Everyone is dressed, but I'm undressed. <10

——People should get undressed all together, then there would be no shame.

——Since he is undressed, they have the *de facto*[1] right to be haughty and superior.

——They took away his shirt without his permission. He didn't even pretend to ask, but said forthrightly: no, we will take it away.

——Wait: that's a little too long to wait.—

Final[2] $\begin{cases} \text{If I lived for twenty years, I wouldn't understand as much as} \\ \text{I have in this single terrible night of my life.} \end{cases}$

---

[1] *De facto* is in Latin in the Russian text.
[2] *Final* is so written in Roman characters in the Russian text.

Undressed $\begin{cases} \text{We have done in this case all that we could} \\ \text{couldn't stand Grigory} \\ \text{His lips trembled—enough!} \end{cases}$

BEFORE—I will show you everything. Mitia got tired, got weak, morning, rain—Something sort of was unhinged in his head. They blew out *the candles.*

Here $\begin{cases} \textit{Confessions about the money.} \text{ Yes, I wanted to kill myself and} \\ \text{thought that I could stand the idea that I was thief. But it} \\ \text{doesn't matter, I'll kill myself, and nothing therefore will} \\ \text{make any difference. But it wasn't like that, it turned out that} \\ \text{things do matter! It is hard to die dishonorably. One should} \\ \text{die honest and free.} \end{cases}$

Oh, I've learned a lot that night.
I learned, I would not have learned as much in twenty years . . . etc.

Here $\begin{cases} \text{[Enough] Tell <me> what is your ring made of?} \\ \text{——Smoked topaz} \\ \text{——He took it and threw it, not needed—} \\ \text{[He covered his eyes, his lips trembled. Overcame]} \\ \text{Gentlemen, about Grigory. Could he have stood.——} \end{cases}$

Witnesses: In the shop they said that he showed 3,000—

⟨7⟩   ——AND WHY DID I CONFESS TO YOU! IT'S YOU, PROSECUTOR, THAT BROUGHT ME TO THIS! SING, SING YOURSELF A HYMN IF YOU CAN, IF YOU KNOW HOW! BUT CONSCIENCE, CONSCIENCE! MAY YOU BE CURSED—YOU GOT IT OUT OF ME!

Yesterday it was still possible to think of suicide in the black of night, in the vulgarity of ignorance, passions, and unawareness. But now, now, how is it possible to tear oneself away from the world. Now live as quickly as possible, live, the light that calls, knowledge.

——And never heretofore did a man enter prison more filled with hope, thirst for life and faith—

N.B. THE INVESTIGATION HAD NOT YET FINISHED
Mavriky Mavrikich—

Don't drive the horses, please.
[I'm going to struggle with you, and there as God wills.]

About Grushenka.   <10

Here I thank God that you have shortened,
    You are all so honest, all such honorable people.

From the window (waved his hand)
About Grushenka. Gentlemen! But she isn't here, you won't take
her will you, you don't suspect her do you—
[Prosecutor. It's very possible that he killed the old man acci-
dentally, in great anger]
——And yet all the same one pities human nature, pronounced
Mikhail Makarovich.
——We'll get to it . . . We are working on her.
——But one must in the city.

And they had a fine lunch.
Perhaps to be silly or to make someone laugh, or from stubbornness, but he will not say anything against his conscience for anything
in the world, he will never lie. Believe that. He'll go to his death before
he lies.
——[I thank you Agrafena Aleksandrovna, one soul knows very
little.]

They questioned everyone in great detail
He noted only—Two points: 1,500 and Smerdiakov.
On the string of nobility.
——Acted naïvely
    (be quiet, quiet!)
He was disgusting.
——And I think that you don't have <the right> to ask me about
that and I don't have to answer you.

42) but not on him, but above his head, fixedly and even strange, <1
motionless . . . ~~Some kind of astonishment~~ A kind of astonishment
suddenly expressed itself in her face, almost fright.
——Mitia, who is that looking at us from behind the curtain? she
suddenly whispered to him.
Mitia turned around and saw that really someone had parted care-

fully the curtain ~~carefully~~ and was looking at them, as if ~~carefully looking~~ examining ~~them.~~ And he was not apparently alone.

He leaped up ~~quickly~~ and quickly went toward the person looking . . .

——This way, please, this way, someone's voice said not loudly [but firmly] and urgently.

Mitia ~~went forward~~ came out from behind the curtain and stopped short.

The whole room was filled with people, not with those who had been there before but with [completely] new people, a chill ran over his spine for a moment and he shivered. He recognized all those people in one instant. That tall and plump old man, in an overcoat with [epaulets on his shoulders] with a hat with a cockade, was the police captain ~~Mitia knew him only too well.~~ And that large, pale, and thin ~~prosecutor~~ was the comrade prosecutor, and that youngish boy [very young but portly man in glasses] ~~in a hat~~ in a hat with a cockade, that was . . . Only he couldn't remember his name . . . but he knew him also—that was the investigating lawyer, the judicial investigating lawyer . . . And farther, who was it: that was the district constable Mavriky Mavrikich, and those with emblems ~~that~~ who were they? not ~~soldiers~~ And still two more of some kind, and there at the door ~~farther off~~ Kalganov, and Timofei Borisych . . . ~~also~~

——Gentlemen—what is it, you gentlemen? murmured Mitia, but suddenly as if he were beside himself, as if he were not himself, he yelled loudly, at the top of his voice: [Mavriky Mavrikich stood and sort of was watching them]

——I un—der—stand!

Do you understand? Do you understand? Almost louder than him and reproachfully, the old police captain, stepping up to him, yelled suddenly—have you understood?

——Mikhail Makarych, Mikhail Makarych, that's not the way, not that way . . . I beg you with all my strength to restrain yourselves . . . the youngest little man with a hat with a cockade said in a lively fashion, and turning to Mitia, he began hurriedly and mumbling somewhat suddenly:

——We have to speak with you . . . In short I beg you to come here, here, to the divan . . . We have to clear up things a bit.

——I especially beg you, dear Mikhail Makarych, the friend of the prosecutor began to the police captain, but he didn't finish.

—The old man! yelled Mitia in a frenzy, the old man and his

Notebook Page 108. Handwriting is clear and of various dimensions. Featured prominently are geometric figures and the drawing of a male face. The lines of writing are almost geometric in their regularity.

blood! . . . ~~the blood has cried out! I have understood, I've understood~~
~~everything! . . .~~

. And like someone who had been cut down ~~fell~~ he sat down, as if he
had fallen on a nearby chair.

——Yes, monster, yes father-killer. The blood of your father cries
out before you! . . . The old police captain roared at him, once again
not containing himself. [He was beside himself, became purple and
trembled all over—drunk with a disreputable girl in his blood. Delirium, but it must be delirium!]

——But this is really beyond measure, Mikhail Makarych! I beg
you to permit me alone to talk! the youngish small man yelled in a
firm fashion, and turning to Mitia he said firmly and gravely:

——Mr. reserve lieutenant Karamazov I am obliged to tell you
that you are charged with the murder of your father Fyodor Pavlovich
Karamazov, which took place this night . . .

He ~~seemed to say~~ continued to say something yet the prosecutor
also ~~said~~ began to say something, but even though Mitia listened, he
no longer understood them. He looked at all of them with wild eyes—

[Psychology]
To convince oneself then whether he is living or not.
Yes,
How did you become convinced?
——I realized that he was dead.
——And then you ran away
——destroy a witness Why would one behind whom the blood of
his father cries out jump over a fence? He would have looked at that
as secondary. But he leaped over to convince himself, and once con-
vinced ran away.
Alas, Mitia did not speak about the words of pity.

The Police Captain. Pardon me, dear girl. I don't want to accuse
you, I see that you are not guilty
——Permit me. How was it. Sit on the fence, on the chair for example: how he grabbed you.

——Fine, beautiful, excellent! (to every word) Am I permitted to
speak? Or am I not already permitted <to speak>? Finding himself
on the couch, he does not remember. So the old man is killed, who
then killed him?

What old man The old man Grigory has not been killed.

Not killed, thank you, oh Lord. Oh, how you frightened me, but, permit me, he leaped up as if to run—permit me—

This person.   <11◄
I know well that you will imprison me for Grigory—one can't permit fighting really without punishment . . . But a year, perhaps two—and there—I myself want to go to Siberia—

——You have cheered me up, I thank you—[and although much tormented, tore ~~this~~ his soul, at that moment his whole being irresistibly concentrated itself only on her, on his queen, ~~on his fateful creature~~ on her ~~he ran toward~~ toward whom he flew to look at her for the last time and there, well there to attend to all the remaining decisions ~~and up to this moment he tried to push away from him everything, turn away from himself~~]

——The gray, the gray then hold on to (Mitia suddenly)
——Don't worry, said the district constable.

——Imagine this lady . . . (Mitia recounts an intimate and free anecdote about Khokhlakova) Absolutely.

The prosecutor—Can't you remember at least someone else whom you showed, or at least hinted at (about the borrowed money)
——And so absolutely no one?

——Since you had already kept 3,000—then what special shame was there in it?
Mitia. This money (thief—you know tormented me all night more than anything. Not that I killed the old man—the servant and that Siberia threatened <me> and when—when my love was crowned and heaven opened up for me again—nothing, nothing tormented me as terribly as the consciousness that I had torn finally from my chest that cursed money and had spent it. Thief, thief and dishonorable—that's what I said to myself every second this night! Oh, yesterday I condemned myself to death and I thought that it was a matter of indifference to a condemned man whether he unsealed <the envelope>. It turned out that it was not a matter of indifference. It means that not only is it impossible to live like a scoundrel, but it is also impossible to die as a scoundrel. Impossible to die or to live as a scoundrel. At least for me it is impossible. Particularly now, particu-

larly after what has happened this dawn. Do you understand me, gentlemen? This is the cry of an honorable man. The confession of an honorable man to honorable people! Can it be that you don't understand? Oh, in that case, I'll shoot myself! Why then have I disgraced and dirtied myself with the confession.

(drink some water)—

Mitia to the investigating lawyer. It seems to me that I had the honor, the honor and pleasure of meeting you once at my relative's Miusov.

Mitia to the prosecutor and the investigating lawyer—I understand that you are driving me into a corner, you have to after all, that's your job. I wouldn't like your job, gentlemen (ha-ha), etc.

[It's impossible for you not to be convinced of what is obvious in the matter, but you are doing your duty, your sacred duty, and therefore you are persecuting me, I understand really, I understand.]

15—Gentlemen, I listen to you and it seems to me . . . I see sometimes in my dreams someone following me in the darkness, looking for me, and I know that he knows where I have hidden, but he looks for me on purpose so as to torment me—that's what you are doing.

Conclusion. Oh, yes! What's to be done, one has to submit—[Suffer, be humble, and keep quiet]

The investigating lawyer: I consider you to be an honorable person, carried away by your passions (a small fop. Mitia looks on strangely)

Oh why did I sully myself by telling you about it.

——But it is astonishing that you did not feel these torments while you were carrying <it>

——I felt them but not such as these, for I had not yet spent it. I could have gone the next day and given it back.

——But since you spent half, how would you look returning <the other half>?

Etc.

Not comprehensible. We will all do what we can for you. How is it possible: to want rather to kill another and to steal so as to give the money back.

——Oh God, life, life, gentlemen, life, life—

————Why did you try to bribe Bem[3] with three thousand.

————I wanted to show her his baseness.

————Why did you think that he was so vile.

————I could tell by his eyes.

————Where would you have taken the other 2,300, since as you say you don't have it.

————I wanted to give him the rights to my property, sign a document.

————And you think he would have accepted that.

————For pity's sake, but it's a question of not only three—but of four, of six thousand that one can get for it. These Poles are masters at that: he would gather together a bunch of little Polish and little Jewish lawyers and would have gotten the whole of Chermashnia from him, and not just a small part. Surely, he would have agreed!

MAY I LOOK THROUGH THE WINDOW, GENTLEMEN?

THE POLICE INSPECTOR TAKES MITIA AWAY.

HE REMEMBERED GRUSHENKA AND HER CRIES: THE SPIRITUAL PURIFICATION BEGAN (EMOTIONALLY AS IN THE CHAPTER ON THE CANA OF GALILEE)—

————Such contemptible foolishness.   <1]

————I am a wolf and you are hunting me, yes and persecuting me, ha-ha!

————Mitia. Who then killed him? (About Smerdiakov, sick, sick). And then: who then killed him? *Perhaps Smerdiakov.*

————One can really be purified by evil! cried out Mitia. You are not crushing me, you have raised my spirit, gentlemen (to his accusers)

Most Important

Grigory shows that the door (from the house into the garden) was open.

The suppositions of the Investigating Lawyer: Dmitri Fyodorovich pretended that he was going to the civil servant with the packet of money (he did not hide, but pretended).

---

[3] A variant of the name of Grushenka's former Polish lover. He is called most frequently Podvysotsky and occasionally "Mussialevich."

The Investigating Lawyer: The question that arises from the first glance: did he kill through the window or through the door . . . Are you acquainted with this envelope . . .

The Police Captain (alone)—And suppose it is Smerdiakov, gentlemen?

Mitia says good-bye to the Investigating Lawyer and the prosecutor *familiarly,* tomorrow everything will be cleared up, but the worst is that he himself in a certain depth of his soul feels that they are no longer his comrades, that he is *no longer* their equal, that they are his judges, *his formal judges.*

He is riding with the district constable also, the thought flashes through his mind about Fyodor Pavlovich: Well, the old man died, have to forgive. It may well be that I am as guilty before him as he was before me.

Mitia (after the confession about Katia's money) Gentlemen, I see with sorrow that you don't believe me.

Mitia: Oh, gentlemen, how is it that you can't understand that. I wear the money, and tomorrow I can decide to give it back and I'm no longer a scoundrel, but I can't make up my mind to do, that's what: *fine, fine?*

Or: Fine, fine. Let's assume that you are completely just—and yet at the same time: a bonnet for a bonnet and a rag for a rag.
——bonnet or rag? N.B.!
——Gentlemen you are tormenting me? I'm speaking to you of the sufferings of a fallen angel, and you of an old woman's bonnet. *Passons,*[4] I say to you *passons,* let's talk of what is essential.
——But turn the page, gentlemen, otherwise we won't get to anything.
——No gentlemen, you have not wanted to turn the page, and that's why things have turned out as they have.

The prosecutor keeps at the same thing: how, when, and why? Mitia yells at him: oh, gentlemen, one must stay with trifles: how did you

---

[4] French: "pass over" or "let's forget about that."

go, where did you go, when did you go? . . . Hold on to the essential, follow the essence, otherwise I'll get all muddled. Otherwise it means skimming God knows what.—

Mitia Gentlemen! An honorable man is talking to you. Don't lose sight of this most essential fact. A man who who has done much that is bad, but who has always been nevertheless an honorable creature in essence (forgive me the calembour that came out, but I'm not a literary man) I have suffered all my life just because I've always thirsted for honor, I have been, so to speak, a sufferer for honor, and (a searcher for honor) and yet all my life I created did only base things—and that is all of me, and that's what has tormented me all my life. But one must make distinctions in all of that gentlemen!

Mitia—Gentlemen, I see that you definitely don't trust me.—Who opened the door—Yes, who opened it? It didn't open by itself. Smerdiakov? but it was impossible for Smerdiakov, this man by his feelings is a chicken, a chicken, epileptic, and besides he is after all his son . . . The Holy Ghost—but it cannot be that the Holy Ghost decided to do such a base thing, and such a banal thing besides, a banality! That's a base kind of sorcery, but in our positive century of science, so to speak (which I have always acknowledged) there cannot be any sorcery. Smerdiakov—but he is his father. But you wanted to kill him? Yes, I wanted to, oh, gentlemen, I did want to. And perhaps I might have. . . . Yes I wanted to kill! In truth I wanted to! There were moments . . . Yes man is vile, gentlemen, in truth he is vile—in general and in particular. . . . except for rare instances, but it is base for you to remind me when I have already revealed to you my feelings

Chapter 1. Story   <11!
Chapter 2. Mitia gives testimony. He refuses definitely to say where he got the money.

Before that the Investigating lawyer asked about the door, but he didn't say anything about Grigory's testimony.

When Mitia refused to say where the money came from (mine, I have it) then he asked: how much money there was.

Not three thousand, but half that

Are you acquainted with this envelope?

At Khokhlakova's 3 (the testimony of Perkhotin)

——At the shop they also give testimony (perhaps I've said <that already>

——Trifon Borisych.

——Bem.

——Grushenka (at Katia's) Grushenka upset Mitia.

I must tell you of the testimony of Grigory.

How is it that the door was open?

(Did Smerdiakov kill?)

N.B. {
The Investigating Lawyer: In view of the fact that you re-fuse to say where you got the money and the precise testimony of Grigory what are we supposed to conclude?

Mitia is terribly upset: Gentlemen, I'll reveal to you the whole secret (soften the punishment)
}

Interrogations—How is it that the door was open?

Prosecutor Yes, certainly, if you had killed the old man Grigory, then there would not have been this testimony.

[N.B. On learning that Grigory was alive, Mitia *suddenly* changed the tone of the testimony to something cheerful, and happy—I have the honor to meet you.]

Grushenka's yell. The Police Captain and Grushenka.

Khokhlakova—Oh God! you are giving me an idea: he could really have killed me.

——But he wouldn't have killed you.

——Killed! Killed!

A note to the police captain: I never gave him any money.[5]

The Investigating Lawyer repeats often: *I thank you!*

Mitia about who killed at first: That really confounds me! That positively confounds me!

Mitia in the carriage: I will not become more honest . . . I am not one of those who can lift themselves and save themselves, incorrigible! But I will dedicate my whole life to her, to her alone, and in the rays of her holiness, in her honesty, I will purify myself.

Look, I am now good, but now it is impossible to be good, I don't dare reveal my feelings, I am a prisoner.

The conversation after Mitia is taken away.

---

[5] Verb indicates that a female is talking, probably Mme Khokhlakova.

The Prosecutor: The door is the overwhelming fact. What was he really thinking of? He thought that Grigory, who threw himself after him, had not seen ~~forgot~~ that the door was open. Then it would be easy to suggest that it was Smerdiakov. When he learned—became completely dazed—Oh, he fought cunningly—

——After the undressing: Realism, realism, realism of real life, gentlemen.—

Before the witnesses, it became light, morning,
—— ~~Before~~ After the interrogation of the witnesses, when for the suppression of all means, etc. [after the signing of the interrogation]. Gentlemen, I am a monster, I would never have raised myself, would not have changed no matter how much I might have sworn to do so— People like me need to be pushed, to be thrashed. I accept suffering, unhappiness will purify me, but—I am innocent, I wanted to—wanted to and that's why I accept. But it may be yet that God will save me. I am innocent—and I am firm in hope. In any case I thank you gentlemen, you have been humane with me—*hands*.
Where is the money that was taken away?
——Search? Take off shoes?

The prosecutor and the Investigating Lawyer order of interrogation they interrupt one another.

The doctor of the province (what is his name)
——Any doctor or the doctor of the province.
——Do they take a doctor to Mokroe with them?

——Do they make the witnesses swear?
——Can the prosecutor reveal facts of the interrogation to the accused, for example, the interrogation of Grigory.
About what measures and rights the prosecutor must propose and explain to someone who doesn't know the laws.

The witnesses in the first chapter
Clerk (uniform)
Did the witnesses sit in the room?
Who drove him away, the district constable?
——The search of Mitia's pockets.
——Can he say good-bye to Grushenka?

<3>   ——The Investigating Lawyer: for what special reasons [principles] did you hate your father so much? jealousy?

Mitia—I did not hide my feelings, everyone knows them . . . in the tavern. You know, gentlemen, I believe that you don't have the right to ask me about that. That's my affair, my inner affair . . . But since I spoke to everyone and in the tavern, I will not make a secret of it now. It's known to everyone. [I said . . . I admit that there is quite a bit of proof in this instance. I told everyone that I would kill <him>, and suddenly he is killed, how could it not be me in such circumstances? *I excuse* you, gentlemen, *I excuse* you *completely*.

——Why then? jealousy?

——Yes, jealousy, but not it alone.

——Property—

——Yes property too. But enough, gentlemen, enough. You see: I didn't like the way he looked, something dishonest, braggart, trample everything underfoot, dirty, disgusting. . . . But now, since he is dead, I think otherwise.

——How otherwise?

——Well, not otherwise, but I'm sorry that I hated him so much—

——Do you feel repentance?

——No, not exactly repentance. . . . I myself am not good, gentlemen, what the hell! I myself am not very good—And therefore I didn't have the right to consider him disgusting.

[Oh misfortune, misfortune, he cried out, leaped up again to run.]
——About the murder, *Mitia* suddenly: That's a wild thought, gentlemen. That's a wild thought. I will prove to you that it is a wild thought.

The Investigating Lawyer: Why did you have to have 3,000 so much to the point of looking for them so late at night and in such an eccentric fashion.

Mitia. That's my private life, gentlemen, that's my private life and I won't allow anyone to interfere with it. And even though you are *authorized,* still all the same it would be dishonorable for me to permit you to interfere ~~in my private life~~ in those episodes where [my] honor at least was at stake. I won't permit it.

Mitia That's superfluous, gentlemen (that is, these questions). They are not necessary, they are superfluous. I tell you: follow only what I'm saying and you will know all.

——The Prosecutor. . . . But wouldn't it have been better *first of all* to take the 1,500 to Miss Verkhovtseva, tell her precisely what you have said, that is, that you are weak, perhaps, and a scoundrel, but not a thief—and then look for as much money as you would need.

——*Mitia.* No, gentlemen, not better!

——Why? You could have even asked her for this money: You see, you could have said, I'm not a scoundrel, I'm returning <half of it> and will return <the rest> but lend me the money . . . at least under the guarantee that you offered to Mr. Samsonov and Mrs. Khokhla-kova. You could have offered precisely the collateral for the old debt and the new since you considered this collateral so valuable?

——Oh, how base that would have been?

——But why?

Mitia: Gentlemen, gentlemen! Do you know gentlemen, that you are tormenting me, gentlemen! But I will tell all, all, all! [What a hellish matter I am admitting to you] Do you know really that I had that thought, do you know that I even almost *decided on it.*—So base is man. But to go to her, reveal to her my betrayal, and on top of this betrayal, in fulfillment of it, to *beg* her for money (beg, do you hear, beg) money, so as to run away from her with another—that would have been such a disgusting act, that would have been such a stinking act, that I really don't know what to say!—Yes, of course, if it was a matter of jealousy, etc. mumbled the prosecutor.—But you know, do you know—She might have really given me, given that money, gentle-men, and I would have taken it too and then . . . all my life, oh God! Gentlemen, I have made this confession to you, this terrible confes-sion, in all my baseness—oh value it, gentlemen, otherwise—other-wise you will say straight to my eyes that you don't respect me, that I am a scoundrel!—Oh God, don't torment me, don't torment. I am a scoundrel, yes I am a scoundrel. And since I have confessed to this, I have revealed to you my secret,— so don't call me straight to my face a scoundrel because of that—that would really be too cruel.

Calm down—drink a little water—

Wait, gentlemen. I'm still more of a scoundrel than you think and than I thought of myself. Why didn't I take Katia the money before I began looking for <more money> for myself. Because if I gave back 1,500, I wouldn't have it anymore. I would begin to look for my money at Samsonov's at Khokhlakova's, but suppose I didn't get any. And here I already had it if the moment came to run away with Grushenka. [And suppose she were to say suddenly: we're going]— the money would be there! I thought that way, gentlemen, I did! Tell

me, gentlemen, did I have that thought or didn't I? You are con-
noisseurs of the heart, you are prosecutors, it seems to me that the
thought was not there, but maybe it was, it was, it was! Oh why is it
that man is capable of such baseness!

4>   7. The prosecutor wants to write down the testimony (that is, that
he kept the money and did not repay the debt because he wanted to
have it in his pocket in case he needed it to carry away his mistress)

Mitia yells out. Gentlemen! Don't write that down! Have a shame!
[Don't write down that I wanted to go to her.] I have, so to speak, torn
apart my soul, into two parts, and you take advantage of that and
forage around with your fingers in the torn place and in both halves.

We were writing it down for ourselves, you yourself will read it
later, but now let's get back to the matter at hand. [Everyone knows
about it. Everyone most definitely knows about it. But words still
mean something, yesterday still before the hut, about 3,000, and not
1,500. The amulet I will shoot myself]

——Witnesses. Trifon Borisych: Said that he brought 3,000

Mitia: Did I really say that Trifon Borisych? It seems that positively
did not say that I brought 3,000?

Trifon. You said so, Dmitri Fyodorovich.

Discussion of the judges alone. The colonel objects: Yes! (goes out)
Prosecutor. *He said it to the whole world, to the whole world.*

The speech of the investigating lawyer to Grushenka (after that)
serious and penetrating.

The Police Captain: says *scamp.* The prosecutor smiles.

——The boy-investigating lawyer: Gentlemen, you don't believe
in the most sincere transports of the human spirit.——

Mitia I am one of those who, no matter how many promises they
make to reform, with tears, beating themselves in the chest, they
nevertheless continue to do nasty things and that's the way the whole
life will pass. Now, gentlemen, now, I thank the blow of fate, it will
bring me to my senses, because for our brother an external force is
needed, an exterior blow . . . And then perhaps he will be twisted . . .
into reform. I accept it, gentlemen, I accept the suffering of accusation,
the torment of my shame before all—and perhaps, [you see,] I want to
suffer [because] I will be purified ~~suffering purifies,~~ gentlemen, you
know the thought.

The investigating lawyer—We take you for an honorable man in
essence, but one carried away with passion.

A small figure, but Mitia was deeply moved and though something scraped his heart (on seeing the small figure), he wanted to grab hold of his hand and he cried out

I ~~know~~ do not doubt that you are an honorable gentleman—

20) *Mitia* . . . You cannot not believe a criminal. . . . Or an accused tormented by questions. But you must by all means believe an honorable man, gentlemen, believe the very honorable transports of his soul.

Mitia (in the carriage): Be patient, be humble, and be quiet!

Mitia. With words from Schiller:
Only that palace ~~union~~ is strong—
Gentlemen, We weren't strong at that!

Prosecutor (afterward) Yells: Trifles, *passons,* he makes himself out to be such a *naïve officer,* that he doesn't understand where he is sitting and what kind of evidence he is giving.

The investigating lawyer. Yes, yes, He even disgusted me at that moment.

Prosecutor. I observed him simply with curiosity like a subject. He wanted to deceive us with the appearance of touching naïveté.

The investigating lawyer: Oh there are tricksters of that kind from among the people, as that Snegiryov in July, the matter of the petit bourgeois Snegiryov, I don't know anything, I don't know anything. . . . And then it turned out really mathematically and that he did the murder and the theft.

The prosecutor analyzes the soul of Mitia it might have been criminal at first only <in tendency> half-deliberate and half-premeditated, he might have decided to kill only in general, but that was still far from the actuality <of killing>, from the moment of the crime. 2) He might even have changed his mind. But the minute influenced him. One can understand the 3,000 and having done that he might really have intended to shoot himself because he had a passion for that woman. But when she smiled at him 3) he fell into anguish . . . and when we thundered in on him suddenly, and perhaps even during the interrogation, perhaps even while he was sitting at the table the idea came to him about the money sewn on to his bosom.—

The police captain: It seems that you are attributing to him a very strong firmness of spirit, prosecutor, and resourcefulness.

Prosecutor. He has it: He is sitting on the fence and according to his

own testimony, he jumps down to Grigory. It would seem that after
the father—this would be a matter of tertiary importance, but he
jumps down in order *to be sure*. Is the only witness dead. I see in that,
in my opinion, not so much firmness as, so to speak, animal cunning ...

The investigating lawyer: Bravo, prosecutor (connoisseur of the
heart, you!)—But now the purchase of wine and the sweets, and he
had his hair curled.

The investigating lawyer: and furthermore money has a drunken-
ing effect on these dissipators, when they get their hands on these rain-
bow-colored notes, these 10-ruble Catherine notes[6]

5>   ——Oh, afterward, perhaps he becomes anguished (from loss of
nerve) (from loss of nerve, Prosecutor, isn't that an apt expression),
but for a while still he is drunk from the money—he gives everyone
three-ruble notes. And furthermore he might have really wanted to
shoot himself—and in that case this drunken poem has *quelque chose
de grandoise*[7]—isn't that true, isn't that true?

Well grandeur or no grandeur—

The investigating lawyer.—a little interesting matter, but prosecutor—one can carve oneself a brilliant reputation throughout Russia
(ha-ha).

The prosecutor. I think that someone may come to his aid, they'll
hire a lawyer—Miusov, that Vershonskaia . . .

The investigating lawyer. Yes, but you'll crush them Innokenty
Semyonovich,—one has to serve truth, the public weal, (etc., Shchedrin, kn. Urusov) and runs off to Grushenka, *the scapegrace.*

The investigating lawyer: Oh, you'll carry it off Innokenty Kirilych,
I can foresee it: This will be a work of refinement and we here in our
godforsaken little place—will shine! Bring on even the lawyer Fetiukovich from Petersburg ~~bring him on~~ we will crush them here.

——But why this godforsaken place.

——Oh, patriot!

The investigating lawyer.—That's the way it should be, the way it
should be, Mikhail Makarych, I respect it, as young as I may be, I
value such flights of patriotism, and I respect them sincerely, if you
must know

---

[6] Notes of 10 rubles carried the portrait of Catherine II.
[7] French: "something grandiose."

——Yes you are a fine young man, but . . .

——What?

——Rascal

——Ha, hee, ha—Oh, yes, about that, that person—[Tomorrow]

(The prosecutor about Mitia: firm character

The investigating lawyer. Unstable. . . .

~~The investigating lawyer after the prosecutor finished~~

The prosecutor about how he leaped down to Grigory: I don't know whether he's stable or not, but at critical moments he doesn't lack decision and cleverness.

The investigating lawyer: Bravo, Innokenty Kirilych, I simply would not have noticed that. What a psychologist you are! Frightful to be at your side: You could take out my soul and cut it up anatomically! You will be brilliant!

They have their tea: Well, then, gentlemen, we have earned our tea

After Bem's testimony: Well, now, that whole love affair will become clear—I understand.

Grushenka. Believe what he says.

——How did you believe: Did he spend *three* or one and one-half thousand that first time?

——I believe it was 3,000—

——And did he speak of you?

——He did.

Mitia—You are telling the truth, Agrafena Aleksandrovna, I did say it, did say it, said it to the whole world—

Mitia—It was the devil who opened (the door)

Prosecutor. Well, then, perhaps . . .

About Katerina Ivanovna:

You aren't even worthy of knowing that, gentlemen.

But I saw that *she hated.* That's why I gave her up, gentlemen.

The pestle. Write it down in this way: Perhaps with the intention of killing the old man—there you are, gentlemen, you see—

The prosecutor's avid questions when the interrogation of the witnesses began. It was apparent that the prosecutor wanted to get at Mitia's psychological state that night in Mokroe by the lines of his face.

This is Important
{ Scoundrel but not a thief!
You make such a distinction about that.
Yes, such a distinction.—

——Anyone can be a scoundrel, and indeed everyone is, but not everyone but only an arch-scoundrel can be a thief. But then I can't make my way with such subtleties . . . Only a thief is more of a scoundrel than a scoundrel—that's my conviction.

The prosecutor: One thing is clear to me now:
——He's playing his fantasy on the tune of nobility and will not cease playing that tune. That's rather clever, when not a single substantive piece of evidence, not even a doubt, supports him, that is, literally not a single bit, but on the contrary everything is against him. And it is not a few tens of some kind, but a hundred, two hundred—against him. But he won't wriggle out of it.

6> The day before yesterday I gave you twenty-five kopecks and you drank them up, and now you are crying. It's just that I'm surprised at your goodness with our vile people, Mavriky Mavrikievich, and that's all I have to say!
——Why do we need another troika? intervened Mitia, we'll go in one, Mavriky Mavrikich, it's not likely that I'll mutiny, I won't run away from you, what's the point of an escort!
——Would you kindly, sir, learn how to talk with me, if you still don't know, kindly address me with the formal pronoun, and keep your advice for another time . . . Mavriky Mavrikich suddenly ~~yelled~~ answered fiercely, as if he were suddenly glad to get things off his chest.
Mitia fell silent. He became completely red. In a minute he felt suddenly very cold. The rain stopped, but the turbid sky was covered over with clouds, a sharp wind blew straight into his face. "What is it, do I have the chills," Mitia thought shaking his shoulder. Finally, Mavriky Mavrikich climbed into the carriage too, sat down heavily, and as if not noticing it, squeezed Mitia forcefully. It is true that he was in a bad mood and he did not enjoy at all the mission which he had been charged with.
7> ——Good-bye, Trifon Borisych! Mitia yelled again, and he himself felt that he had not cried out from good feeling, but from ill feeling, had yelled out against his will. But Trifon Borisych stood proudly, his arms folded behind his back, and stared directly at Mitia, looking at him severely and angrily, but he didn't answer Mitia.

——Good-bye, Dmitri Fyodorovich, good-bye! Kalganov's voice suddenly rang out ~~suddenly yelled~~ having suddenly leaped up from somewhere. Running up to the carriage, [he] stretched out his hand to Mitia. He was without a cap. Still Mitia managed to grab hold of his hand and to shake it.

——Good-bye, dear man, I won't forget the breadth of your heart! Mitia cried out [warmly] ~~with a trembling voice~~ But the carriage started off and their hands parted. The little bell rang out—and Mitia was carried away.

And Kalganov ran to the vestibule, sat down in a corner, bent his head, covered his face with his hands and broke into tears, he sat there and cried for a long time,—cried ~~as if completely~~ as if he were a small boy, and not already a twenty-year-old young man. N.B. *Oh, he believed* completed in Mitia's guilt "What kind of people are they, how can they be people after that!" he kept exclaiming in a disordered fashion and in bitter sorrow, almost in desperation. At that moment he didn't even want to live on earth: Is it worth it, is it worth it! the hurt young man kept exclaiming ~~poor . . .~~

The end of the third part.

F. Dostoevsky

Book Ten

These notes are dated approximately at the end of January and the first part of February 1880. Dostoevsky originally planned to include the chapters on the boys in the book "Ivan." This is why notes on Ivan, especially on notebook page 118, are mixed with notes on the boys. In a sketch of a large section of action we get, for example, the following:

> Ivan at home after the second meeting with Smerdiakov. Smerdiakov suddenly calls him. He confesses and returns the money. He hanged himself. Alyosha comes to Ivan and tells him at night that Smerdiakov had hanged himself. Ivan went to see. He returned home.
>
> Ivan, alone—

One might note that in the final version Ivan did not return to see Smerdiakov after he had hanged himself.

The notes on the boys cover in a fragmentary way the important events and dialogues of the final version: the loss of Zhuchka, Kolia's training of Perezvon; the cannon, Iliusha's sickness, and Kolia's swaggering and his statements on various subjects. Although we have fragments of dialogue between Alyosha and Kolia, we have very little of the complex attitude that the swaggering yet timid Kolia Krasotkin has toward Alyosha. Similarly, even though we have fragments of scenes about Iliusha, we have very little of the desperate love between the sick father and the sick boy.

Dostoevsky apparently planned at first a larger field of action for the boys, because on notebook page 120 we find notes referring to a variety of incidents that did not find their way into the novel: torture of a four-year-old boy, an eldest son who kills himself, the suicide of a small boy, a shot from a window, the theft by boys of money from a trunk.

Plan for the 4th part. <1]

[AT HOME]

Mitia with Rakitin. Socialism. Rakitin laughing about Mitia to Alyosha.

The boy is a rascal. He came to Iliusha. Alyosha with the boys, the rascal-boy does not want to become friends.

He came, saw Iliusha, fell into tears.

Alyosha, Katerina, the family and so forth.

Alyosha at Mitia's. The social mood. *Mitia begs him to go* [to Katerina Ivanovna and to find out if she wants to talk at the trial about the bow down to the earth. *So that she would not speak.*]

Alyosha to Katerina Ivanovna. She submits mildly I don't love <him>, but I'll save <him>.

She told the lawyer about the bow and suddenly to Ivan Fyodorovich in Alyosha's presence: But did he murder, did he murder? I went to Smerdiakov's. And then, irritation, sarcasms, hints,

——Ivan came out and was astonished: why did he go only once to Smerdiakov's (description of this first time). And then he goes the second time. The second meeting with Smerdiakov—A quick meeting with Alyosha.

2

——Iliusha's death, funeral. On the eve of the trial, Alyosha at Grushenka's. She is afraid of Katerina Ivanovna. Alyosha to Katerina Ivanovna: they don't receive him. Ivan at home after the second meeting with Smerdiakov. Smerdiakov suddenly calls him. He confesses and returns the money. He hanged himself. Alyosha comes to Ivan and tells him at night that Smerdiakov had hanged himself. Ivan went to see. He returned home

Ivan, alone—

3

The trial—

At the trial—Proper people will not go to you, every respectable person ought to have a dissatisfied air. Liberalism shields the bribe-taker and the scoundrel—because, because he has the appearance of something European.

Alyosha knows the secret and *keeps it to himself* (Kalganov, they live together).

The boys love Iliusha. Krasotkin knows about Zhuchka, says that <11 he disappeared (N.B. the boys explain this to Alyosha.) Krasotkin wanted to come. The boys go to Iliusha. He awoke. Walk a little. The shoes are worn.

——Krasotkin (goose). I say instead of a plan.

——Smurov was whipped. Because of the goose. The story about the goose. But Smurov for what reason? And he came and laughed. I, he says, was there and saw. Ah, you were there then too? No, he says, I lied. But it didn't matter, they thrashed me. That's not allowed with me. If you were there, he says, then you should have been thrashed, and if you were not there, why did you lie. Logical.

——And will you be whipped?

——Me? the boy looked proudly—

——Krasotkin said that Zhuchka disappeared.

——Krasotkin whistled. Zhuchka began to scratch. They let her in.

——Her?

——I didn't say anything then on purpose.

——They fed Zhuchka, gave her bread.

~~the boy~~ Krasotkin got up and made his peace. I, brother, don't like effusiveness. They showed him the little rabbit (He looked on haughtily)

——Krasotkin looks at Iliusha: "Nothing."

——There is a good cannon

Smurov was whipped because of the powder—24 of saltpeter, 10 of sulfur, and 6 of birchwood charcoal.

They made it in a pomade pot, it burns.

They wanted to explode me, an old man, they whipped <him>—

They want to whip Shiriaev because of the goose.

——*Krasotkin.* Good-bye.—Good-bye Krasotkin.—I'll come.—Ah, come. Here's a whistle.

Krasotkin (You'll be whipped too) I wanted to spit on that. (and then he gets up proudly); I wanted to risk it [at home]

Krasotkin <says> to Alyosha alone: I like that boy. Will he die? Will he die.

Scoundrels. Who?

~~yes~~ All. And he threw a stone at some sparrows.

Krasotkin <says> to Iliusha: you remember we made a cannon. I'll bring a cannon to him: can I? Cannon with a key, they fired it. How could one get powder? Alyosha got some small shot in the window.

In geography I'm better than Ivan (the teacher). In arithmetic, I'm the best.

N.B. At first Iliusha was under the control of Krasotkin.
What do you think about America? (Run away to America) As far as I'm concerned that's stupid.
Krasotkin leaves, Alyosha accompanies him ~~Kr~~ Alyosha returns. Iliusha to his father: papa take a little boy. If I forget you Jerusalem.[1]

Either we will become friends or we will part enemies, blushed   <1
(perhaps he said something stupid).
N.B. Boys. Good-bye. You may become a man.
You think so . . . There's a lot of mysticism in you, but reality will cure you.
Krasotkin (about the woman). I'll tell you what: a mug such as ~~impossible to imagine~~ you've never seen before.

——Kolbasnikov. [the teacher,] is getting married—a mug as you can't imagine possibly. In love.
——Krasotkin: We are like other people. I don't like that.

Look up 3 Krasotkin recounts how a boy lay down under a railway car and the car ran over him. That was Krasotkin himself. Strange— Well, not particularly.—And in America they burned it and went away. I read it in the newspapers. Perhaps they lie. They lie a lot in newspapers.
——Men of antiquity lied a lot too—Cassandra lied 28,000 times. How old was she and when did she have the time.
[Under our zodiac]
——Everything changes, consequently there's ~~no such thing~~ as good, wants to shoot himself.
4) Torture of a four-year-old boy.

———————————————

[1] Compare the words of Capt. Snegiryov in Book X, chap VII of the final version: "I don't want a good boy! I don't want another boy!" he muttered in a wild whisper, clenching his teeth. "If I forget thee, Jerusalem, may my tongue . . ." And Kolia's questions to Alyosha: "What was that he said about Jerusalem? . . . What did he mean by that?"
"It's from the Bible. 'If I forget thee, Jerusalem,' that is, if I forgot all that is most precious to me, if I let anything take its place, then may . . ."

6) Sold the cat.

7) The eldest son wants to kill himself [in my opinion] to run away to America[2]

(Krastokin with Alyosha)

7) The boys stole a trunk with money. Krasotkin: I detest that.

8) He shot from a window. The suicide of the small boy.[3]

Krasotkin: Mystification.

Krasotkin: the company rushes to the girls' pension.

22. 23. The boy with the penholder, no, he has a good character and drinks a little.

N.B.—If I forget you Jerusalem (in the vestibule). Suddenly he doubled up and started crying, climbed under a bench, is trembling.—[4]

Here—The Captain went to get the puppy and brought back another puppy, and the children came to say that Zhuchka had got lost (Krasotkin told it that way). *About the puppy.*

A black nose, that means he is bad.

Teucer, Dardanus, Ilius, and Tros, founded Troy. Smurov, having said that, felt guilty (he looked it up in Smaragdov). Krasotkin did not get confused.[5]

21> He looked haughtily: Well, how did they found it? What does it mean to found something? Four fools came and founded. Smurov could not explain that.

Here—An ass of the first order and last degree—The teacher Dardanelov.

---

[2] Dostoevsky narrates in his *Diary of a Writer* about two school boys who planned to run away to America to escape punishment for a crime of some kind. *The Citizen*, 1873, No. 50. Also Kolia says to Alyosha in the final version: "I think, too, that to leave one's own country and fly to America is mean, worse than mean—silly. Why go to America when one may be of great service to humanity here? Now, especially, there's a perfect mass of fruitful activity open to us. That's what I answered" (Book X, chap. VI).

[3] The episode of the suicide of the small boy is not to be found in the final version.

[4] See n. 1 of this section.

[5] From the final version: "Kolya had read of the founders of Troy in Smaragdov, whose history was among the books in his father's bookcase."

——I don't believe Darwin. The origin of the dragonfly.

——On the other hand take even God—all that is hypothesis.— One would have to invent him.—

——I'm not saying anything against God. He is needed for order.

I'm not a mystic and I will admit that I can't stand to enter into all these discussions. Moreover one can love mankind without believing.

——I read Candide[6] (Voltaire for example, loved mankind and did not believe in God).

——No, he believed.—

——Did he really believe. I moreover . . .

——Did you read Voltaire long ago

——I read a little. I read *Candide*.

——And did you understand everything?

——Oh yes . . . everything . . . that is, I don't understand why he expresses obscenities. I understand of course that it is a philosophical novel and was written [to carry out] to prove an idea, but . . .

——And have you read Schiller?[7]

——You know, all that is sugary. Schiller is an idealist.

——26 page   (the dreamer)

——27 page (to the children about the battle of Kulikovo).[8]

——28 Katerina gave birth. Not a husband but a child. Krasotkin comes and listens: Let's go. You'll enter and you'll say: Krasotkin came.

29) The seminarian about Gurin and Varsonofin.

---

[6] In the final version Kolia brags to Alyosha about having read *Candide*: "Have you read Voltaire? Alyosha finished.

"No, not to say read. . . . But I've read *Candide* in the Russian translation . . . in an absurd, grotesque, old translation . . . (At it again! again!) Book X, chap. VI.

[7] Schiller was favorite reading of the young Dostoevsky, and references to Schiller abound in his creative works. By and large, a Schiller-like soul is one who is idealistic and unrealistic.

[8] Important and perhaps even decisive battle in Russian's successful efforts in throwing off the Tartar yoke. The battle took place on 8 September 1380 between the forces of the Moscow prince Dmitri Donsky and the Tartars.

31) Krasotkin with Alyosha about the backwardness of the Russian people, but all the same one ought to strangle those Germans.[9]

33) Not pedagogy but the pedagogue.

2>   [Kolia] That cost me a lot

The boy sort of was ashamed. But if you knew how that was bad for him, his little heart.

grew pale

Everyone started to praise Kolia—

——KOLIA SWAGGERED

——He will begin to howl and you will be unhappy—

——I DON'T WANT THE BOY—

——How did the *new doctor* talk (about me) to you

——The ear is cut exactly as you told me. It was by these marks that I found him. *No one's.* I locked him up at home so that no one would see him, and didn't tell you—

——And to establish a social commune on rational principles.—

[I AM AN INCORRIGIBLE SOCIALIST KARAMAZOV, AND IN THIS SENSE I WILL NOT BE LAUGHED AT.]

——But I refused. We too can show what we're worth.

——Kolbasnikov himself told us that.

---

[9] Compare with the following from Book X, chap. VI of the final version: [Alyosha talking first]: "Not long ago I read the criticism made by a German who had lived in Russia, on our students and schoolboys of today. 'Show a Russian schoolboy,' he writes, 'a map of the stars, which he knows nothing about, and he will give you back the map next day with corrections on it.' No knowledge and unbounded conceit—that's what the German meant to say about the Russian schoolboy."

"Yes, that's perfectly right,' Kolya laughed suddenly, "exactly so! Bravo the German. But he did not see the good side, what do you think? Conceit may be, that comes from youth, that will be corrected if need be, but, on the other hand, there is an independent spirit almost from childhood, boldness of thought and conviction, and not the spirit of those sausagemakers, groveling before authority. . . . But the German was right all the same. Though they are so good at sciences and learning they must be strangled."

——Iliushechka, make me a gift of that little cannon
——no, let it be completely mine and no longer yours.
——Twelve o'clock—

Ninochka.—Come to Iliushechkas's—
——No, come to us everyday.

Teucer, Dardanus, A kid who got caught.

——Kolia about the hunchback woman. Is she good, good?   <1!
——Ah, very good.[10]

I will not say anything about Dardanelov, he is a well-informed   <1!
man, very definitely well-informed, I respect such men.
——Still, you put him down as to history—about who founded
Troy.
——Were you really put down by that—about how Troy was
founded?
——He knows everything, papa, he is only pretending, but he is
the best in his class.
——But that is really nothing but foolishness, and I myself con-
sider it to be an empty question.
Dardanelov. He mumbled something, hesitated, and I didn't under-   <1!
stand anything. And then he blushed.

Kolia, powder, pulp, a bit of soot, a trace of soot.

You wanted me to blow up an old man,—showed off, I won't let them
do that to me. ABOUT THE GOOSE.

Dardanelov: He is well-informed. He had precise knowledge.

——He does not take off his coat: *I've come only for a minute,*

——History: Old wives' tales, the study of mankind's follies.
And consider those classical languages: everything is really translated, etc.

---

10 The rest of the notebook page is filled with calculations pertaining to his
novels and the diaries. These are apparently numbers pertaining to the sale and
distribution of his books.

Madness.

——No that's because it is boring. Well, how to arrange it so that it would be even more boring. Turn a wheel. For the sake of discipline. Beat the water.[11] [But that is doubtlessly impossible, and that's why they invented the classical languages.]

——[But I am not falling behind.]

——[He's first, first, and he's only talking that way.]

——That's true, said Smurov.

——Man is made in the image of God and he beats the water.

——No, Ivanov said that, the teacher—

——The twelfth year. Soon, 12. My age is no one's concern. The question is whether I am judging rightly or not, and not how old I am, [right?]

Kolia to Alyosha. *Mysticism.* Agree that the Christian faith has served only the rich and the powerful so as to keep the lower class in slavery.

6>   I am not against Christ, he was a humane man [individuality] and if he lived in our times and [had] had received a modern education he would have immediately joined the revolutionaries.[12]

[That's clear.]

[*Alyosha.*] Thus a beautiful nature like yours, which has not yet begun to live, is already spoiled by convictions.

——I'm still not that much of a revolutionary. I consider, for example, that to leave [one's fatherland] for America is vile

——~~Even~~ worse than vile—stupid

——But [didn't] you want to run away?

——I admit that they were inciting me to do so, but I refused.

[This] is between us, of course, Karamazov, listen and don't tell anyone a word. I don't want to fall into the hands of the third section and take lessons . . . at the Bridge of Chains.[13]

——Do you remember, you will recall the building near the Bridge of Chains. Beautiful.

---

[11] The Russian is *vodu toloch v stupe* which means to beat the air in vain.

[12] See n. 32, Books I and II.

[13] The Tsarist secret police (the third section) had its offices near the Bridge of Chains (*tsepnoi most*).

——Christ. And perhaps he would not have completely played the ultimate role

——Where did you get that?

——For goodness' sake you can't hide the truth.

[the old man] Belinsky said it already

——[Where did he say that?]

——[They say that he said that.]

And have you read Belinsky—

No, I haven't read all of him . . . but I have read [the passage] about Tatiana—[14]

——And did you understand everything.

——Really, I think you take me for Smurov

——Look at my convictions and not at my age.

——But I've read about why Tatiana did not go off with Onegin.   <12

——How she didn't go off with Onegin? Did you really understand that?

——Really, I think you take me for Surov.

——[But you still aren't 12 years old.]

——[I'll soon be 13, 13, and not 12, but finally what difference does that make to anyone?]

——Why go to America when one can be useful here. And especially now. A whole field of the most fruitful activity.

[HERE] Kolia and Alyosha. Happy to make your acquaintance, sentimentalities.

[Kolia. I'm a socialist, Karamazov, a socialist by conviction.]

Kolia, this is the dog Perezvon. And it is not Zhuchka. I know that you would all like it to be Zhuchka, I heard it all. Listen, I'll explain the matter—

I didn't go . . . because of a certain reason, you'll learn soon.

——And how happy he will be

Yes, I heard that he mentions me. He will die.—

[*Alyosha:* He dreams of Zhuchka, the boy cries, find Zhuchka for

---

[14] This is a reference to several articles Belinsky wrote on *Evgenii Onegin* for *The Fatherland Notes* in 1844 and 1845.

me.] It's a pity that Zhuchka has not been found, you were the last
hope. The father was counting on you. Yes, it is a pity. [puppy]

Kolia (bursts into tears). I can show you the cannon. Kolia what
does a goose think?—I like to talk to the people at the market. We
have separated ourselves from the people, and certainly we must raise
the people to our level—

I am always ready to admit to render justice to the people, but without spoiling them much. That *Sine qua.*

8> [HERE? Fyodorchenko wrote some poetry, it begins

Our third-graders were struck
By Kolbasnikov's marriage
And what follows is very amusing.

to all dogs

——But I think there's something foul, and it must be smoked out.
Onegin. I'm against the emancipation of women . . .

——You're taking me for Smurov.

——[But you are only 12!]

——What are my convictions, and not how old I am.

——From a starry sky

——That's charming, that's a German, that's good [Therefore, an
independent spirit, and not a spirit of German slavery—Strangle the
Germans.] So they're strong in science, but all the same they deserve
strangling. Corrupted and atheist.

Charming character.

——I'm not against Christ—he would have joined—I'm not so
much of a revolutionary

To America
at the Bridge of Chains—
I'm not a mystic—one can learn from you
If I forget Jerusalem
Illiusha and Kolia kissed
——Papa Take the boy
If I forget—

There's a slander going around that I played robbers *with the kids.*
It's true that I played, but it's a slander to say that I did it for my own
amusement.

——And yet suppose you did it for yourself?

——But for myself at my age!

——But look here, in the theater where they show the adventures of great heroes, at times at war—isn't that the same thing? To play at war or being robbers is the beginning of art, the need of art in a young soul.

[Consequently, why be ashamed of it?]

——Do you think so? Is that your conviction? Well, I'll think more on it, I'll exercise my brain on it when I'm alone . . . But you know you said a profound thing; one can learn things from you. I intend to learn from you, Karamazov—

And I from you.

——No please, let Perezvon stretch out.

4) Liza and brother Ivan (don't forget)

Krasotkin: I hate my name Nikolay,—   <1?
——Why
——Very official and government-like.

Iliusha Papa, buy a little bird and set it free.

Kolia and *Smurov:* nonsense, perhaps. [All these things with Karamazov. I don't understand Karamazov. Aleksei Karamazov's activity.]
Zhuchka is a trivial name.

What is—If I forget Jerusalem . . . This is what does it mean? . . . such a character, he became a clown and even in tragedy remained a clown . . . Doesn't forget his eccentricity.

Kolia—You've said that well. You know, you can learn something from you Karamazov.

——And I'm learning from you, from the children.

——N.B. After the burial the father ran and called Zhuchka.

Teucer, Dardanus—*Krasotkin*—I'm not much interested in that. Today the natural sciences are more <important?>

The septenary system . . . Yes, and I don't know how to solve it, but have only posed the question. But Dardanelov definitely had trouble answering.

You are a smart peasant
——I know I'm smart.
——He is in any case a smart peasant.

I am always ready to admit that the people are intelligent.

Krasotkin They don't try that with me. For some reason I'm dangerous for them.

Iliusha said to his father: That's why I'm sick, the dog Zhuchka—

That's the same Zhuchka I can guarantee it, only now it is *Perezvon*
isn't it a beautiful name? It's Slavic and I myself found it.

Kostia to Alyosha: I have two fledgling on my hands now at home.

Iliusha [here] answered: as it pleases him, tell him that I will throw
<such an object> again to the dog and that I will do the same to all
dogs.[15] I would have become reconciled earlier. But it was necessary
to train (Zhuchka).

---

[15] A reference to the pin Smerdiakov had taught Iliusha to put in a piece of
bread and throw to dogs. Iliusha had thrown such a piece of bread to Zhuchka.

Book Eleven

These notes were written for the most part in June and July 1880. The first five chapters were published in the July (1880) issue of *The Russian Messenger* and the other five chapters were published in the August issue. There are also two dates in the text: 16/17 June and 30 July.

Notebook pages 132 and 133 are composed of a short sentence outline of the entire book. The order of events is not the same as in the novel itself, and there is some intrusion of facts from other books.

In the conversations between Smerdiakov and Ivan, Dostoevsky states openly and baldly the point of each conversation. We get in the notes, for example: "(63) 2d meeting (You too wanted the murder)." And: "And at the 2d meeting, I threatened you and you went away with your tail between your legs. Then I realized too that you were not dangerous to me." Dostoevsky masks somewhat such frank statements in the final version for psychological and structural refinement.

A simple phrase like "Hoffman's Malt Extract" is repeated several times in a long paragraph about Satan's concern for his health. Dostoevsky also reminds himself several times that Satan has a wart: "Satan. He has a wart. When leaving Satan looks for his handkerchief." Both the malt extract and the wart are details Dostoevsky is determined to use to emphasize the everyday, literal, unromantic nature of Satan: "Satan would cough from time to time (realism, wart)." Dostoevsky's intent seems to be to humiliate Ivan with the shabby romanticism of the devil and with the contradiction of the materialistic-spiritualism of Satan. In essence Satan taunts the atheist Ivan with his reality (like the liberal philosopher who, in Satan's anecdote, disbelieved and was astounded that there was life after death), and it is possible that the mixture of shabby materialism and supernaturalism is the kind of vulgar mixture Ivan suffers from.

In a note dealing with the tangled relations between Dmitri and Katerina, Dostoevsky adds motive and explanation to what appears in the notes. In the notes we get: "He sends word to Katia not to testify in his favor about the bow to the earth. I don't want it. She is capable of dishonoring herself before everyone for me." And in the novel we get: "And there are some people who are better as foes than as friends. I mean Katerina Ivanovna. I am afraid, oh, I am afraid that she will tell how she bowed to the ground after that four thousand. She'll pay it back to the last farthing. I don't want her sacrifice."

30>   He harnessed up the carriage. Krasotkin—they heard that.

S. Smerdiakov

——Krasotkin: I gave him what for.
Krasotkin to Alyosha: I'm astonished how you find time for everything. Tomorrow your brother is being judged and you <are bothering about> [such trifles] with the boys.
Here—Then, you want to influence the younger generation.
——You are not proud, that's clear.

——Grushenka calls Alyosha and tells him in agitation that D Mitia is talking rank nonsense—he wants to change the people, and Rakitin is with him.

Mitia $\begin{cases}\text{F—Mitia about Rakitin: There's something dry about} \\ \text{them, just like when I was coming up to this prison. But it's} \\ \text{the truth. What can you do if it is the truth.} \\ \text{——Do you believe that it is me?} \\ \text{——I did not believe it even for a minute—}\end{cases}$

[Alyosha—F. Leave Ivan.] There's something here I don't understand.
He sends word to Katia not to testify in his favor about the bow to the earth. I don't want it. She is capable of dishonoring herself before everyone for me. The lawyer hinted at it.

Katia—to Alyosha: I thought at times that it would be as horrible for me to touch him as it would be to touch a toad (father-killer). No, he is still human for me.
Alyosha to Katia: *Spare yourself* (at the inquest)

——Katia with blazing eyes: You still don't know me, and I still don't know *myself*. It's possible that after the examination you'll want to trample me underfoot.—

——A woman is [often] dishonorable.

WHERE DO IVAN AND ALYOSHA LIVE? ~~On guard.~~   <1

Ivan's sick face.

Ivan to Smerdiakov: —You are sick.

Smerdiakov But you are no better. It's been a long time since you've come.

Have you talked to Aleksei Fyodorovich.

——You don't have any need to know.

——Have you spoken or not, I beg you

——I didn't say anything straight out, but I said something. Could I have said it to him straight out?

~~Well he's just a snot nose. All he can do is talk. Meat.~~

16/17 June

Katia (Follows after Ivan. But despite the fact that she hates Mitia,   <1
she wants to save him. She believes that Mitia committed the murder)

II Katia and Ivan

——Grushenka supports the Pole

——III and IV Satan

——IV Katerina Ivanovna with Mitia's letter at the trial.

——V Fetiukovich's speech

——VI Satan

——VIII Satan

——Mitia X. So that the baby would not cry.

XI (Mitia's letter to Katia).

Mitia XI about Grigory's testimony (Rakitin's thought)

XIII *Mitia* in prison.

XIII Mitia in prison. Mysticism.

XIII Katia. Prays to the Mother of God. Hate for Mitia. Confession to Alyosha. I must overcome myself.

——XIV The brother Ivan

——XV Satan

——XV F. *Mitia about the woman* (under the slippers).

XV Satan. I.

XV F. Ivan about conscience. Satan

XV *Mitia*. Some are better as enemies than as friends

XV Mitia. The son to the father: Why should I love you.

2

33> ——XVI Satan (wart and so forth)
 ——XVII Satan (I am becoming superstitious)

XVII—F. Mitia. The Karamazovs are not scoundrels, but philosophers. About thought *non est disputandum*.[1]

——F. XVII Rakitin's poetry. The little foot.

XVIII Mitia about Rakitin. He is publishing a little brochure, brother.

——About Iliusha: the environment is at fault.

3F Mitia about Rakitin: *They are dry*

3F About the deep bow. wants to tell it in my favor.

4 Liza and the brother Ivan.

5 Testimonies against Mitia have multiplied (with Khokhlakova)

Khokhlakova about Katia: I know one bit of evidence that she is concealing and with which she can kill him immediately.

---

[1] The Russian is *de myslibus non est disputandum;* the Russian word for "thought" (*mysl'*) has been latinized.

5 (Ivan and Smerdiakov)

6 (Ivan and Smerdiakov)

8 *Mitia* word to Katia so that she would not tell about the deep bow

8 F Katia to Ivan in Alyosha's presence: But did he kill? Did he kill? Sarcasm.

9 ~~to Alyosha~~ Alyosha and Katia. *Mitia* (EVERYTHING IMPORTANT).

10 11) everything important ⎫
12   everything important ⎬ Mitia

12 About Grushenka passionately and tenderly.

12 The course of events. THE MOST IMPORTANT.

13 Mitia (love Ivan[2] (Satan) Ethics and so forth. EVERYTHING IMPORTANT.

14 Mitia (small tails. Pity of God. Don't forget about someone else. Bernards.[3]

14 Satan (much).

15) F. Ivan Who killed?

Alyosha. Not you.

15 F. Mitia.

He doesn't feel contempt for anyone, that's why   <13

If [AT THE END] he doesn't believe, then of course he feels contempt.

——And me, me too? but

——And you.

I want him to take me aside, beat me and then go away (at the end).

I didn't believe that it was good to torment a small boy.

To be held in contempt.

[Not completely]

[That's Alyosha]

[I'm coming immediately.]

[She asked.]

---

2 The parentheses are not closed in the notes.

3 Claude Bernard (1813–1878), celebrated French physiologist who developed and applied the experimental method to medical science. He was an important influence on Emile Zola's introduction of the experimental method in his theory of diction. For Dmitri and Dostoevsky "Bernard" is a term of contempt for those who would reduce the soul to material causes.

4 The scene on this notebook page corresponds to the scene in chap. III, "A Little Demon Visit to Lise."

He answered, arose, and left
——He acted honorably.
Again I'm not ashamed. Alyosha
Why is it that you don't like me at all
No, I love. Not at all
there was nothing better

——Dream about devils
I also had that dream.
——Really? Alyosha that is terribly important. Is it possible that different people can have one and the same
——Apparently so
Alyosha said that it was terribly important
the dream is not important but your ~~wanting~~ lying is—that's the truth.
——The truth.
——Alyosha come to me, come to me
——I will always come
——I am telling you after all

5>   Mitia—Be careful of asking forgiveness of a woman. And keep you They are the angels without which we can't live.—
——It's not only Smerdiakov . . . I don't want to—
——and I don't want to say (both, something)
Mitia said good-bye and kissed Alyosha
——Love Ivan—
Alyosha astonishes Me
No, don't be astonished. You see, Rakitin doesn't understand, but you, you understand. You see—

——Mitia about the lawyer. He seems to think that I <killed>
In that case why is he defending me

The little foot.
A Pig came from the son of the dog. ~~agree that you yourself~~ pure pig.
And really he set in motion a civic tendency

6>   ——Everything in a feverish state, and everything *as if in its synthesis.*
——Alyosha asks Katia: Why are you saving him if you are convinced that *he* is guilty?

——*Mitia* is sort of in a feverish state the night before.

——Mitia is interested in the relations between Katia and Ivan.

——Mitia says about Ivan mysteriously—There's a man for you . . .
He's a superior man. Not like you and me.
——Katia [is afraid] doesn't want to appear as a witness.
——Mitia is jealous of the Pole, because Grushenka is helping the
Pole.
"You believe that I committed the murder," he says to Grushenka.

N.B.—*Mitia's secret* he announces it to Alyosha, that Ivan is pro-
posing that he run away.

And yet he himself believes that I committed the murder (never
before had Mitia insisted to Alyosha that he had not done the killing,
It was a question of some kind of pride.)
And so saying good-bye to Alyosha: My arms on his shoulders: Do
you believe that I committed the murder?
Thank you.

——He became suspicious.

——About Grigory's testimony.

Mitia speaks of the resurrection of another man within him: he was
imprisoned in me and he would never have appeared if it had not
been for this circumstance. He says to Alyosha: What difference does
it make to me that I will spend twenty years in the mine beating ore
out with a hammer? You can live fully there too. You can find the
human heart in the person of the prisoner and murderer under the
earth, by one's side, one can come together in love, one can be reborn
and be resurrected.

10)
this is a lost, frozen heart, watch over him for years and bring to <137
light a lofty soul, a suffering consciousness, of a lost hero. And there
are many of them, hundreds of them. Oh, yes, we are in chains and we
are not free; but then resurrected by our great suffering and having
acquired the consciousness of new men we will sing a sad, tragic hymn
from the bowels of the earth—to nature, to the mysterious and in-
evitable genius of fate, to God finally. No, life is full, there is life

under the earth too. You can't understand how much I want to live, what a thirst I have for life and consciousness! And what is suffering? I'm not afraid of it, even if it is boundless, I seem to have so much strength that I will overcome everything, if only to say to myself every moment that I exist, I exist while suffering a thousand agonies, I exist while writhing from torture. Though I sit on a pillar. You know various philosophies torture me, for example the idea: The more intense the sensation of life (it seems that it would be healthy), the more I pay with my death. I never had such ideas before, but everything has fermented in me, remained hidden. Perhaps I drank and raged around just because such suppressed ideas remained hidden and stormed inside me and I wanted to quench something. I spoke to Rakitin in this vein, and he smirked. He is a clever man.—

——And do you see Rakitin often?

——Hmm. But our brother Ivan is not Rakitin, no, he's a sphinx. He is superior to us (his gaze is loftier) He is hiding an idea. But there is only one thing that is tormenting me. You know, God torments me, the idea of God. And suppose he doesn't exist? Suppose it's an idea that man has made up. Then if he doesn't exist, man is the chief of the earth, of the universe. [Great.]

11)

38> But how will he be virtuous, without God? [Because whom will he love then. Whom will he be grateful to, to whom will he sing a hymn?] Question! But maybe then there will be a different kind of virtue. For what is virtue? The Chinese have one kind, I another—it is a relative thing (consequently) Or not? (Or Not? [Or not relative] An immense and insidious question. [I am surprised how people can live and not think anything about it.] You won't laugh if I tell you that I couldn't sleep for two nights from that. Ivan doesn't believe in God, but in an idea, he remains silent, he doesn't reveal himself. I asked him ~~I didn't speak about that~~ He's a Mason. I wanted to drink some cold water from the spring <of his soul>. He is silent.

——What does Ivan talk to you about?

So, nothing, <I'll tell you> later. I haven't talked to you about this up to now. When my business finishes here and they pass sentence, then I'll start talking to you, but now don't begin about that. [Talk about the trial.]

——Good, tomorrow's the trial, are you ready?

——Do you know, would you believe it, I myself know what a nightmare it will be, the settling of my fate, but I hardly think about it. I keep thinking about these matters [and questions. Questions.] But is it true that you know something about that?

Then a conversation about the lawyer, the doctor, about Katia (about the fact that she knows that I called her a woman of great anger) about Grushenka, jealousy. About the accumulated testimony. About Grigory's testimony. You know, it's perfectly possible that I will not speak at all. And yet. About the rumors in town, about the town, about Russia: A parricide, they say. ~~You know.~~ I read in the newspapers that I was sentenced in the newspapers before being sentenced. ~~You know Ivan wants me to run away, there's plenty of money. I will tell you a secret.~~ I intended to reveal it to you later (because you are important to me, you are everything for me). Even though I say that Ivan is superior to us ~~man,~~ but you are a cherub for me. Your decision will decide everything. [Perhaps you are a superior man.] You see there's a secret here that is so important that only you can settle it. It is a question of conscience, a matter

12)

of the highest conscience. That's why I put it off until you decided, <139 because I can't decide it myself. In comparison with you I am infernal, a demon, and you are a cherub and you have to decide. But you will decide afterward . . . after ~~their~~ sentence, that is, together you will decide my fate. They won't decide, you will decide. I have not revealed myself to you, but look now, that is, shortly I will do so, [I will tell you everything, but I will not tell it in detail,] but I will tell you the IDEA right now, but on condition that you listen through it silently, and don't say a word as to what decision you will make afterward. Listen, but without the smallest question, movement, you hear, agreed?—And yet, Lord what will I do with your eyes? I'm afraid that your eyes will speak out your decision. Well, it doesn't matter, I will speak out, you will see: to escape. Be quiet, don't decide.

About Grushenka once again. Fiery.

(N.B. About Iliusha)

1) Course of events. The accumulating testimony. Summoning of the lawyer and the doctor.

2) At Grushenka's (at Khokhlakova's)

3) At the prisoner's.

4) At Katia's. Ivan at Katia's.

5) Katia and Alyosha.

6) Ivan goes to Smerdiakov (All the other times)

7) Ivan at home. Alyosha at night, from Iliusha's.

8) Ivan alone. Satan.

Mitia to Alyosha about how he hadn't made up his mind yet about
God, about the fact that God disturbs him and so forth.

Shorter.

And then to live with Grusha forever. I can't live without Grusha,
I can't live and that's that, can prisoners marry? And one's conscience?
And a hymn from under the earth? He ran away from suffering, then
He ordered me not to talk to you under any condition. Ivan says that
with good will you can be more useful in America than you can be
underground. But the cross, the cross—I would be running away from
the cross! Don't decide. We can wait for the trial. I see after all how
you are looking at me. You have already decided. Let's wait for the
trial. I can't live without Grusha, but do they let prisoners marry?
That's the way Ivan talks.

Does Ivan insist on it very much?

Very much. Very much. He is urging me with all his might. 10,000
he says for your flight, and 20,000 for America. One can arrange a
flight beautifully for 10,000.

What's to be done, a pity a little. Pity. Nothing else to do, step aside,
Your Reverence.

Have you asked whether he believes or not?

——No, I haven't asked, I can't ask, but I see clearly that he does.

1) You are right, you will decide after the sentence, Alyosha said.

——You will decide, you, you will decide, and not me! You are the
decider. And now good-bye, You have to go, and I do too! You hear,
not a word about the secret. But I don't have to tell you that.

2) My brother Ivan believes that I committed the murder and
wants me to run away

——Yes, he does believe, said Alyosha sadly and reflectively.

Good-bye, embrace me, kiss me. Make the sign of the cross over me
Alyosha for tomorrow. Good-bye.

3) Alyosha, come back, you believe?

——Completely

——Thank you. You never lie. Would you believe it, I was afraid of
asking you that up to now. I put it off until now . . . Well, you have
brought me to rebirth.

He had to, had to very much see Ivan. Ivan tormented him as much
as did Mitia.

Love Ivan.

enter into relations, he says that one can do everything with money. Flee to America.

Ethics.

——Secularize

In order to settle this question, it is necessary about everything to place one's individuality in opposition to reality.

Mitia

     Why the poor child—*an ardent speech.*

Alyosha

Mitia (at the trial) 700 poodles, I am a poodle.

     Alone. Satan enters and sits down (a gray old man, warty).
Ivan Conversation. You are a hallucination. *Satan.* I advise you
Satan take the cure. An embryo from a butterfly, orangutan and
     man. I advise you to take the cure.
He gets up and he suddenly leaves. And so forth. I see with my senses, but whether or not it's correct I don't know. I lay for a 1,000 years. Thunderous cry of joy of the Seraphims, two truths and so forth.

Ivan at Katerina's. Ivan is irritated. To Alyosha while leaving: I feel myself to be very sick. Alyosha arrives and brings the news that Smerdiakov hanged himself.

Satan. He plays the liberal in our fashion. Finishes pathetically. Ivan spits. Satan laughs at himself.

Satan.—Rien de nouveau.[5]

——Satan to Ivan: Yet you believe that I am
——Ivan: Not for a minute (I would like you to exist)
Satan: Hey!

Mitia. Well, brother, man heeds his own mind less than anything. I know that. (It goes without saying that if he is a decent man, a Russian decent man he will always heed the mind of another, even

---

[5] French: "nothing new."

though he might be very vain. As for the dishonest and the stupid ones, well they value their own minds, but they always mix it up with their stomach, so that in the final analysis they listen only to their stomachs. [Subtle perhaps, but clear for me.]

Mitia (several times in conversation): I love you. And once while letting Alyosha go: "Love Ivan." [But what's wrong with you Mitia.] ——A speech.

14)

41>   ——*Mitia*. Imagine: It's there in the nerves, in the head, that is, the nerves are there in the skull (but the devil take them) ~~doctors have discovered all that,~~ there are little tails, the nerves have little tails, and well when they quiver, [the tails,]—that is, you see I look [at something] with my eyes, and they begin to quiver, and when they begin to quiver, a picture appears, but doesn't appear immediately, but an instant of some kind, a second goes by, and [such] a moment appears, that is, not a moment, the devil take the moment, [an image], that is an object or an event, [well the devil take it]—well that's why when I look, then there's a thought . . . and not at all because I have a soul and not because I am [some kind of] image or resemblance <of God>. All that is nonsense. Brother, all these things have now been explained to me . . . (Rakitin) and I have been like set on fire by it. [Really.] [I understand that] And yet I miss God.
Mitia. Pity for God.
Alyosha Well, that's good too
Mitia. That I miss God? Chemistry, brother, chemistry. What's to be done then. Why regret it. Rakitin doesn't love God. God and as he writes, place in opposition to reality.

——Rakitin: so as not to forget what's mine.

Mitia: Don't forget what's not yours.
Rakitin gets angry.

Mitia—Man with voluptuous saliva on his lips, and the lips are fat and red.
Mitia and Karl Bernard[6] was there (This suddenly after Grushenka and Katia)

---

[6] See n. 3 of this section.

Alyosha: What kind of Bernard—

Mitia, that is, you see either ~~baron~~ Klodt or Bernard, I don't know, but chemistry alone . . .

Alyosha: Claude Bernard probably?

Mitia. Yes ~~who~~ is he doubtlessly, who is he?

Alyosha: I have to admit that I know little about him. I've heard only that he is a great scholar, but precisely what kind I don't know.

Mitia. Well the devil take him, I don't know either.

You see (N.B. And he begins about something completely different, about the trial or about Katerina Ivanovna).

Mitia—You see they are all scoundrels. These Bernards . . . We have our Bernards also. That lawyer—he [also] is a Bernard, and what a Bernard yet!

Mitia. And then afterward: Bernard! (instead of scoundrel).

Ivan to Satan. Trash! (in answer to his speech). I see in you the filth which has come out of me. *Satan*. Well that's an extremely amusing thought.—And objectivity doesn't trouble you? the fact that you can take me, almost feel me: and perhaps, he says, he does exist! Ivan beats him and he appears on different chairs.

15

<142

——Testimonies accumulated against Dmitri. *Dens of iniquity.*

——Smerdiakov to Ivan. 1st meeting: Sinner that I am I thought that you wanted it too. How could you not have wanted it

Smerdiakov. 62 (when the epilepsy came so naturally)

1st meeting 62 pages. What would I have said if I had spoken only simply and directly. I talked really not knowing what and you could have become suspicious of me too, but *I spoke only with great fear.*

——If you were afraid, then you were waiting for something?

——How was I not to expect something. Just at the time when Grigory Vasilievich fell ill I told you all about that.

——Why is it that you wanted me to go Chermashnia, if you suspected?

——But I thought that you too had suspicions and that I had alerted you enough.

——So you thought that I wanted to commit murder in accord with Dmitri?

~~For God's sake, what are you saying! On the contrary I thought that~~

~~after what I said you would never leave and that's why I was suggesting to you . . . .~~

~~—— How suggesting? How not leave, what's the matter with you?~~

~~—— What's the matter with you? I thought precisely that you felt that the murder would doubtlessly occur and that you would stay to protect the life of your father.~~

~~—— But you would have done better to ask me directly to stay?~~

~~*Smerdiakov* (timidly after reflecting:) to ask you directly was fearful . . . .~~

~~—— Why?~~

~~—— But suppose you had become angry?~~

——But why the devil would I?

——I didn't know your thoughts then and I wanted to find out.

——What? What does that mean?

——Forgive me, I am at fault and suppose you yourself wanted to have your father killed?

——How dare you . . .

——Forgive me, I am at fault I was in such a state, I had become so completely frightened, I was shaking and I suspected everyone—

——And me too, that I would kill?

43>

16

[*Smerdiakov*]—Please, for God's sake, never did that enter my thoughts, for God's sake, what are you saying?

——But then I don't understand you.

——You see [in order] to kill him, you couldn't do it at all, but in order to want him killed, well, I am guilty of thinking that.

——But why would I want to, why?

——For the inheritance—Grushenka, marry, then nothing, I'm sorry, I thought ill of everyone then.

——How did I give you cause to think thus?

——God knows, you said to Aleksei Fyodorovich that you sort of wanted. [Everything is permitted, you said] (Ivan reflected, remembered, there actually was something of that kind)

——Ivan—What you must have thought of me when I sat in the carriage—you said then, I remember: it's interesting to talk.

——Smerdiakov—I remember. (lowered his eyes).

——What did that mean?

——I said it out of spite, I thought you wanted—

——And why did you say that you know how to pretend an epileptic fit.

So that you would think your brother and I had thought up the murder together, that we had plotted together.

——And since you remained silent, it meant that you yourself wanted it, pardon me for having thought that. I was filled with fear then. I should have had my mug smashed.——

I said it from naïveté—in order to praise myself. Simple stupidity. I liked you then very much and I was with you out of pure naïveté.

[If I wanted to commit the murder, would I have told you that I knew how to pretend.]

N.B. (Ivan went away, called him a fool, but became convinced that *Smerdiakov* was sincere and innocent.)

In the second meeting Smerdiakov spitefully insists that Ivan knew and wanted to murder. (I was afraid that if things went wrong *that you would denounce me,* but now you won't, you will be afraid to do so).

The epileptic fit was natural. [Across the mug]

N.B. 63 (Second meeting).

Iliusha XIII, XII, XI, VI, I.

1st meeting., 57, 59, N.B.   <14·

51 Consider! *Reason for the second meeting*

DS) Consider for the 1st meeting.

Add: I said it from friendship (lowering his eyes)

Why would it have been better to go to Chermashnia.

Chermashnia is closer, ~~sort of~~ it would be handier if you were closer, you would be able to defend me. And if you were to go to Moscow, you would have given your brother an entirely free hand.

Ivan He accuses you.

Smerdiakov: He has nothing left to do. Grigory Vasilich saw the door.

Ivan And how is it that you told me that you knew how to pretend an epileptic fit?

[62 pages, to present an epileptic fit]

Smerdiakov. I said it out of naïveté . . . and then he fell into silence [as if remembering that he spoke, that he can]) Judge for yourself, look he (Dmitri Fyodorovich) wanted to push the murder off on me, but you yourself can be my witness after this [and testify to the authorities in my behalf] for would I have told you [beforehand] that I know how to pretend if I really wanted [to do something?] [Our conversation now.] No one knows about our conversation, about the fact that you said that if one intended to murder—one would not be so naïve as to give clues beforehand. You can testify in my favor.

You said that to the examining magistrate

No, I didn't say that.

——I was afraid that you would go away to Moscow, Chermashnia was nevertheless nearer.

Ivan—You lie, you were simply inviting me to go away.—No, I wanted you to go to Chermashnia. Out of friendship, I—

Smerdiakov. But I thought that you would guess yourself, I didn't dare say it [all] straight out.

Guess what? What is it you didn't dare?

——But suppose something had happened. If I tried to turn you away from Moscow toward Chermashnia, then that meant I wanted your presence [nearer.] I thought you would guess it yourself and would not go away, but would defend me [and your father].

——But you should have come right out with it?

——I thought that you would get it without my coming straight out.

Ivan—Yes I would have remained if I had guessed it.

Smerdiakov. And I, imagine, thought that you were not only guessing it all, but that you even were going out of reach simply so as to get away.

Ivan You think that everyone's a coward like you.

Smerdiakov. Forgive me, I thought you were afraid as I was and where could I go. And I thought, well there's a free man and he's going away—Remember: I told you then: it is interesting to talk to an intelligent man. I told you that then as a reproach—

——What kind of reproach? Because of what.

——Because you were not staying to defend me and your father.

——Then I was glad, I wanted it?

Smerdiakov (after a silence) You were happy to get away. You *wanted that sincerely*.

He began crying again.

Look, I don't suspect you and I consider the suspicions to be laughable. I won't say anything about our conversations at the inquest. . . .

Smerdiakov. As far as I'm concerned, do what you want. If you don't say anything, I won't say anything . . . with an intelligent gentleman.

——Devil take it, say what you want. I'll protect you

——Kiss the hand

First tries. He saw Mitia. Everything is permitted. Smerdiakov did the killing, but the testimony was turned away. The fool talked disconnectedly, *became confused*.

2d meeting. Reasons (don't explain). You once spoke of 3,000. Katia <14
was it he or not?
N.B.?? (think up the reasons)

At the 2d meeting: *Ivan* you said something different before.
Smerdiakov. I said the same thing before.
Ivan You are lying you spoke then only about my fear.
Smerdiakov. That's true. I didn't dare speak to you what you know too. I was testing you. I wasn't completely convinced myself that you knew. It was from bitterness that I said that it was interesting to talk to an intelligent gentleman.

Reason for the 3d meeting (when he got up to his bell) Jealousy of Katia. And [the fact that] he was a coward.—

After the 2d meeting document: Tomorrow I will kill my father as soon as brother Ivan goes away and I will give you back your 3,000.—

——Katerina Ivanovna's document cheered him up, but a terrifying doubt appeared: "Did I really desire it?" The railway, scoundrel (Alyosha in a conversation reminded him of his words: that he reserves the right to desire it for himself) He hadn't seen him since.

He himself asked Alyosha: do you remember I said that everyone can desire, and perhaps you might have thought that I desire . . . Why are you quiet?
Alyosha I thought that you desired it.
Ivan interrupted the conversation, but then avoided meeting Alyosha.
3d meeting. Smerdiakov: Everything is permitted—you taught <me>.

DOCUMENT
The first letter that he will kill his father for the 3,000 was a month before.—[It was this document that she decided not to present at the inquest and she did not present it but kept it from everyone in secret.]

The second, on the eve. He got drunk in an inn, they took him away from the inn the next morning.

Tomorrow I will get the money and I will give you the 3,000 back, fateful Katia. [And then quits.] Good-bye woman of great anger, [and good-bye also my love. Tomorrow I will pester everyone <for it>] ~~but tomorrow you will have your 3,000~~ And if I don't get it from anyone, [then I give you my word of honor,] that I will go to my father and kill him by simply breaking his head.

[Before the 1st meeting
Katerina Ivanovna gave her testimony in tears in Mitia's favor.]

[When Ivan leaves, provided that your Ivan does leave.] I will take it from my thief. ~~. . . .~~ I will give back the 3,000 and will go to prison. Wait! And good-bye to you. I bow down to the earth, because I am a scoundrel before you. Forgive me. No, it's better that you don't forgive. It will be easier ~~for me.~~ [For I love another ~~the insulting one.~~] Better to go to prison [than your love.] ~~I will kill the old man and I will go to prison.~~ How could you then forgive? I will kill my ~~old man~~ thief and I will go to prison. I will go away from everybody, not know anyone. Her also.

I am writing a malediction, but ~~do you know~~ I know that I love you. A chord remains and it vibrates. [I understand.] Nothing better than a rent heart. I will kill myself. But first the dog. I will tear out three and will throw them to you. Even though I am a scoundrel ~~before the world,~~ I am not a thief ~~before you~~ before you. Dmitri Karamazov is thrice a scoundrel, but he is not a thief. Wait for the three thousand. They lie under the mattress of the cur, a pink ribbon. [I will kill my thief.] Don't dare look at me contemptuously Katia. Dmitri is a murderer but he is not a thief. He killed his father, destroyed himself only so as ~~not to be a thief before you~~ [to stand] and not suffer your pride, and not to love you.

I kiss your feet, good-bye.

Garrulousness of a drunkard.

Katia: Pray to God for someone to give me 3,000—then my hands will not be bloody, and if I'm not given the 3,000 they will be. ~~Just so you will not disdain me as a thief.~~ I am going to spill blood so as to return <it> to you!—

Dmitri　Oh, kill me! Blots. Finished <it> on all the margins, garrulity of a drunkard. Cut off because of shortage of paper.
1) Smerdiakov: that it might come into being—on the contrary, absolutely never.

Smerdiakov: There's no God on earth, let it be that you are right, but conscience exists.

Smerdiakov and Ivan.　　　　　　　　　　　　　　　　　　　　　<14
——Look up D. S. and on the other page.

——(14) French conversations.[7] I am preparing specially.

——(37) Herzenstube that Smerdiakov is not in his right mind, after the 1st meeting.
Ivan was sort of *ashamed* that he went the second time to see Smerdiakov.
2d meeting—(57) Why did you want me to go to Chermashnia if you had a presentiment?

——(59) So that they would not suspect about the envelope (I was afraid)

——(60) For the 2d meeting.

(61) (At the third meeting) *The most important* 2d meeting
You committed the murder *together* with Mitia.
(62) 2d meeting and 3d (Forgive me, I thought that you too desired the murder.—

(63) 2d meeting (You too wanted the murder.)—

(65) [THE MYSTERY OF IVAN IS HERE] Before the 2d meeting, the *Reason* why he went the second time to see Smerdiakov.

(65) 2d meeting. Ivan is dumbfounded. Wanted to report it. But Katerina's document, but the conviction that Smerdiakov couldn't have been with Mitia [that night] (he visited Mitia for that) Testimony of Grigory. Attributed it to Smerdiakov's spite and madness. (Herzenstube). He didn't visit Smerdiakov again and even *tried to*

---

[7] This is undoubtedly a reference to Smerdiakov's learning French.

forget about the conversation *from terror,* that Smerdiakov would really denounce <him> that he killed.

Here N.B. At the third meeting Smerdiakov said directly to him, as had *Alyosha:* You have asked yourself several times whether or not you killed him (Ivan shivered).
Here—And at the 2d meeting, I threatened you and you went away with your tail between your legs. Then I realized too that you were not dangerous to me.
——After the 2d meeting?
——Yes, after the 2d meeting.

——He became frightened. Kill oneself. Resolution to prove <it>
——I like her.

48>[8] Even if there were a perfect republic here.—
——Smerdiakov.
Ivan Now they don't beat you over the mug.
Smerdiakov It is true that in ordinary conditions of life beating has stopped, but in exceptional conditions, not only with us but all over the world, even in the most perfect republic, beating nevertheless continues, as at the time of Adam, and it will never stop (Doctrinaire and reflective Smerdiakov) (even if it were a republic)

Even if it were a republic—

Smerdiakov As at the time of Adam and Eve
[1st meeting] Ivan insists on asking why the epileptic fit came precisely then and he *fell into the cellar,* as he said? He had asked Herzenstube. Answer: Possible. Smerdiakov explained how. (Herzenstube said ~~that~~ to Ivan that Smerdiakov was not in his right mind) (Smerdiakov about the epileptic fit: from anticipation)

——I am crawling down the cellar, will it come or not, and then I fell, and as I fell I hit myself and it came.

---

[8] The following beginning of a letter appears on this notebook page:
Petersburg
   10 April/80
     My dear Madame,
       Most respected Katerina Fyodorovna
        Forgive my inexcusable tardiness

Smerdiakov (3d meeting) Important because everything is permitted, and because an infinite God does not exist. If there is no infinite God, then there is also no virtue, and we absolutely don't have any need of any money that's the way I reasoned. [and everyone for himself].

———Ivan. That's where you go to, bastard, with your own mind.
——With your direction.
——[And now you believe in God]
[——No. then why are you returning the money.]
[There's no God, apparently, and yet you are getting angry.]

Yes, of course, he is right.
But his Smerdiakov's spite astonished him.
[But the inheritance was nevertheless useful to you.]
[Ivan went out shaken. And then he stopped: It had all happened just like that.]
[If Mitia of course did the killing, but if Smerdiakov did the killing, then I killed along with him.]
[Then another investigation: Did Mitia commit the murder?—]
[The document]

Even though the strict girl had not sacrificed herself despite the unrestrained desires of her new lover

Ivan—He's terribly stupid. He is stupid like me. Exactly like me.   <14*
[But that's how he's able to act.] He took everything stupid from me and embodied it in himself. I am looking at my portrait. And if you want the image is pleasing from an artistic point of view.

Alyosha Satan.
Ivan What kind of Satan is this! It's a devil, a simple devil, I can't really believe that he was Satan. Undress him and you will probably [search out] find a tail a long, smooth tail as Danish dogs have, an arshin and a half, brown.

3d Conversation
——Of course—I. As if you didn't know it.—
The Reason. Katia's words: I was at Smerdiakov's. Self-love. There was still another reason. (Satan)

Ivan. After the 2d conversation he conducted his own investigation—and Fenia and everything—and still he didn't know what to say, then Katerina Ivanovna showed him the letter.

He became convinced: but the question: wasn't it he who committed the murder? *He wanted to kill.* Sometimes he laughed, sometimes he was in despair

Alyosha: "wanted to."

The thought that Smerdiakov thinks that he encouraged him to commit the murder.

Smerdiakov's threat.

Smerdiakov 2d meeting.

——My mug should have been smashed.

——Now they don't thrash.

In ordinary conditions they have ceased to thrash, because it is forbidden, but in *exceptional* conditions it's as it was at the time of Adam and Eve.

KATIA, OF COURSE, TOLD ALYOSHA.

3d meeting, At the bell (reason for the meeting). Yes there was the idea that if Smerdiakov committed the murder, then I was certainly at one with him. Why did I propose to Mitia to flee? From pity and Katerina Ivanovna (he thought). No, because I felt myself morally to be as much a murderer as he, because of those feelings of regret that father's money would be spent on the devil knows what, on Grushenka, and would miss him. [The document.] It was only the fact of the murder that he had not committed, but he had urged Smerdiakov. *Yes, urged* . . . If Mitia had not done it, then Smerdiakov had done it, and in that case, of course, he would be with Smerdiakov. Ivan was surprised that he was saying this to himself, as if for the first time, but that was nonsense, for it was not the first time, even though he had never said it to himself, but during this whole month, something was speaking in him by itself, even though not in words, and even though not consciously, and why had he felt such a hatred for Mitia, precisely because of the murder, why had he insisted so that it was he who had committed the murder? Because the conviction that Mitia had murdered was the anchor of his salvation. If Mitia had not murdered, and Smerdiakov had, then he Ivan was without doubt a murderer, for he had urged Smerdiakov to do it without any doubt. But had he incited him, really? I don't know.—

Such were his thoughts up to the bell, but having grabbed hold of the bell, another thought: she had visited Smerdiakov, and he had not known it. Why did she go? Isn't it because she doubts that Mitia is the murderer? And the document? Is it that she doesn't believe in the document? What could Smerdiakov have told her? Does she feel contempt for me? And as if I had convinced her that he was the murderer. I did not try to convince <her>, but only spoke contemptuously of him. What could Smerdiakov have told her? Why had the document appeared to me up to now like mathematical <proof>—why had he gone to Mitia with the proposal of running away? A disgusting Smerdiakov-like thought—he tried not to think about it—perhaps he was happy about Mitia's 40,000

Sine qua   <1

——Ivan still in a nervous excitement with Smerdiakov and Satan. Peasant. He laughs with Satan.

——I made the decision, therefore the peasant[9]

——He tells Alyosha that he loves Katia passionately and senselessly.

I like Lisa.

Then he cuts sharply:

I like that girl.

——Are you talking about Lisa? Asks Alyosha staring at him.

——Without answering: I'm afraid that I am walking directly in Fyodor Pavlovich's footsteps. In a certain respect at least (he laughs).

——Not looking at him . . .

——Do not look at the corner . . .—

Ivan—Tell me about your Elder: the cry of joy from the Seraphims, Seraphim? Perhaps a whole constellation or world? But a whole constellation may be only a chemical molecule of a certain kind, according to chemistry, somewhere on Sirius. Don't look *at him* . . .

Alyosha—You have said three times not to look at him? At whom at him?

Ivan—At my delirium, Ivan grinned suddenly.

——No I am *looking at* your delirium with all my strength.

---

[9] This is a reference to the peasant that Ivan had knocked down while on his way to see Smerdiakov for the third time. On returning Ivan transports the peasant to the police station and spends an hour caring for him.

Ivan. Seriously: you don't see anything there in the corner? There in the right corner on the couch? etc.

He, he said that all was permitted.
[Ivan's secret]

1> ——*Satan*—Is there God?
——Good grief, I don't know. There I've really said it now.
Alyosha⎫
and Ivan⎭ ——Who committed the murder?
——Do you want an answer: *Not you* (that is, you didn't murder).

Satan—Hoffman's Malt extract also helps.
Ivan—Shut up you imbecile.

Satan. The cry of ecstasy of the Seraphims.
Ivan. Keep quiet, I know all that, that's all mine.
—Yes, of course, you studied in a university.

Satan. 150 degrees below zero. Rheumatism. Honey with salt.

Satan. He has a wart.—When leaving Satan looks for his handkerchief.

Satan.—I'm surprised as to why you are talking with me.
——And did you notice that we are on very familiar terms of address

—Amfazniki[10]
Mitia. Why are you looking at me with such a critical air?

Mitia Formerly I threw out that kind, and now I listen to them.

——Satan. My friend, I am becoming superstitious in your presence. I love dreams.

Ivan.—That's stupid.—Satan: No, that's not true, that's rather witty.

---

[10] An incomprehensible word.

Mitia. Who killed—Smerdiakov. Do you believe, the lawyer believes I did it.

And then to Alyosha: Do you believe that I didn't commit the murder (and so forth).

Mitia about Khokhlakova. The old woman was in a frenzy. You know that he wanted to make his career, and well he looked around, but Perkhotin won out.
Poetry
Look I will show you, I have it written down.—
The archimandrite and the Section of criticism.

<152>   *Satan*   30 July
Because you believe that I exist. I would perhaps want you to exist.
——And a little while ago you yelled out to Alyosha: It is from *him* that you learned about it. You remembered me. For a small instant you believed.
Ivan.—And you, do you believe in God.
——Satan. Good grief, I don't know.
Satan—It's the custom to say that I am a fallen angel. I am on the contrary a proper man. (who am I if not a hanger-on?)

——Satan. Life clings to what is negative
——Now, everywhere it is figured by kilometers.
——Satan. Now. But that oughtn't to confuse a real philosopher. 30 years.
Satan—We are using the familiar form of address and you permitted it.
——Ivan. You don't see *blue* rays.
——Satan. Why a short time ago didn't you go immediately to the prosecutor?
——Satan. Everything is permitted. The geological unpheaval for you has taken place.
N.B. Satan—Your decision to find proof is a consequence of the fact that you have become frightened.

——Satan. There isn't any virtue or there isn't any immortality. That's what I have to say to you.

——To be duped.
——Rheumatism. Hoffman's cure and so forth. Newspapers.

——Without suffering what kind of pleasure can there be in life. A perpetual hosanna.

——Eternal religious service.

——If I were *to join* and yell hosanna, then there wouldn't be any negativity and criticism. Everything is based on criticism. The play of faith and doubt. Suffering, but *in return they live*. That's the *mystery* . . . My truth, my truth.

—Look you say that I'm stupid. A good heart. Scapegoat. I have much more morality in me than is supposed.

——And you also didn't ask Smerdiakov about Katerina Ivanovna.

——*Sarcasms.*

——Only intelligence and intelligence, that's all you care about—

——The play of ideas and contradictions.

——Burned by the fire you took him to my place. Satan. That only does me honor.

Ivan to Alyosha. I went to the doctor. He hold me that visions are possible—

——*Et qui frisait la cinquantaine.*[11]

——And join the choir.

——Well then, let's read "From the Other Shore."[12]

——He lay then for a 100 years.

——Spiritualism. The absolute shows its horns.

——I would be happy to go to paradise, but they won't let me in. I am nourished by the consciousness that I am indisputably useful.

Satan would cough from time to time (realism, wart)

——Liberal 1,000 years.

Wanted to cry hosanna, it will go out.

53>   ——Satan You are expecting something great and exceptional from me.

——You yourself don't understand your significance

——*Ivan and Alyosha.*

——I sold it for what I bought it for.

——Malt extract.

---

[11] French: "And who was touching the fifties."

[12] Alexander Ivanovich Herzen (1812–1870), *From the Other Shore* (1847–50).

——Frost 150 degrees. (If there were anything there to freeze, everything would be frozen. (Spirits don't freeze, and I had just then put on human form and was hurrying to earth. Stupidly I didn't want to change clothes and I took the risk of flying off in the form of a human being and I caught rheumatism.

——*Satan*. About realism and about dreams. In a dream you accept as a fact someone dead for 15 years. Join an ideological society.

——Beware of rheumatism. Very trite.

——You are not well? Keep quiet, you fool.

——Reconcile yourself with the absolute. 1,000 years. You intend to sulk. Finish as soon as possible.

Did you tempt Mary the Egyptian The constellation. Nose. And so forth.

——How stupid you are. *Satan* On the contrary how intelligent you are.

——The point of your appearance is to convince me that you exist, and not my nightmare, not my imagination (Hegel. Iv. Kuzmich)

——You believe in a small drop. Homeopathic. A little seed—oak. An oak grows up. You will go off to the fathers of the desert and the uncorrupted women. *Ivan*. That's to convert me. Satan. One has to do a good deed sometimes.

——After the Seraphims. *Ivan* I know all that and it's all nonsense.

——Hide and seek. You don't believe in me and you beat me. *C'est bête mon cher.*[13] That's in the feminine manner. We are, you are, they are.

We will reconcile ourselves with papa.

——150 degrees of frost.

——Cook eggs on a candle.

Satan. You wrote a poem the great Inquisitor. Noble passion.

——I got to the point of negating myself, I went further than you.

——Catarrh of the respiratory canal. Berlin professor I will live 15 years. And imagine two times fright: I had myself vaccinated two times. *Satan sum et nihil humanum a me alienum puto.*[14]

——Ivan. *Humanum?* That's not stupid for Satan. Well, I didn't

---

[13] French: "That's foolish, my dear."
[14] Latin: "I am Satan and nothing human is foreign to me."

think that up. Where did you take it from. (In dreams reality of every-thing, but awake you won't think anything up.)

Ivan Idiot. Satan: How polite.
——Satan (about Alyosha) He's nice.
About Zossima. I was busy at that, brought such scenes.
Those ladies who are coquettes stink the most in their graves. I took a bouquet from each.

54>   ——Ivan. What kind of torments are there in the other world. Satan. Before they were like this and that, but now they are more moral. It began with Jean Jacques Rousseau, pangs of conscience, so that those who don't have much conscience have even gained.

Chief sarcasms.

XVII *Ivan and Alyosha.*
——Ivan to Satan: you are stupid. Satan Alas I always suspected that. Stupid that I showed you ~~so~~ to yourself.
——Satan I love dreams.
XVII—I advise you to stay with this idea (Hegel). Otherwise, we will have a fight. Well, we will have a fight perhaps in imagination. *Satan.* Ah, *c'est charmant.*[15]

XV and XVI *Ivan and Alyosha* That's he.

XV Ivan. We make our own conscience. Satan. Why are you tormenting yourself?
——I have got used to doing so. When we lose the habit we will become gods. Satan. Well at least that's a solution of some sort.
——Satan. God alone knows who *He* is and he doesn't die from that knowledge.
XIV—*Ivan and Alyosha.*

VIII I am the most glorious of the Seraphim. Do you think it was easy for me to tear myself away from you?
——*Satan and Michael.*

VI *Satan and God.* You would have forgiven me immediately. But

---

[15] French: "that's charming."

common sense . . . my most unfortunate quality, no I would not have invented that, how many curses these good people hurled at me.

——two truths, mine and yours.

IV Sulfuric hydrogen. Gas. That's why their little souls smell like that.

——How many souls was it necessary to lose in order to gain one just Job on whom I was so cruelly set on in time of yore.

Chapter III Satan and God (After he wanted to yell hosanna)—

II If everything on earth happened rationally, then nothing would happen.

I eavesdropped on confessors. Nose.

Cela lui fait tant de plaisir et à moi si peu de peine.[16] Why do you go with anybody?—Satan.—I retreated. That is perfect innocence. I retreated and the confessor then took it up. He made an appointment for that very evening through his little window. Meeting.

Satan to Ivan. Wherever I might sit down, ~~I always~~ the first place   <1!
will always be there.

N.B. N.B. Satan. Sarcasms. *I hope I am still talking to the author of the Grand Inquisitor.*

Page 15. Rheumatism. Honey with salt.

——Warts. He looks for his cigarette holder.

Satan. My friend I am becoming superstitious with you. I'm not grumbling, I'm not grumbling. That's very nice. I've gotten vaccinated two times. *Satan sum et nihil.*

Page 15 *Sine qua. Ivan and Alyosha.*

I like Liza.

——He is crazy, crazy like me.

——He's simply a devil

——A tail 1½ arshins long.

The molecules and the protoplasm put their tails between their legs.

Hatchet. If there happened to be one there? It wouldn't stop turning around the earth without knowing why.

---

16 French: "That gives him so much pleasure and me so little pain."

Ivan. Keep on talking nonsense, I'll let you. I have a holiday today (he walks)

Satan—Ah, yes, you have made up your mind, tomorrow at the trial. *C'est noble, c'est genereux, c'est chevaleresque.*[17] I didn't expect anything less from you.

——Fool.

——But why are you abusing me, but let's leave that. You aren't well?

——Fool. Spin out some kind of nonsense.—

——Please.—attacked by rheumatism.

Katerina Ivanovna.

Alyosha believed a little drop. (He is nice, why are you so. I before to the Elder Zossima—)

The realism of the Lion and the Son.

Prejudices, Superstition.

Two times vaccination.—

Ivan. At times I *cease* seeing you, and only hear your voice.

Satan. I know a rogue, a nice ~~young~~ Russian lord from among the young thinkers, the author of a poem, the embryo of the Grand Inquisitor, which . . .

Ivan. I forbid you to talk about the Grand Inquisitor.

Satan. *Passons,* but that poem, that passion, that energy. (theory everything is permitted)

<6> After *the word* and everything.

Be quiet, fool.

And I thought I was expressing that pathetically, in a literary fashion. There you see I invent something at times, like about the Word, for example, and even cry.

Fool—

And I thought that you loved literature.

The Grand Inquisitor—

Ivan's secret

Little devil

——I also all kinds of vaudevilles. <not clear>

---

[17] French: "It's noble, it's generous, it's chivalric."

I think you are taking me for a grizzled Khlestakov.[18]
——Mephistopheles I want to do evil and I do good
Well, as it pleases him—
And I precisely to the contrary.

I am perhaps the only person who loves the truth, and [sincerely] desires good, and nevertheless [only] evil comes out of me—[Why?] Simply because of my social condition. [I have a thirst for new institutions, but in the meanwhile I have decided to sulk] I am good and I want to go to paradise, and I am told to go to the Critical Section because without you there won't be anything. And how I've been slandered, how I have been held in contempt, and why? simply because I've been chosen to be a scapegoat. I was there when the Word—

---

[18] He is the hero of Gogol's *The Inspector General* (1836).

Book Twelve

Book XII, which is entitled "A Judicial Error," was first entitled "Trial." Except for the first two notebook pages, which go back to May, these notes date from about August 1880. The first five chapters were published in the September issue of *The Russian Messenger* and the remaining nine chapters were published in the October issue.

Most of the notes for this book are taken up with the proceedings of the trial. The interrogation of the witnesses and the summations of Fetiukovich and the Prosecutor are given quite fully, and a disproportionate time is spent on Dr. Herzenstube's testimony. But the reactions of the audience to the speeches and the proceedings, which form such an important part of the final version, are for the most part missing in the notes. On the other hand Dostoevsky devotes a considerable portion of the notes to explaining to himself what legal protocol involves: what the duties of the various members of the court are, what happens to witnesses after they finish testifying, and under what conditions a witness may be excused.

As in the other books many scenes are sketched in with a few words, as for example: "Rakitin. Brochure about Zossima." Katerina Ivanovna's first testimony, recalling her first meeting with Mitia, appears in these notes in a fragmentary and schematic way. Nothing of her timid yet firm manner, her black dress, the look on her face when she enters the witness box, nothing of the tone of her voice—all of which is expressed in great detail and precision in the final version—are to be found in the notes. The story of Mitia's first generous gift to her, and the tone in which she tells it, the effect on Alyosha and on the court are all absent in these notes. We get only the essential facts: that she had given him the 3,000 to send by post because she knew that he was in need of money, that she would have gladly helped him out and that, despite his difficulties, she was in such a position that she could not have called him to see her. The analysis of motives, the descriptive detail, the tone, the effect on the audience—all that we consider to be the elements that make a situation dramatic—are missing in the notes.

Grushenka's counter testimony is hardly referred to, except for the reference to Katerina's offering Grushenka chocolate and attempting to reap advantage by charming Grushenka. Ivan's sensational testimony is given very sketchily, but his significant statement about desiring his father's death is included: "I myself didn't love my father, I myself desired his death."

Katia's second testimony is given only in a few disordered fragments, but something of the reasons that would have motivated her to give such testimony is given, such as the following: "Oh, he laughed at me because of the bow down to the earth. I hated him."

The last meeting between Dmitri and Katia is very schematic, especially the conversation between Alyosha and Katerina, when Alyosha urges her to go. What we get in the notes is simply Katerina's repeated hesitation and the weakness of her resolve. In the novel we get Alyosha's reasons, his urgings, his explanations of Mitia's feelings and his analysis of the importance of going for her.

3,000   <15

Those who have been interrogated remain.
Supplementary examination.
After every witness the president of the court asks the accused if he has any objections to make?

At the closing of the trial debates, the accused always has the last word.

The local examining magistrate.   <15
——The police interrogation is given to the examining magistrate?
He cannot see his relatives and friends.
Judicial district, local court sessions—
[7-day time limit for the summoning of witnesses.] Court session.
Further step

---

1 Most of this notebook page is filled with the names of people. The names are preceded by the caption: "Visit before leaving."

A copy of the arraignment

List of witnesses

A list of the members of the court and the prosecutor

A list of the jury members

From the examining magistrate to the assistant of the prosecutor for establishing the arraignment for the courtroom.

Confirmation in the courtroom

Arraignment and the end) [the bailiff read the arraignment, guilty or not?]

The arraigning court confirms it and gives it to the regular court.

59>

17 August
Trial Record

N.B. At the trial before Katerina gives her testimony Grusha insults her with her testimony (from jealousy toward me she testified against him)[2] (Answer to one question about Mitia's relations with her and Katerina Ivanovna. Katerina Ivanovna was questioned earlier, and she answered well and briefly, but Grusha got angry and spoke out sharply about her jealousy: She invited me, treated me to chocolate, wanted to flatter me, but I wasn't to be fooled. Since that time she is spiteful toward him. That's why she has testified against him. This after Katia's first testimony. Grusha's insult had already provoked Katerina Ivanovna's anger. And then the catastrophe with Ivan and she showed the document hysterically confessing against Mitia. The story of the bow to the earth in a new light).—

Fetiukovich about the psychology of the prosecutor

——Was Mitia a maniac or a thief?

——Fetiukevich about the fact that perhaps there wasn't any money. The envelope could have been torn by the deceased. Only 1,500 rubles were found. The bed had not been touched. Smerdiakov could have been out of his senses.

The prosecutor bears down on the development of the passion. 3,000 maniac. The envelope on the floor. The accumulation of proof was irrefutable.

---

[2] No closed parentheses.

Fetiukovich. Fathers and children. One has to handle words honestly. I call a thing by its name,

The Bible and so forth.

——Prosecutor. Mitia is a maniac.

——Fetiukovich. He has a sort of disordered academicism.

[Fetiukovich] He had insulted everyone, two of the jury were rejected because they had been beaten by him.

——*Fetiukevich* Don't hurt children, etc.

Fetiukovich. When he was begetting him, did he do it with love?

Fetiukovich about Iliusha you see I don't spare my customer.

Fetiukovich. I'm a newcomer, I've just come, but everyone else here is forewarned.

He was rowdy—whose fault was it?

——Katerina Ivanovna's letter. Does it make sense for a man who has decided to murder to tell others about it. Drunken appearance. This letter is only the result of irritation. The prosecutor points to it as proof, but I look on it as a dream.

Fetiukovich Child to his father: Why should I love you?

Fetiukovich's speech. Whistling rod, about the torn envelope. He <16(didn't kill, but simply made the gesture and hit him. He begot him and transmitted the drunkenness.

Grushenka inflamed the hot blood. You heard her cries.

Prosecutor about Rakitin. We have no control over the relatives life gives us. In return "small division."

Mitia at the trial: I want to suffer, I want to, I invite it and I accept it. I deserve it!

Mitia: I was cruel with Aesop also.

——What Aesop?

Here—But, pierrot, my father

Grusha. He's not the kind of person that would lie because frightened. You don't know him.

One hundred rubles at the place of pleasure? (Trifon Borisovich).

——Mitia. Yes, I wanted to become virtuous from that day on.

——*Fetiukovich.* Father. What is father? And here we have the tender story of a devout doctor (nuts).

You have a [grateful] *generous* heart, because you remembered your whole life long a pound of nuts. I blessed him and embraced him and we both burst into tears . . .

Doctor Herzenstube . . . had the honesty even after the outburst of the famous Moscow doctor to confirm his supposition about mania.—
Nevertheless, he was a noble and generous person, oh, I remember him from childhood, when he ran about in the yard without shoes and with his pants attached by one button.
——The lawyer fastened on to it—
——That was in the flower of my youth . . . yes I was only then 45 years old . . . and I was sorry . . . [why I not] and I asked myself: why can't I buy him a pound . . . I forgot the word . . . of a plant, the fruit of a tree . . . what grows on a tree—how is it called . . . a pound, pound
and he crossed his arms.
apples.
[lemons] oranges—Oranges grow in Sicily and not in Skotogonevsk. There are many of them, but all small, you put them in your mouth and . . . crunch.
[For no one up to then had ever bought the young boy a pound of nuts.]
He loved to narrate. He spoke Russian rather well, but he often forgot the most common words. Besides he would forget in German too and waved his arms as if searching for the words, and then no one could get him to continue his story until he had found the words, because he was very stubborn.

61>   Fetiukovich.
You have seen that I do not possess any expertise in medicine nor any presuppositions about the servant, but I simply accept <the fact> that he is the murderer.

Grushenka about Katia: She has very little true shame.

Prosecutor about the unnaturalness of Ivan's testimony.
[Prosecutor] Unfortunately all are like Fyodor Pavlovich.

Rakitin. Brochure about Zossima.

[*Mitia*] Reproachful To flit about like a butterfly. Amfazniki. Bernards.

——About the quarrel between the prosecutor and Fetiukevich.

Fetiukovich. [HERE] The significance of fatherhood in fact and not according to mystical Christianity. (N.B. Chauvinism) Laughter among the spectators.

Fetiukovich. Disproves the prosecutor: why jump down to <examine> Grigory. Don't ask the impossible from a man. The envelope, no one had seen the envelope.

Katerina Ivanovna about how she gave 3,000 to Mitia.

Grushenka *Svetlova*. Katia: *Rome unique objet de mon ressentiment.*[3]

——Fetiukevich.——Conditioning, development, assimilation, moon and stars.

Perkhotin. Civil servant of the commissariat about Mitia: he was like a madman.

The expertise of the doctors. Looked to the right, looked to the left.

N.B. The testimony of the frenzied one.

——Timofei: he almost killed a man.
——But do you know that you are carrying a murderer?
Contradicting interrogation of the lawyer and the prosecutor.

——Prosecutor. About the squandered 3,000.

——Fetiukovich. If it had been another client, he would have been forgiven, but this one has insulted everyone. But let's be impartial.

[HERE] Temporary section of the St. Petersburg court in the town of Gdov.

[Fetiukovich—prosecutor] Fetiukovich about the discarded but not

---

[3] French: "Rome, the only object of my resentment."

discarded pestle. He murdered then accidently, otherwise he would have hidden it, he was out of his mind.

Also the package. He wouldn't have dropped it, he would have hidden it. A nobleman.

62>   ——Grusha at the trial about Rakitin

Mussialevich.[4] He had served the crown.

Mitia. I'm an admirer of Schiller, I'm an idealist. Whoever decided that I'm a scoundrel—doesn't know me.

——Mitia.—I reject my lawyer.

[Did Smerdiakov give back 100??]

——In answer to a question of the lawyer Grigory says that the *accounting* with Dmitri had not been done accurately and he was still owed several thousands.

——What do you base that on, etc.

——*The prosecutor* seems to speak without premeditation, but not really—because (for such and such reasons) and finally the presented document constitutes a colossal piece of evidence: if Ivan *goes away,* and the clear promise to kill.

The lawyer. But the corpse is quiet and the unavoidable question: who committed the murder. I am not thinking of Smerdiakov. Perhaps Smerdiakov. Perhaps a stranger? There have been odd errors. The cry was heard. The fences are not high.

I give you my client, although I beg you to keep in mind that there be no judicial error. I reject any theft.

The lawyer. He sees his father as a competitor, enemy, sensual appearance, darkness, he calls her—she was to come then truly—I will destroy the nightmare, the terrible vision, he raised the pestle, flourished it, but he did not murder.

---

[4] One of the variant names of Grushenka's Polish lover. Usually called Podvysotsky, but also referred to as "Bem."

Don't ask the impossible of a man, let's be Christians, not only because we go to church and observe the rites . . . No, you will *free* my client.

——And it was the end of the vacillations that had so terribly <16?
tormented him continually during the last days.

Grigory. He was self-willed (extremely self-willed).
Lawyer. How did he show his self-will?
The lawyer. Can you tell me at least what is the current year?

The lawyer. Do you know for sure whether or not you were sleeping at that moment (the open door)
The lawyer. What was the composition of the medicine which you took?

Grigory I am an underling. If my superiors think it fit to laugh, then I have to suffer it.

Fetiukovich. The testimony of two jealous women—which is more plausible?

Herzenstube *forgot the word.* German surname beginning with K.

The testimony of the junior captain. He was a little drunk he burst into tears, was thrown out.

Fetiukovich—You received 200 rubles? (reproach).

Fetiukovich (It is exaggerated a 100 times. Gleb Uspensky)[5]
The prosecutor. The press has rendered a service in showing an uninterrupted series of monstrous phenomena, by comparison of which the present affair is a joke. Why? No institutions. We are not Europe. Everything with us has been in movement.
The significance of the Karamazov family, the whole of Russia.

---

[5] Gleb Uspensky (1840–1902). Populist writer whose works and articles described the life of peasants and artisans in somber colors. Most important work is *The Power of the Soil* (1882).

Mitia at the trial. I break my own sword and go into the abyss of shame and nastiness!

[Convictions—that is life!]

There's no order in me, higher order!

700 poodles.

Grusha at the trial. I'm guilty, I brought him to it.

Mitia. Well, it's not very smart sometimes to be a Russian.

Grusha. I ran about without shoes. No one loved me. I became nasty.

Mitia. It was all done quietly and secretly.

——Did you make a gift of 100 rubles to Fenia (no)
——Sent to Fenia—

——The testimony of Samsonov was read. The barefoot woman. The dyer.

64>   [Here]—*The prosecutor* to the jury in the peroration of his speech: And whatever you might hear from the talented and famous defender, who has come from St. Petersburg,—remember all the same that you are the defenders of Russia, of truth in Russia, of her foundations, and of everything sacred in her—You are the representatives of Russia at this moment.

The prosecutor added from fear of what Fetiukevich was going to say.

The prosecutor. He reminds them that Grushenka began to shout when they arrested Mitia and called him a murderer: together, together! I was guilty, I caused him to do it! He told you then that he was going to kill his father, or you suspected him strongly?

——Grusha I don't remember my feelings. He talked to me about spilled blood and about some kind of old man, that I remember.

Mitia 700 poodles. I'm a poodle.

Mitia. A Russian man listens to his own mind least of all, that even

I know. As a consequence he listens to his own feelings more than anything, and his [passions, passions, especially his passions!] We know that too.

Mitia THE PAYMENT OF THE WHOLE SUM.

Mitia. I break my own [saber] sword, but I preserve the pieces with benediction for my whole life!

Herzenstube. Petrov? Peterson? Pestlotsy? Miusov—
Miusov? [I've known Miusov for 20 years, and I know but I've forgotten. I know his surname, but I can't pronounce it because I've forgotten—]
~~Idea~~ Where to put it? Wallet? Cigarette case? Drawer? Oh, no, the drawer is in the table, that's in the frock coat. Pocket? Pocket.
—He had . . . he had . . . I forget the word, what he had. Money? . . . No! Passion! Oh, no, the complete opposite. Religion? That . . . that let's say, But [let it go], I wanted to say, idea . . . but it's not necessary . . . I'll go on further. Ah, yes! Conscience ~~honor~~ ! He had ~~honor~~ conscience [conscience and then honor] and honor and then he didn't have it, because the Russian proverb says: preserve your honor.
——Preserve honor from your youth?
——Well, yes, in your young years. That's all the same.
Because the Russian proverb says—If you go off to find something, then you'll find [what you're looking for] on your path.

Final

A man who gives his last 5,000 and has bestial thirst for 3,000 that presented the matter in a sort of new light. About the 3,000 sent off by mail. [Mitia to send off] I didn't give him <the money> directly to send by post: I had a presentiment that he needed the money [very] much [for some affair] . . . and I didn't know how to ~~give~~ propose <it> to him more delicately. He [despised] tormented himself so in vain. I was always firmly convinced that he would always manage to send the 3,000, as soon as he received it from his father . . . [I knew that he had had differences with his father, but I have been always convinced and <am> even now that he had been insulted by his father. I don't remember any threats from him toward his father.] At least in my presence he said nothing, no threats. He was firmly convinced that he would receive <the money.> And if he had come to me, I would have quickly allayed his anxiety. But he didn't come to me. [And I . . . I was put in such a position that I couldn't call him ~~then~~ to see me.] Even more I had no right to be demanding, for I myself had received from him on another occasion a much greater financial favor, and I accepted it despite the fact that when I could not foresee how I would be in a position to repay my debt to him.

She was Mitia's fiancée up to the time that he himself left her. Left her for whom—the prosecutor's staff did not touch on this point out of delicacy. ~~She considered herself~~ They began to ask her [among other questions] about the three thousand.

That was before you settled here, and at the beginning of your acquaintanceship? Approaching the matter carefully Fetiukevich began, he had a presentiment of some favorable fact. [(N.B. Remarkable that] even though he had been engaged by her up to that very minute he didn't know anything about the 5,000 rubles that Mitia had given to her.
——Yes, it was not here. It was still there . . .
——No, never enough strength to forget those minutes.
Excitement resounded and muffled sobs.
The confession was news in any case.
Still unknown whether that was very honorable, and whether [in any case] an innocent girl should have acted that way.
But K. I. from her first words resolutely answered one of the questions.

It was because of me that everything happened, he fell in love with me, and he left the young lady. She offered me chocolate yet, and wanted to charm me—She has very little shame in her, that's what
The president of the court said impressively—
To reply snappishly
let herself be pulled along further and further
when I still ran about barefoot.
I didn't know anything about that.
She let drop some questions.
The prosecutor when they arrested
shouts

66>   Assimilate
Prosecutor. That is the false image of Christ.

Prosecutor—Nothing in common, no culture, all disunited in their basic elements.

Prosecutor. He would have remembered the cap, precisely how he had stolen the cap.—

——How will we save society from unbridled passion if not by collective decision. Don't let yourself be seduced by Fetiukevich (his cracked voice resounded).

When could Smerdiakov have committed the crime?

——If it was Smerdiakov, then it was <done> with Mitia. But look Grigory finds Mitia alone, and hears the other groaning behind the partition, three steps from his bed. And if together how is it that one against the other?—

Do you hear all these improbabilities?

HISTORICAL COURSE
I learned by accident that just then he had changed two 5,000-ruble notes.

——About the cap.

——Toward the end: document. That's an actual program, if Ivan goes away. That was formed also in a sober and not drunken mind. How could there not be premeditation, how <could there> not <be> calculation?

Expertise has shown—

——Let them give us some kind, even the smallest positive evidence. We are thirsting for it.

Fetiukovich The crucified one, who loved men, said . . .

Fetiukovich. How is it possible to guess how much money someone had in his hands by sight alone, without counting it. The chunk seems to be always great in someone else's hands. The landlord Maksimov has testified that he saw 20,000. The Poles say categorically that they saw 7,000. Given the uncontrolled character of the accused, as he has been described by the prosecutor, he would have offered not 700, but three thousand, or if the money was necessary for the continuation of the orgy, then 3,000 if he had it. He is surely not the kind of person who would stop [and calculate.]

67>   *Fetiukovich.* Where <will one> find on our [dirty] square after twenty-four hours a piece of cotton from a hat. Why the first peasant who would step on it would carry it away on the sole of his shoe.

The man bribing the Poles no longer wanted to shoot himself.

——He had killed, tomorrow they would take him and so much energy, I understand <all that> if he still intended to shoot himself: he would have danced to the end and then put a bullet in his forehead. But no, he had by then already a hope—

   Fet. Crush him with your pardon because of the inadequacy and ambiguity of the proofs.

   Fet. But suppose he had murdered. I am not affirming it. On the contrary I reject categorically that he murdered, but suppose he had murdered, let's consider that proposition, let it be our fantasy, let it be our dream.

Fetiukovich. So he yelled in all the taverns that he would kill his father, that alone shows that he didn't want to murder him. If he intended to kill and with premeditation yet, would he have talked against himself? At the very least he would not have talked so much, would not have yelled it at all the crossroads. And don't children say to each other when they quarrel: I'll kill you! Don't drunken peasants cry out when quarreling and when leaving a tavern: I'll kill you. And after all he practically lived recently in a tavern! But the most colossal proof is: when will Ivan leave.
2 abysses.

——But those sitting behind applauded and the presiding judge restrained himself.
[Fetiukovich. If we happen to receive money, do we value it? And then an episode takes place (Katerina Ivanovna and the document) take care of him, I have formed such an understanding about him. 2 abysses.]

Fetiukovich. Yes, I agree the mass of testimony against the accused in its entirety is terrible, that blood, the blood dripping from the fingers, the linen soaked in blood, that dark night with the resounding cry of the father-killer and the one who yelled falling with his cranium cracked by the bronze pestle! By the way: That pestle, he grabbed it at the last moment, grabbed it almost unconsciously. If the murder had been firm and premeditated, *he would have seen to a weapon.* If he had talked to the servant in the vestibule then there wouldn't have been a pestle and he would have run off unarmed. [Let's say it is a trivial thing] but take them, put them all together and they will make a strange mass of contradictions. Besides that is not a trivial thing.

Ivan—Smerdiakov hanged himself. He won't give his testimony <16: from the other world.

Fyodor Pavlovich—I think like everyone (the same) one reptile will devour another reptile. Everyone desires the death of his father.

I think that this crowd would disperse in great sorrow if there had not been a murder.

(Eccentric. The president of the court did not have the presence of mind)

——You are not well?

——Yes, I'm not well,—but besides that's not your affair.

I saw the money.

——You saw the money,

There it is.

I must make one declaration—

He went bad because he wanted to save that monster. He tormented himself: I myself didn't love my father, I myself desired his death. He visited Smerdiakov two times and each time he came to me completely convinced that his brother had committed the murder and not Smerdiakov. Once coming back from Smerdiakov: If Smerdiakov had committed the murder, then I would be guilty, because Smerdiakov had not understood my words and that I desired the death of my father. Then I brought out that letter for him, and then he became completely convinced that his brother was guilty.

What caused you to give testimony, despite your oath, in another sense.—

I wanted to save him. He tormented me. He took the money looking me straight in the eye.

N.B. (disconnected)

Oh, he laughed <at me> because of the bow down to the earth. I hated him.[6]

Mitia. Recollecting himself. Well, now I'm lost!

Katia had destroyed <him> Katia's testimony.

Mother-in-law,

Mitia cries out bitterly

Hysterics

Grushenka—

They took her away also.

The doctor came in

Continuation.

The arguments began at 8 o'clock.

Grusha after the second testimony of Katerina Ivanovna.

Look, she showed her true colors, Mitia, Mitia!

And she rushed to him. They took her away in hysterics. The reading of the document.

——*Fetiukovich.* I suspected that he felt insulted that they had not communicated everything to him—

69>   Amulet: That never comes into their minds.

PROSECUTOR

——A man with money—is everywhere a man.—

—[If he had not put 1,500 rubles away, the idea was not strange to him nevertheless and he had considered it.

——I am good only when things are going my way "when I'm in a good mood, if not—watch out for me, oh, watch out, I'm terrible. And he is terrible.[7]

He is always entirely <absorbed> in the <present> moment.

Prosecutor. Well you'll keep me in prison for 6 months because of Grigory one can't go about breaking the heads of old men with impunity that's what he says, his words—but without any deprivation of

---

[6] Fragments on the notebook page which do not fit into the context: "I know that later when the matter was analyzed—the judicial staff."

[7] No closed quotes.

rights, do you hear this anxiety, this Karamazov-impatience, this anticipation of events?

Final[8]—How will we stop this troika, change its horses, how will we stop this troika, change its horses, how will we repair the carriage.[9]
 Not to change horses, not to repair the carriage?[10]
 [The last time everyone saw an important sum of money in his hands here in Mokroe, a month ago, well, then he put aside <the sum> from it.]
 [For how else? One has to remember and imagine the money for that to be probable if not 1,500 and he himself sells his watch, pawns his pistols.]

The horror consists in the fact that it has almost ceased to be a horror for us.

——Model of disunity. Let the whole world burn, so long as it is fine for me.

About Ivan. But the reason of a very powerful mind was not able to come to terms with reality.

About Mitia.—To look cynically at her generosity.

——He didn't know anything about the door, when he found out, he yelled that it was Smerdiakov—

About Rakitin

Prosecutor
——He showed more talent than they had supposed.
[It seems that he had written her beforehand and then talked as if he were reading it.] He gave his whole heart to the affair. He demonstrated civic feeling and patriotism. *Chef-d'œuvre.* [to die]
 Who would have thought that he was a thinker?

---

[8] *Final* is in Roman letters.
 [9] Reference to the celebrated conclusion of Gogol's *Dead Souls* (Part I) where he compares Russia to a troika before which all nations give way.
 [10] Fragments on this notebook page which do not fit into the context "Incomparable more talent" "At the beginning" and "The latter lays the foundations."

——This current affair thunders across all of Russia. Why be surprised? The horror is that events of this kind have practically ceased to be horrible for us. The press has been helpful. A brilliant officer cuts the throat of Vlassov, kills the mother, and brags that she consider him like a son.[11] And about debauchery—then Fyodor Pavlovich is still a child. Where are we going, where are we hurrying to? The great writer of a recent age in the finale of the greatest of his works says: troika like a bird, troika who invented you? The troika represents for him Russia. *It flies by and peoples step aside in respectful perplexity.*

[Don't the nations step aside in terrifying perplexity?]

<170>
And other nations are astonished. So it is, sirs, but the great writer either because of [beauty of spirit] simplicity of spirit or because he was afraid of the censor. If Chichikov, Sobakievich, Nozdryov, Skvoznik are harnessed to the troika, then no matter who the driver is, you won't finish up with anything good. Wouldn't it be better to repair the troika? And to do that you have to look deeply and examine.

Well, then, let's examine closely our troika, for the troika before us is, if it is not all of Russia, it is the emblem and picture of it.

——Actually the Karamazov family represents for me a sort of image in which much that is similar to everything and perhaps to all of Russia is pictured in reduced and perhaps microscopic form (for our fatherland is great and immense). This family, the father at the head of it, who is the father? We all remember him. He lived among us. At first a hanger-on, a petty cheat and a clown ~~whom~~ and most of all a usurer. With the growth <of his capital> he became confident. Capital. *Après moi le deluge.* Voluptuousness is everything. Complete disunity. Education of his children, lice. (I won't let others do the defending, I will show how Mitia grew up). Then his children. The eldest. Strong philosophical intelligence but not yet having grown up [already] denying everything. Smerdiakov cried: everything is permitted. He and Fyodor Pavlovich. Oh, I don't dare talk, but there are moments of social significance when we ought to raise ourselves above the fear of insulting people. And besides, where is the insult? Spiritual cynicism. But nature still struggles. You heard here a confession. He had gone mad because of his brother, he wants to save him. He is convinced that Smerdiakov is right, but he has died. And he decides. But to lie even against a dead person is shameful. To purify his con-

---

[11] The Russian reads "mother," but the context demands "son."

science, he sacrifices himself. He brings three thousand (he had changed notes of 5,000). It is true that all that is done in madness, in hallucination, God preserve him from that in the future. But that is the model of the intellectual layer of our society, which has rejected everything already in an abstract and philosophical way, and it is only in a practical sense that youth and the good seeds of knowledge and enlightenment still struggle. May God preserve, but . . . Oh, Oh, so often the cynicism of life stifles the cry of nature and a Fyodor Pavlovich emerges, but only in a better appearance. We are all like that, all intellectual Russia. Another son, mysticism and chauvinism. Elemental Russia remains. Picture. Mitia. I will not give to Herzenstube. I am good only when I feel good. Give, give <me> all the good things of life, and especially do not pose any obstacles of any kind to my temper, and then I will be very good and beautiful.

In the inn the junior captain. The good moments, we saw the sacrifice   <17]
for the young girl: he gave his last, gave everything, without any hope of recouping. But we have heard also the other cry of that girl. Oh, I don't judge, I don't dare. That is not appropriate to my task. That is, causes. But the exclamation burst out from her: "All his life he despised me for that bow." Isn't the truth somewhere in between. It could have been one thing and another, we are Karamazovs.

Maniac, but to a certain degree. Avidity and generosity. Seized by passion. About Grushenka (she laughed at the father and son). He betrays Katia, he takes 3,000 from her and they looked into each others' eyes. He took <it>. Demonic lack of restraint! In one instant he squandered it, but he pleased <her>. Because of the hatred for his father, jealousy and a thirst for money come next . . . Yes, I agree that he could have tormented himself also from honorable shame before Katia, I agree to the highest degree. But money was needed. His father is enticing Grusha with three thousand, and he owes him exactly 3,000. It is with his money that he is taking his treasure (taking Grusha). Jealousy and frenzy. Beat him up. He tells Alyosha that he will commit murder. Then that 1½ thousand. That's his fantasy— we have all the proof. Thousands of witnesses that he squandered it all. You have heard <it>. He even said to her, to Grushenka, *but we will talk of that later.* He writes a *document* from a tavern in town. It is a fateful document. It is a program. He writes it hoping for impunity after the quarrel between the two women. But it contains one terribly important line: *If my brother Ivan goes away.* Premeditation. Oh one will point to how he shouted. But the firm intention of killing did not arise immediately, but he shouted before. But once it had arisen, what difference did it make to him that he had shouted. As long as he attained his aim. There was complete premeditation. He secured the signals. Observation post. True there was jealousy and passion, but also money.

——Tie with Smerdiakov. Signals. Kissed the boots. Chicken and epilepsy. But we will return to Smerdiakov later. Having written the letter, the next day <he went off> in search of money. Agreed, he used every means to get it. If he had got it, he would have returned it to Katia. No. Later he had it, and he didn't return it. In order to go away ~~pawned~~ sold his watch. Description of the day of the journey. Came, jealousy, She was there.

72> He is not jealous of Samsonov. He pawns his pistols to Perkhotin. He goes to Mme Khokhlokova. Reasonable advice . . . Almost killed. No, now where would he get the three thousand, he possesses the signals, and furthermore he had sworn to Katia that he would kill his father if Ivan went away. Well, Ivan went away. Leaving he learns by accident that she is not at Samsonovs. He flies to her, but she is not at home. Grabs the pestle. Let it be unconsciously, but his nature knew well enough for what purpose. He goes. Smerdiakov is sick, he must have known that. Under the windows. Possessing the signals, restrain oneself? And how could he see that Grushenka was not there. (Description of the room, the curtain, she could be behind the curtain.) No, he knocked on the window at first, and then sneaked in through the door. He murdered. Broken precisely with the pestle. The envelope, torn open. Lack of habit of the nobleman, did not destroy the evidence. Ran away. Grigory, jumped down to him. Ran away. There news awaited him, she had gone away with her former lover!

But before, about Smerdiakov, the whole episode. Are they together or each on his own? In that case why did he tell about the signals? Together then. But he is lying there . . . The door. Groans. In order to hamper?

[If they acted together, why the epilepsy?]

[Perhaps they had so agreed] Then they did not act together. Got up: suppose I kill the man. (but suppose Mitia came?)

Absurd. I saw him killed. He finished up by going mad.

[If he is alone, why communicate the signals?—If together—he goes to be just then. In order to hamper? Perhaps together, but as a passive being, he would not have dared accuse. But Mitia declares categorically that it was he, that he was alone. He communicated openly to me that he gave the signals. Alone then. But if alone, then why was he lying there knowing that Mitia would come. Why was he pretending? After all Mitia would take the money before him. By chance: suppose I kill the man. Now each accuses the other. He had written that he would kill himself. Why hadn't he added that he was a murderer. Fairy tales in comparison with reality.] [that terrified he let him be killed, but testimony that he did the murder. He could have told. And why the epileptic fit? He could have slept in Mitia's presence too. So that he could say that he was sick and so that there wouldn't be any suspicion. But Grigory couldn't sleep.]

———But let's return to the hero. He gallops off. Wanted to shoot himself, that's true. But in the Karamazov fashion. Not a single Hamlet-like question. To the driver [Andrey]: you are carrying a murderer. There he says flatly that <it was> the sixth thousand. Witnesses without number. But circumstances change: the former <lover> is driven away, moral state. ~~but for a Karamazov~~ He didn't think that they would discover it so quickly, he thought that Grigory was killed. Until tomorrow—for a Karamazov that is an eternity.

Drunk and passion, he might have killed himself with the pistol, hides 1½ thousand for any eventuality. He bargains with the "pan" he is in her embraces, but the murder torments him. *But the embraces are for all that stronger.* And then God's thunder. *Not me* (self-preservation).

Interrogation. He is cunning about Smerdiakov, how is it that he doesn't remember about the cap? . . . — — —

———Look at it—all the evidence is against <him>— What is there in his favor? Alyosha by his face.

We will save the troika.

[Ivan. We see that the elemental power of truth still lives in his young heart, that his deep sense of conscience is still not stifled by lack of faith and negation, acquired more by inheritance than by suffering of thought.]

[Certainly there is an extraordinarily great number of minds, firm and well-intentioned who are waiting for rejuvenation from Europe. But such as Ivan F———ch don't believe in Europe either. And there are many such and perhaps they have more influence on such an important matter as the course of events than the great number of firm and beautiful minds who are waiting for rejuvenation from Europe. The most extreme youth from among these dangerous negators are rushing into socialism, but the most advanced of them don't believe in it, and live practically in despair. This despair is not far from what was embodied in Fyodor Pavlovich: as long as it's good for me. Then elemental Russia. Because they exert a kind of higher fascination on those who simply believe in rejuvenation from Europe—from education and our innoculation with European civilization.]

[Goodness of the soul degenerating into obscure mysticism and in blind chauvinism, menacing a nation still perhaps with greater evil than early decay and inborn cynicism of the opposing party.]

73>   [But then the little bell resounded and the long-awaited F——ch stepped up to the podium. All became quiet. Fly.]

——*Fetiukovich* spoke less correctly but more precisely—[half-bending his long back.] [TROUBLE]

About Katerina Ivanovna's letter.

——But that is really a romance, an alien romance breaking into our domain. And what do we know about this romance? [But if he said that he would kill—and then suddenly a man turns up dead, why <does it mean> precisely that he did it?]

Fetiukovich. Why didn't Smerdiakov leave a note? He had enough conscience for one thing, but not for another?

——Permit me. conscience, that's already repentance, but the murderer could not have had repentance, but only despair. Despair and repentance are two different things completely. Despair may be malicious and unappeasable. . . .

Fetiukovich . . . But then there is the father—that's the misfortune. Yes, misfortune, Some fathers are misfortunes. Let's examine more closely this misfortune, gentlemen.

Fetiukovich. There is a young girl in Finland. In a trunk three children. Is she the mother, gentlemen? Yes, she gave birth to them, but is she a mother to them, gentlemen? Will anyone of us dare knows say pronounce the sacred name of mother over her. [To call her a mother is more than a prejudice, it is a crime]

After Fetiukovich's speech: Threads.

——What will our peasants say?

Fetiukovich. I am new around here. I received impressions without preconceptions. The accused, unbridled and riotous in character, did not insult me beforehand as he did perhaps thousands of people in this town during his stay here, which is why all are prejudiced against him. Oh, prejudice is a strange thing. Because I am not prejudiced <against the accused> and I have not been insulted by the accused, I can see the truth easier ~~than many~~ than for example, the very talented accuser, in whose truth I believe deeply and whom I respect but who is too nervous and ill. There is much that is personal in his speech. You must agree with that. Easier perhaps than even

On my way here I knew that I would meet a psychologist. I was warned. I listened to this speech so deep and [containing so many psychological generalizations.] [I listened to this speech with deep respect. Coming here] Argument that cuts both ways.

Fetiukovich In such a case love for a father which is not justified by the father is an absurdity, it is a prejudice. [Where will he get this love.] Man can't create something from nothing. That is God's lot.

[Fetiukovich He could have also avoided beating the petit bourgeois in the inn.]

Fetiukovich. Why should I believe your fantasy about money hid-   <174
den at Mokroe and not believe in the testimony of Aleksei Karamazov, so sincere, so unprepared, so sudden, so naturally escaping from him.

Crush him with mercy: and he will say, he will say, *people are better than I.*

If he is not guilty, he will say so.[12]

Punish him and he will say: You are scoundrels yourself and are judging me. We are quits.

PROSECUTOR
You will be measured by the measure you use, isn't this in the Bible?

[But to forgive and to turn one's cheek]

Not to do so, but to avoid doing so because the world, [the evil world] does so, the world of evil people does so.

[That is what God taught us ~~and not~~ the crucified ~~only~~ lover of men whom you call the crucified lover of men.]

[You say the crucified lover of men and we say: you are our God.]

---

[12] Various arithmetical calculations are to be found also on this notebook page.

But what difference does the Bible make, we glance at it on the eve of our speech so as to shine with our eloquence.

——He did not order that
The lover of mankind did not command that.
Fetiukovich. Dangerous Insinuations for my personality as a citizen.
Prosecutor: We have heard the great truth [two words were lacking for the great truth] that it was a prejudice to forbid the killing of fathers.

75>   *Final.*[13]
Mitia—Fateful Katia, I forgive you!
Friends, brothers, spare others. [People. Listen] I swear by God, [with my life and with eternal salvation] that I am guiltless of <my father's> blood.
——I didn't kill my father! Katia, I forgive you! Friends, brothers Help have pity on your fellow man!

Before the jury.
I thank the prosecutor, he has said much to me about myself, but only it is not true that I killed my father. The prosecutor is mistaken. I thank the defense attorney, I cried listening to him, although it is not true that one may kill fathers [and to assume so was not necessary.]
I will not be a Bernard.
I will break my sword over myself and I will kiss the pieces.

Ipolit Kirilovich would have said a lot more, but the presiding judge interrupted him and cut the prosecutor short.
Exaggeration within permissible limits.
Fetiukovich objected, placing his hand to his heart.

Prosecutor—Crush—When that's all he asks for.

Mitenka's career was finished.
——And suppose he was destroyed unjustly.
——Perhaps so, the devil take it!
——[The devil, yes, the devil.] One couldn't get around the devil. Where ought he be if not here.

---

[13] The word *final* is in Roman characters in the Russian text.

[And don't you have pity. Yes I have a little sorrow.]
Let's assume that it's eloquence. But still one can't break the heads of fathers with impunity, otherwise where will we end up?
——The chariot, the chariot, do you remember?
——Yes the chariot.
——From a cart he made a chariot.
——Always as necessity dictated.

Mitia.—I will pray for you. I will be better. [I promise it] Similar to a wild animal.
[The day of my judgment has arrived, severe and unjust.]
[I was dissolute, but I loved the good. No matter what I did to become better, I lived like a wild animal.]

I feel the hand of God on me, but how will I confess to God—
I tell you for the last time: No, innocent, I am innocent of my father's blood!
My soul is heavy
I will not protest.
Do not believe the doctors I am completely sane.
[Have pity, do not deprive me of my God, I may revolt.]

——No perfection in this imperfect world.   <17(
——And if?
——And we will close Kronstadt and we won't give them any bread. Where will they get it?
But that isn't so terrible. In America.
You are lying.
Prosecutor. 2d speech.
But isn't the defense attorney too modest in asking only for the acquittal of the accused? Why shouldn't he ~~ask~~ establish a stipend in the name of parricide, to perpetuate the memory for posterity and for the young generation.
[I will talk about the important things only briefly. He talked more and more going deeper. Really, the facts, did not defend himself but most important the idea that there wasn't any money at all interested many and left a trace in memory. But suddenly the 2d part of the speech began]
——Pestle—

——Romance and romancers, meanwhile you lose the man. It's clear from the document that you are giving the romance a significance.

——Think of it, even up to today the prosecutor, according to his own words, was uncertain about premeditation, and now, he, if only Ivan would go away.

Give me a chance and I'll get to it—A man shouts in taverns, is that premeditation? then he runs—runs completely by accident, not at all for that: if there hadn't been a pestle, there wouldn't have been any crime. So having erupted into his father's, he murdered and then stole *from under the bed*.

About the money forthwith, but about Smerdiakov beforehand about 5 men entered and then suspicion fell on Smerdiakov. And why must it necessarily fall on Mitia—Why not: all appearances point to him, he shouted, wrote the letter, he was seen in the garden, he hit Grigory, grabbed the pestle—

But the prosecutor cries out at what moment could Smerdiakov have murdered—

Continuing about Smerdiakov—

How is that worse than your supposition.

Gentlemen, all that is fiction, there are no hard facts.

At Tobolsk. [But the important thing is that there was no money. He killed the money changer.]

~~But~~ he entered and saw his father. Then they didn't find the money. He hid it in a crack. A chunk in someone else's hands. Maximov, the Poles. Cap! So much psychology about a cap. WHO DID THE KILLING? ~~on trial.~~

Fetiukovich's speech. The fence, the pestle, when Ivan goes away— I will take the liberty of touching on (Katerina Ivanovna). Smerdiakov—But what is important—there is no money.

Then about the cap (how could he forget it?)

Karmazov couldn't sew—but you yourself said *two abysses*.

N.B. He examined precisely in that way also the other points— cap and so forth.

A romance is constructed and a man is destroyed—all for the love of psychology.

[Waste so much psychology for an old cap]

But here is a fact that hits you in the face (there is no money).

Who did the killing? Ilinsky and another case.

Two peasants, two godparents—
He manages to reflect, Ilinsky—[14]
In any case there are no firm facts except that if it were not Smerdiakov then <it was> Mitia.

Why didn't Smerdiakov leave—
[*Pestle.* Agree that if he had not taken the pestle, there wouldn't have been a murder.]

———Mitia: I will be a good man, I will, have pity on me now.

Fetiukovich. Psychology. And suppose that it is not the same   <17ᵉ
person?

Rakitin. Prosecutor: Did you tell the civil servant Perkhotin that you are awaiting a catastrophe—What prompted you to say that? Answer—Landlords, etc. Relationship to Grushenka. Yes, she attracted.

The Defense Attorney. Still before that he asks Alyosha about Rakitin. Deep religiosity? And so forth. Did he take 25 rubles for Grushenka? Alyosha gives an answer in a confused fashion.

The defense attorney asks Alyosha, and Grigory and everyone about the envelope. (Who saw him?)

Why didn't you declare it to the prosecutor?
Ivan. I said it to Alyosha.

N.B. When they carried off Ivan, the prosecutor and the defense attorney ask permission to interrogate Alyosha for the second time. *He* did not see the money, and his brother did not tell him about the money.

[About the strokes of the chest]—

———The prosecutor and the defense attorney interrogate particularly Herzenstube and Varvinsky about Smerdiakov.

———They interrogate Marfa Ignatievna and Maria Kondratievna particularly about whether they heard anything from Smerdiakov about the envelope. *Nothing.* [The bed was not touched] [*Fetiukovich.* There is no one proven fact!]

---

[14] Ilinsky refers to Dmitri. See n. 25, Books I and II.

Smerdiakov gave back 100 rubles.

[Lawyer] Crush him with your forgiveness.

The junior captain. God be with him. Iliushechka did not command. Papochka, papochka how he humiliated you.
The lawyer—What's that, near the stone, near what kind of stone?
Junior Captain—Nothing, not necessary— Good-bye, began (drunk) to [say good-bye by bowing]—

The lawyer. Forward! (with these ideas, with this spirit (that is, not only the letter)—and Russia is saved!)

Prosecutor. He had got hold of the most precious ideas of the Russian spirit and dragged them along the street, just so to win, an unjust and dirty business!

78> *Alyosha.* Smerdiakov did the killing. I don't have any proof, this is only my conviction.
——At the preliminary inquest I answered only the questions <asked of me> and I did not myself accuse Smerdiakov.
——I am saying what my brother (Mitia) has said. I believe my brother to be innocent. No one other than Smerdiakov could have done the killing.
——How he did it—I don't know.
——The door was apparently not open.
[Smerdiakov was honest.]

I knew about the existence of the envelope from Mitia.
——Yes, Mitia said that he would kill.

——Did you believe that?
——I am afraid to say that I believed—but with the conviction that a higher feeling would save him at the given moment.

Alyosha. I did not consider Smerdiakov crazy, neither did I consider him a fool. But his mind was certainly damaged. (From religiosity? Yes from religiosity also) Exaggerated self-confidence. Conviction that he could fill an incomparable greater role. Hate for Russia. Not roots in his native land. He was born of Stinking Liza. I arrived and found him with the idea of fleeing to a foreign country. He kept asking about France and about America.

Prosecutor to Alyosha. If this matter was Smerdiakov's, why did he have to communicate about the envelope and about the signal knocks to your brother? *Or do you suppose that they did it together?*

[N.B. No I do not think so.]

But it is strange that one and the other immediately began to testify against one another? And about that we have precise testimony that the supposition about joint action was impossible: Just when Grigory got up and went to investigate the cry in the garden he saw Smerdiakov lying peacefully behind the screen and groaning.

If Smerdiakov had been an accomplice, then he wouldn't start talking [communicate to us] about the signals and about the envelope which he had communicated to your brother. He would have said that only if he had confessed completely about the complicity. He communicated these facts without confessing at all to any complicity, *consequently* <he was> not afraid that he would be accused *because of this confession* of this complicity. Only a completely innocent person can do that.

[What kind of accomplices were they when they immediately began to testify against one another? *They might have waited a little.* To begin to confess immediately after dividing the spoils is, to be sure, absurd.—]

Prosecutor. Ivan proposed money, but we know that he changed 15,000 only 7 days before.

2 Abysses   Here

Fetiukovich—The lover of mankind readying himself for the cross   <17
said: I am the good shepherd, the good shepherd sacrifices his soul so that not a single sheep perishes. (Crush it with mercy (forgiveness) and you find and resurrect the lost sheep.)

Fetiukovich. The immense power of tying and untying has been given to you. Let's be careful. The stronger the power the more need for prudence. It is better to justify 10 guilty men than to condemn one innocent man. Listen to that great voice from the past century. And suppose he is innocent? And what if he is a criminal, but not guilty?

Prosecutor (2d speech). And what if it's not that, and not that, there you have all the arguments of the defense. It is odd to imagine *a stranger* to be the murderer.

The Prosecutor Defame everything that is sacred, just to win the case.

If parricide is a prejudice, if the son asks his father: Why should I love you and what will become of us? What will happen to the bases of society?

[What will become of the sacred family, the foundation of society?]

Fetiukovich. Why would he leave the money if he went to shoot himself?

Prosecutor. But he did not leave it in the town. Perhaps he hid it somewhere in Mokroe.

Why would he need money if he was going to shoot himself? But then he had already changed his mind about shooting himself. Face the trial or run away, in either case the money would be highly useful. For a Karamazov the money would be very useful. The demonic nature of a Karamazov. After all he once put aside 1,500 as he himself assures <us>. If he did not put <the money> aside, well then such an idea that he might put it aside was in his soul. He was already avaricious with the Pole. And finally even if he had put aside the money that does not all the same dispose of the suspicion that he also took the 3,000. The defense attorney says that no one saw it. Well, then that's to swim in the most baseless suppositions. Fyodor Pavlovich himself unsealed <the envelope>. How can one prove that.

The bed was not disturbed—but why crumple it. He had put the money under the mattress. Did not bloody it? But then one can't base oneself on such a fact. All that is only if and if, if the cabbage did not grow and consequently there wasn't any garden.

80>   *Fetiukovich.* Not only punishment, but also the salvation of the human soul.

—Fetiukovich (about Katia) I will permit myself to touch on it. The cry of an irritated woman. It's not up to her to reproach someone else for betrayal, because she herself had committed a betrayal, she loves another brother and having sensed a danger [for him] in his testimony and struck by his sickness she testified differently from an hour before. If she had had even *a bit of time to think about it,* she would not have testified that way. That testimony is unjust.

One word simply: If only Ivan were to go away.

Prosecutor. about Mitia, after having described his return from seeing Liagavy: His self-love was suffering although . . . this person has less self-love than many have, that's strange. He thirsts for justice. [LIAGAVY] He becomes angry if you look down on him. But if suddenly you show him respect, he will become your friend and he will forget entire years of contempt. Raise him with your praise and he will suddenly start to lower himself immeasurably and to feel ashamed of your praise. Yes, this animal nature is well-disposed, I can't deny that.

Fetiukovich. A father fighting over a mistress with his son. There's something disgusting about that.

——The prosecutor was accusing: that's pitiless.

If it wasn't his father, perhaps no killing would have occurred. Everything surged up in a single minute.

The passion of nature, avenging its eternal sacred laws without restraint, unconsciously.

[Fetiukovich. There are souls which in their limited natures accuse the whole world. But crush such a soul with mercy, show it the light in a different aspect and it will foreswear its affair, for it has so many good rudiments. The soul will become broader and will see that God is merciful and how people <are>.]

Such parricides are even less than simple killings, for it is precisely the memory that the enemy is my father which moves my hand perhaps. 23/IX, 1880

and moved my hand all the more powerfully.

Fetiukovich This complete denial not only of the theft of the money but also of the existence of it struck everyone with its unexpectedness —all the more so because it was very logical.

Fetiukovich. He did not kill—he waved the pestle. If it weren't for that unfortunate pestle he might have simply killed him.[15] I dare to affirm that this killing was accidental, without intention to kill.

Prosecutor. The feeling of abasement, of a fall is just as necessary to such souls as the feeling of a high triumph. Two abysses, two abysses, gentlemen, two abysses in one and the same moment—without that we are unfortunate and our existence is incomplete.

---

[15] The text reads "killed" (*ubil*), but Dostoevsky probably wanted to say *izbil* or *pobil* "beat up."

These two abysses are the basis of the Karamazov character.

81>   Prosecutor. Oh, he is not avaricious, but nevertheless, give him money, more and more and as much as possible and you will see how generously we squander it in one night in an unrestrained orgy. And if they won't give it to us we will butcher for that orgy!

[But I do not anticipate our thought]—

Oh, we lovers of poetry, Schiller!

Give, give me means (Lend me, lend me cries Khlestakov).[16]

Prosecutor (in the 2d speech) With this demonic nature, with this desire to throw money to the winds, can we possibly suppose that he carried on him thousands for a whole month and was satisfied to spend twenty kopecks for drunkenness, or went to pawn his pistols, when everything depended on money in order to save himself).

Here Prosecutor Let him return 1,400 to Katerina Ivanovna, but he could have put aside 100 rubles and so with that 100 everything. *That's how it could have been.*

Like plucking the leaves of an artichoke.

Prosecutor—The best minds will perhaps someday occupy themselves with the psychology of Russian crime.[17] Now we are either horrified or like children we chase [the sinister specter,] we wave our arms and hide our heads in a pillow, just so the horrible nightmare does not confront us. But it is necessary to think it through sometime. One must start sometime—I am determined to do so. Because in the affair before us the whole terror of our time is in a certain way concentrated.[18]

That is Smerdiakov! and he had already used Smerdiakov completely without calculation, and without any sense.

(Would you believe it, I even took pity on him at that moment.)

---

[16] The main character of Gogol's *The Inspector General.*

[17] These fragments, which do not fit into the context, also appear on this footnote page: "Shoots himself—cynicism. Hamlet-like question. That's the way it is with us."

[18] The following fragment does not fit into the context: "The open door."

Cap—all the details will be extinguished, but the green roof will remain in the mind—

They were taking Marie Antoinette,

she didn't turn her attention to the insults but to a sign on which something was written.

Fetiukovich—Just like about the cap. Well, then he remembers perhaps the green roof, but he forgot that—

[Fetiukovich. First of all the accused comes off very badly because of his feelings toward his father. But what is a father?]

Maniac: He needs money. He kept on dreaming about giving it back. He is an appropriator, but he does not want to be an appropriator.

I am not a thief, I am a scoundrel, but I'm not a thief.

Fetiukovich—The torn envelope: I swear to you that I heard about   <18 it from Smerdiakov himself, he *suggested* it to me. Didn't he suggest it to my talented opponent? I conclude so because it was too *familiar*.

> *Fetiukovich.* My opponent says: I will not let only the defense attorney defend him, I myself will defend him. And yet he did not remember that if he had been grateful for a pound of nuts, he could not have forgotten that he ran around barefoot, without shoes, and with pants hanging on one button.[19] He remembered the good but he did not forget the bad.

Fetiukovich. Father why should I love you. And if the father can prove to him, *has something* to prove oh, then he is a father!

Fetiukovich. Parricide compared to murder is a prejudice. That is only an old, terrible word,

Prosecutor. In his speech—about the signals.

Mitia. In the last speech about Bernards.

Prosecutor Inviting the Poles to go away—he was imagining his future. Fragments of thoughts. He was completely in the present. Put aside money. In any case he did not expect that so swiftly <. . .>

---

19 The Russian says *na odnoi pokupke* (on one purchase), but Dostoevsky obviously means *na odnoi pugovke* (on one button).

Fetiukovich. Psychology. Jumped down to Grigory. He still had room for a good feeling, for the conscience was pure.

——*Prosecutor.* We have here a mass of words, sayings, gestures—all confirmed by witnesses.

——Fetiukovich. There are unseen threads which tie the [defense attorney] orator and the jury. I have felt them.
The case is in the bag.

Fetiukovich. Character is created for you as a novelist <would do it> as a narrator, and you are supposed to believe in my novel. The play of art, psychology, and eloquence. And because of such a toy the fate of a man can be lost! Are we gathered here to judge the novel of a fashionable writer or the fate of a man.
[A character is created, thoughts and feelings are given to him, *it all turns out neatly.* And yet suppose it is completely different.]

——[MITIA IS FINISHED.] They have finished off Mitia, those leaving the hall said.
Fetiukovich. Smerdiakov was an ardently envious creature, spiteful hating his masters. Why didn't he say in a note—he carried off his vengeance to his grave.[20]

83> ——Katia's testimony. The image of the officer giving his last 5,000 rubles and respectfully bowing before the innocent girl came out as completely sympathetic and attractive.

Alyosha, without being sworn in of course, need not answer, but then an unexpected episode occurred, by which the defense attorney knew how to profit immediately.

The document produced a most gloomy impression and in reality the victory of the prosecutor was complete . . . The testimonies that followed after this blood, Fenia, Perkhotin, the driver
the prosecutor's speech.—

The prosecutor. If it had not been for that woman, he would have

---

[20] Fragments which appear on this notebook page but do not fit into the context: "Fetiukovich. You ask the moment: Well, then and then."

confessed in Mokroe already, but she had just . . . she was in his embrace, he was embracing her with his arms covered with blood . . . And then he decided to defend himself. The amulet, very cunning.

———After Katia's testimony (2d time) Mitia jumps up
Deserved (hard, hard, but deserved!)
Katia, Katia, why are you hounding me!

. . . What can be seen not only from many of his former actions, but also now.

When [really) the witnesses began *à décharge*,[21] that is, called up by the defense attorney, then Mitia's fate sort of smiled a little.]
[Herzenstube, so that suddenly an impression appeared in Mitia's favor. The lawyer grateful that Mitia had not spoiled the matter with his exclamation. Thank you German—Gott . . .] [And] Something like a factual proof in favor of Mitia flashed in Alyosha's mind and that occurred [almost] completely by chance [for the defense attorney.]
    Alyosha
But the most important impression in Mitia's favor [(although only in part)] was produced by Katerina Ivanovna's testimony. It was something stunning and unparalleled especially such an eccentric girl, such a lofty and frank testimony, something akin to a self-sacrifice was hard to imagine from her.
[I do respect, respect . . . I certainly bow down to. Oh, you don't know my soul. I am a Schiller. Lover. But the defense attorney was content. And really.]

Momentary <18⁴

Portrait of the president of the court, the prosecutor was pale. This was noticed.
    ———The jury—
    ———Mitia's hearing. Clothes. Defense attorney. Portrait
    ———List of witnesses. Smerdiakov, Dog's <death> to a dog. President of the court.
    ———Reading of the accusation. Impression.
    ———No, not guilty. President of the court—
    ———Judicial investigation. Oath. Saw all of them

---

[21] French: this is probably a reference to the French expression *témoin à décharge,* that is, a witness for the defense.

——Alyosha. By groups or not—I don't know? I've even forgotten the order. I'm going to write about the impressions from memory.

Interrogation of Alyosha.

The defense attorney. From the very beginning it was clear that he had a preconceived idea, nevertheless he profited from everything he could.

The same stunning *picture* unfolded. Only concentrated. Irrefutable testimonies. These were no longer rumors, but facts. (I'm not describing everything, for in the prosecutor's speeches). The defense attorney had his own idea. All the same he profited. Mitia behaved badly—Pierrot, 700 poodles.

The same for the expertise, clear that the defense attorney accepted it without believing in the argument for insanity—but in order to define the moral state.

He accumulated facts so as to have them all used. The father deceived Mitia in much.

Although the defense attorney kept Mitia in check, he was rather happy by his frenzy.

He interrogated Perkhotin in detail.

Loaded the pistol.

[I think that] the most important thing at the trial was the unexpected catastrophe which I will tell about and which sealed Mitia's fate.[22] But everything was already spoiled before that. The accusatory side showed from the very first that it had by far the upper hand. It was difficult to imagine how the lawyer was going to struggle against that. But everyone felt that he had already conceived of an idea of defense. Nevertheless, he took advantage of every circumstance. Dirty up.

As a product of serfdom in Russia, suffering from appropriate institutions. Caused by the independence of thought and extraordinary nobility.

You could be interested in turn (the last years). I understand and I

---

[22] At this point in the text there is a drawing of an old man; underneath are the words "these impressions are necessary" and underneath that are the words "but even though it fell to the lot of the lawyer." On the right there is another drawing, this time of a church arch.

spare your modesty, you were interested in a young beautiful woman, gladly receiving at your place the flower of our youth.

Alyosha   <18!
Katerina Ivanovna—
Grigory.

Experts

Rakitin.
The Poles.
The coach driver.
Trifon Borisych.
Grushenka, bad impression. Contributed to the episode.
Ivan—[looking terrible]
again Katia and about the rest in passing.—
He took Rakitin down a peg.
They were astonished (about Fetiukovich) how he could have learned such details.

Prosecutor. *Gott der Vater* I will not permit the defense attorney to profit, and I myself am prepared to defend him.—

Herzenstube. Strained, clumsy, and self-satisfied German wit.

frenzy, but also that which we call mania, that is, the undoubted beginning of actual insanity. There is mania of the 3,000 about which he cannot talk without extreme irritation, and yet he is not avaricious and is even generous.

——So that in addition to the frenzy you find that he is already on the way to insanity . . . and just recently . . . Here I have to contradict my learned comrade—to the right and not to the left . . .

Herzenstube. They are small and there are many of them. I bought a pound and they cracked on the teeth.—Nuts.—

Final

Prosecutor. If Smerdiakov could write two lines so that no one would be accused of his death then why couldn't he write that he was guilty. He had the conscience for one, but not for the other, that is hardly probable.

——He was a little spat on and dirtied (Trif. Borisovich)

Fetiukovich. Not punishment alone, but also the salvation of the human soul.

Fetiukovich. Overwhelm a soul with mercy: that's easier for you to do for in the absence of complete proof it is hard for your conscience to say: yes, guilty. You will lighten your conscience. Grace above all. He will profit from it and you will resurrect a new man. Russian court. Forward!

Forward—and the Russian troika will reach its goal ~~and~~ the Russian carriage—and don't frighten us with your Russian troikas! The Russian carriage will reach its great goal majestically!

Fetiukovich. What is society? [or what society ought to be] Church. What is the church—the body of Christ? Your judgment is the judgment of the church, your judgment is Christ's judgment. And Christ's judgment is not punishment alone but also the salvation of the human soul.

186>   ——What you want to find, you found.

Herzenstube. But yes, yes! What you came for ~~on earth~~ that is what you found. [will find] That's all the same.

The proverb says: one intelligence is good, but if an intelligent man appears, that will be still better (much) better, because there will be two intelligences and not one.

One intelligence is good, but two are better.

——But yes, better, better, and I also say that ~~then~~ 2 intelligences are much better. But another did not come to him with his intelligence, and he let his own go.

How is that? Where did he let it go . . . That word where he let it go . . . I forgot. Ah, yes, *spazieren.*

——To take a walk?

——But yes to take a walk, His intelligence went walking and came into such a deep place he lost himself.

Drowned.

If the pitcher [gets the habit of going] goes after water, then it will break there. The pitcher goes often to the well and there its head is broken.

But yes, I also say Head ~~Head? that is, the upper part~~ For if it goes to the well often, then it will break its upper part, and not its head, because a jug does not have a head, but ~~only~~ an upper part.

Expertise. [MITIA] [Man is weak]. All his actions are contrary to common sense. He himself made known that he would kill, he killed, and instead of running away, he goes off to squander the money. Immobile look, sudden laughter. Strange words. Bernard, Ethic, He entered and looked to the right.

Herzenstube. There's nothing new under the moon.

Herzenstube. I keep talking and then suddenly I forgot the word which I know, but I've forgotten—
I bought him a pound—what is it I bought him, I've forgotten the word.
Goodies—
Yes, but what kind. Yes it grows on a tree—
Apples—no, lemon?
Oh no! Goes crack on the teeth—
Nuts. Yes.—*Gott der Vater*.
23 years afterward. first day he came for nuts.—
Ah, *Gott der Vater*. I remember and I kissed him and broke into tears, he kissed <me> and broke into tears—and I said you have an honest heart, young man, because you remembered all your life the pound of nuts!

Gott der Vater Gott der Sohn, and only forgot *Gott der heiliger Geist,* but I reminded him—and many years flowed by in one morning, he enters.
He fell down in a faint—
The serious part of the public was satisfied.
——He had accumulated a lot of psychology.
——Yes all that was true, irrefutable truth.—He had deduced it as if it had been written down.—
——He had totaled it up.—
——~~What will the defense attorney say?~~
——And he drew up our account, for us, also at the beginning of his speech.
——Yes, he waited a long time, but ended up saying what he had to say.
——But there were unclarities.
There were, there were. And he got carried away a bit. But cleverly done—
What will the defense attorney say?
Those who rely on sentimentality. But he was wrong to take after the St. Petersburgers. Those who rely on sentimentality.

——Yes that was unclever.

He hurried a bit.—Nervous fellow.

A lot of rhetoric,—the sentences were long, long sentences.

He wrote, composed his speech in advance ~~they say.~~

[He spoke as if reading it.—Reading it, reading it. A stiff person.]

[Well, we think it's funny, but how is it for the accused?]

[——Yes, for Mitia how is it?]

[——What will the defense attorney do?]

——[But they put their claws into him cleverly, with Nik. Parfenych, at Mokroe.]

[Yes, he related it once again. Well, how many times already has he told it around here.]

[——He couldn't restrain himself either. Self-love.]

[——An insulted man.]—

[And the troika was good. Yes <the business about> the troika came out well.]—He's given liberalism a boost.—

Gave it a boost.

Yes, it is true after all, When he said that peoples will not wait.

And so? In English. In the English Parliament one member has already interrogated the ministry about nihilists. A barbarous nation, isn't it time to intervene politically? It was about him that Ipolit <spoke.>

No perfection in this imperfect world.

87>   Trial

1) A doctor can sit in the courtroom.

2) The judges enter the hall.

The president of the court asks if all the jury are present.

——The bailiff answers: all except such and such.

The President of the Court asks why they are not present?

The secretary answers: such were given summons, to others no (got sick or simply did not appear)

——Question of the president of the court:[23] what are the consequences for not appearing?

——the prosecutor answers about the legality or nonlegality of the reasons for not appearing (N.B. Legal reasons: no receipt of the summons, sickness, serious illness of the wife)

---

[23] Dostoevsky has *sekretar'*, but the context makes clear that this should be predsedatel' (president of the court).

——The president of the court announces: the case of so and so is to be taken up, accused to be brought in (that to the bailiff)

——The accused is brought in—Interrogation about name, profession, etc.

The accused and the prosecutor can each challenge six jurymen,

The accused if the prosecutor challenges 3 then the accused can 9 (that is, 12 all together can be challenged).

The composition of the jury (if the list is verified by balloting (from 36) 12 jury are selected and 2 replacements.

$$\left.\begin{array}{l} \text{4 civil servants} \\ \text{2 merchants} \end{array}\right\} \text{or in reverse}$$

6 petits bourgeois and peasants

——Then the list of persons called to the judicial inquest is read (that is, witnesses and experts) and they ask: is everyone here?

——The prosecutor at the time of the reading of the charges presents a list of people (witnesses) whom he intends to call. To the judicial inquest.

N.B. If an unexpected witness (not inscribed [written down] earlier) is suddenly called by one side or the other, then the president of the court asks one side or the other whether they agree or not. In case of disagreement the court itself can, if it finds it necessary, have the witness appear—

——The number of witnesses is not determined.   <18

——The secretary announces that Smerdiakov (witness) did not appear because of his sudden death. Police notification.

The deposition can be read in its time.—[Khokhlakova]

——List of charges (secretary reads it)

Exposition of the important facts briefly—

Why he has been arraigned, why he must stand trial according to the opinion of the prosecutor.—

——Do you admit your guilt? (If: yes, I admit it, then the president of the court asks that the circumstances of the affair be narrated) in detail.

——If not: then they proceed to the trial and the witnesses are called one after another.

First the prosecutor's (special order, that is, why one witness comes before another)

but sometimes they are divided into groups according to the decision of the president of the court.

The president of the court—no oath to witnesses who are related.

(N.B. At first they bring in the witnesses together and the priest administers the oath to them all together[24]

The priest's exhortation, the president of the court also after the priest.

(At first name, profession are asked—

———All this immediately after the reading of the list of charges and after the accused's words: guilty or not).—

———At first the witnesses sit all together (as the place permits) but after the oath they are isolated and separated as much as possible (guards, sentinels)—

(The bailiff keeps them under surveillance).

(Communication with the outside world is forbidden for the witnesses. If a child broke his leg, then the bailiff notifies the president of the court)

189> After he is interrogated a witness can remain in the hall after giving his testimony (or he can ask to leave).

(The witnesses who have been interrogated sit opposite the president of the court but not behind a grill.—

———If the witness still wants to say something after having given his testimony, then he communicates this to the bailiff (more frequently to the defense attorney) and they announce it to the president of the court and the defense attorney asks <permission> to ask another question of the witness[25] in view of the new testimony).

(I forgot (the witness) one circumstance that I want to tell about). The defense attorney or the prosecutor immediately intervene and ask the president of the court to have the testimony given).

(N.B. The witnesses are retained in the hall specifically so that further questions might be asked of them.—

[N.B. Place of the Trial.] (club, district court, assembly of the zemstvo, 2, 3, weeks).

Order of the interrogation of each witness.

At first the president of the court asks generally and asks the witness to tell everything he knows about the matter. Then the prosecutor and then the defense attorney (or the other way around)—each time the

---

24 The parentheses are not closed.

25 Dostoevsky has *predsedatel'*, but the context makes clear that this should be *svidetel'* (witness).

prosecutor and the defense attorney[26] announce to the president of the court[27] that they need to ask this question and so forth.

[After having interrogated the witnesses *generally* about the affair the president of the court turns to the prosecutor or the defense attorney (depending on who did the calling) and asks them to begin the questioning.]

And then after an hour break he says: I have one circumstance to add. Second interrogation, the president of the court begins to ask What does he have to say? And he says that it was I who killed.—The president of the court asks him to explain in more detail.

Ivan recounts that he did the killing (he checked himself)   <190

The prosecutor and the defense attorney can each intervene and ask Ivan a question (with the permission of the judge).

When Ivan, not having finished, began to be delirious and then when he began to yell absurdly, he was taken out and the presiding judge ordered the testimony of Ivan to be put in the trial record and to say that the Court had decided to continue the affair. (he can order the bailiff to call forth a medical opinion. He can also <order> an expert doctor.)

The doctor can come in and say that the sick man was taken out in such a state that he cannot remain in the courtroom (through the bailiff) and the president of the court can ask each party . . .

Katerina Ivanovna at first testifies for Mitia

In an hour she gets up and speaks against <him>

The president of the court declares that she did not talk in that way at the preliminary interrogation.

She shouts that she was in a false moral state.

The president of the court says that new testimony will be admitted and asks her to be seated.

But the prosecutor and the defense attorney can intervene and begin to ask questions and interrogate for a long time.

---

[26] Dostoevsky has *svidetel'* (witness), but the context makes clear that this should be "defense attorney."

[27] Dostoevsky has *procurator* (prosecutor), but the context makes clear that this should be *predsedatel'* (president of the court).

Katerina Ivanovna irritated by the words of the president of the court presents also *a fact*. The note. The bailiff gives it to the court. The court gives the note to the prosecutor, the defense attorney and the members of the jury. (as material evidence).

The witness has finished, the trial is finished, the president of the court asks the different parties to sum up.

Then he asks the prosecutor.

The court goes on to the summings up.

It is your turn to speak Mr. Prosecutor.

After the speech of the defense attorney the prosecutor answers him.

The defense attorney has a chance to answer once again.

The president of the court asks the accused after each witness's testimony what he has to say about the testimony.

After the summings up of the different parties the accused has the last word.

The president of the court. The summings up are completed. The court then takes up the character of the questions and asks each side to conclude. (after having read the draft). After the questions the president of the court turns to the members of the jury.

The members of the jury. Yes, guilty. The president of the court to the prosecutor and the defense attorney about the extent of punishment. Then he himself decrees.

Epilogue

‹91›   ——Grushenka kisses the girl's little hand.

[Mitia about Trifon].—Trifon Borisych was so struck by the prosecutor's supposition that Mitia had hidden ~~almost~~ 1,500 r. in his house that he practically demolished his whole house in looking for it (crack, tore a plank, loose floorboard—lift it).

Grushenka to Katia: I *surely* see now whom you love.

Mitia, seeing that all are reconciled: there we are happy now.

Mitia about his brother Ivan, laughing in a friendly fashion: "he wasn't able to carry it off" (but he will. He will triumph over everyone. [he's not like me!]

Mitia. Looks forward to prison but is afraid of the striped clothes.

Mitia. Others already use the familiar form of address. If anyone starts a fight with me, I'll kill him!

No, man is not ready. Wanted to sing a hymn, but he is not ready for anything.

Alyosha to the children. Remember always this minute when you cried.—That will remain with you all your life, perhaps you will no longer believe and your hearts will turn to stone, and yet you will always remember this minute of pure tears, there are not many such minutes, but they are redemptive, they are always redemptive. Even though you will laugh at everything, you will not laugh at them. And if you laugh at them, then you will say in your hearts: no, I did badly in laughing at them, one must not laugh at them.

Coming back from church. Little father, where is that little father, his bed remained there. They made it up.

Hat in his hands

———Put on your hat

———I don't want a hat, I don't want it! yelled the junior captain and he threw down the hat. The boys picked it up, he ran, everyone was going fast.

[Returning from church ~~suddenly~~ he was running with flowers in his hands, suddenly quieted down: little father, little father, dear little father! and he turned around wanting to run back to church, but he was held back. His bed is there; they prepared it.—]

He hurt the mother, wanted to return to the mother, her sore feet, the little bed, the little bed. The little bed pursued him.

The little shoes!

On seeing Grushenka, Katia's eyes flamed up as if saying: <192

———Can it be? Can it be that she is here?

But she didn't say that, went up <to her>: forgive me!

Krasotkin:—Is your brother innocent?

yes—

I will believe you! They say in the city.

You know I want to prepare myself to be a publicist, or something where I could say the truth, always the truth, eternally the truth, in opposition to all the evil and power of this world. I gave my pledge and dedicated myself <to this>.—

———I also—yelled the boy (Teucros, Dardanos, and he blushed)—

———It's hard! God be with them! said Mitia.

——Katia, do you believe that I did the killing?

——I never believed it. Katia whispered in a frenzied fashion. Kill me!

Alyosha knew that she had defamed herself, he knew that she had believed, at least in the beginning, although perhaps there had always been the worm of doubt.

——I don't believe, don't believe

Mitia—And did you believe when you testified?

Katia—Don't torment me, why do you ask?

O—No, one must punish oneself! No, I didn't believe even then. I hated you and myself and believed for an instant, at that instant when I testified.

[Mitia. And when you finished testifying you stopped believing immediately and began to knock your head against the ground?]

[I know, know, Katia!]

[Katia—Yes, yes, yes—there still at the trial, when I said the final word when I began to struggle—that is why I love you, who are so generous!]

Katia to Alyosha.

Oh, only not to her! I cannot ask forgiveness of her. and I, I said to her: forgive me! I wanted to punish myself before Mitia That is why I asked her to forgive me: She did not forgive, I like her for that!

[Mitia: Run after her!]

[Alyosha. Don't worry. She will understand. I will come at 4 o'clock.]

<193> Mitia Will I be honest?—There once again a scoundrel. Fled from punishment. One doesn't become honest all at once.

——Well, then, little by little.

Mitia. I love my native land. I love Russia. America is painful.

——Alyosha to Mitia about his reproaches to Grushenka. Be silent, Mitia, is it up to you to speak <that way> to her?

[Mitia—They will become reconciled, they will become reconciled later.]

——Mitia and Alyosha. Mitia is distracted and dreamy.

About Trifon. About all.

At the church, inside the fence. And as he says all clearly and sincerely.

(Landlady. I will remain by the side of the mother)
Give the little flower. You took[28] his cannon.

I hurt my mother.

[He returned: your little legs are hurt.]
[And he saw the little shoes. Where are his little legs]
[Give me his little legs.] [Little mother]

[Little father! Dear little father!]

Alyosha and Mitia, about Katia. Katia is convinced that Ivan will become well. She does not want to believe in his death.—That is phenomenal.

Mitia—Perhaps because she fears more than everyone that he will die.

Alyosha. Precisely. She is forcing herself to take heart.

Katerina Ivanovna on her knees before Mitia; My joy, my God!
2) I loved you like a God.
Terribly tender and passionate words—
Let me go, I'll come later.
——Now I will get well, now by myself.
Oh, yelled Katia Grusha appeared on the threshold.
You will kill yourself, or they will shoot you!
Appeal lawyer.

At Katia's—About the escape. [At a deportation point.] This will <194 take place in the most natural manner and no one will suffer from it.
——I will tell you frankly, I started a quarrel with [Ivan] him then, [ABOUT IVAN]. I didn't like his running away from Grushenka.
——He left me a note (about the flight) (going to the trial)
——The matter is being pursued.
Alyosha—He knows that you are here.
——I know that he knows. He's afraid of you—of what you will say, is afraid of doing wrong. He has thoughts, imagination, mysti-

---

[28] Gender is feminine here.

Notebook Page 194. This is the last notebook page devoted to this novel. Note the characteristic church drawings in the lower left-hand corner. One may note the insertion of OB IVANE near the top of the page, expressed in the translation as [ABOUT IVAN].

cism: God has sent suffering, one cannot run away from suffering. But is he ready for suffering? Can someone like him suffer? (Bitter word, Alyosha did not contradict him)

Alyosha—No, he is not ready said Alyosha.

Katia—He ought to flee—you ought to support him.

Alyosha—I will say what is needed.

(N.B. Katia not a word about her betrayal. Alyosha, not a word either. Alyosha about the aim of his visit: he calls his brother)

Katia—Can I really? (that is, after her betrayal)

You can: [you will be] all of your life unhappy! Your whole life! [Katerina Ivanonva frowned but did not object]

Alyosha—He is housed separately: We got it, got everything.[29]

Immediately? now, now—You caught me unprepared. I can't leave a sick man. For a single moment you can (You won't meet *anyone* there.)

Katia I'll go but I don't know whether I'll go in or not. It's hard for me.

Alyosha—Have pity.

Katia—Have pity on me. All his life he [has laughed] at me.

Alyosha I'll go and I'll say that you will come.

Katia—No, don't say it. [It's better that you say nothing.] Perhaps I won't go in. Aleksey Fyodorovich, Alyosha, I'll go, but perhaps I won't go in.

Alyosha went. Description of where Mitia is. At *Mitia's*. [Trifon. About Grusha with Alyosha.]

(In prison, in the woman's courtyard.)

Mitia. About Alyosha. Will she come? [They will beat me and I won't be prepared] Alyosha. Perhaps Grusha is in the women's section, at the supervisor's. [She knows. She is not jealous of Katia.] Calls Alyosha to come out. She entered: A wound will remain on my soul for my whole life.

I knew that you would forgive. It's hard for me to be forgiven. [Mitia. I deceived Grusha so that she wouldn't come]

Grusha by chance: I know whom you love, guilty.

Save him, mother!

Katia to Grusha at the threshold: forgive me.

---

[29] The following fragments, which are found on this notebook page, do not fit into the context: "immediately? you can?" and "He said."

~~Katia going away quickly. Did not forgive. Then she forgives. I did a little more than I had to.~~

Mother, save him only.

——We are evil mother, both of us evil. How are we to forgive. Save him only and I will kiss your feet.

But you won't forgive, yelled Mitia reproachfully.

Katia—Enough! Be at peace, I will save <him.>

Mitia—she asked for your forgiveness

Grushenka. The devil she did! [Her lips] her tongue spoke but not her heart. [Her lips spoke but not her heart]. If she saves you, I will forgive everything, then I'll forgive her.[30] And now I kissed the leg of a serpent.

Mitia. Alyosha, Run after her!

Katia—Let's go, I sent some flowers there. Liza sent some also. [Don't talk any more!]

Just so you save him.

---

[30] The following fragment found on this notebook page does not fit into the context: "About Ivan."

Name and Topic Index